THE LAST TALL SHIPS

Frontispiece: The steel four-masted barque *Viking* setting sail off Dover after anchoring to avoid an adverse tide. June 1936.

THE LAST TALL SHIPS

GUSTAF ERIKSON AND THE ÅLAND SAILING FLEETS 1872~1947

by Georg Kåhre

Edited and with an introductory chapter by
Basil Greenhill

With a foreword by the late Edgar Erikson
Chairman, Ålands Sjöfartsmuseum
Translated by Louis Mackay

Introduced by HRH The Duke of Edinburgh

Also by Georg Kåhre
Den Åländska Segelsjöfartens Historia

Also by Basil Greenhill
The Merchant Schooners
Sailing for a Living
Boats and Boatmen of Pakistan
A Victorian Maritime Album
A Quayside Camera
Archaeology of the Boat
Out of Appledore (with W J Slade)
Westcountry Coasting Ketches (with W J Slade)
The Coastal Trade (with Lionel Willis)
Steam and Sail (with Rear Admiral P W Brock)
Karlsson, The Life and Death of the Merchant Sailing Ship
Seafaring under Sail (with Dennis Stonham)
The Grain Races (with John Hackman)
The Evolution of the Wooden Ship

By Basil Greenhill and Ann Giffard
Westcountrymen in Prince Edward's Isle (American Association Award: Filmed: Televised)
The Merchant Sailing Ship: A Photographic History
Travelling By Sea in the Nineteenth Century
Women Under Sail
Victorian and Edwardian Sailing Ships
Victorian and Edwardian Ships and Harbours
Victorian and Edwardian Merchant Steamships
The British Assault on Finland

First Edition, Mariehamn, 1948
Translated from the Swedish by Louis Mackay
English language Edition, first published in Great Britain
1978 by Conway Maritime Press Limited,
24 Bride Lane, Fleet Street, London EC4Y 8DR

Reprinted 1990

ISBN 0 85177 134 3

Design and make up by Jon Blackmore
Setting by Type Out
Printed in Great Britain by Page Brothers (Norwich) Ltd.

Foreword

I am delighted that my friend Basil Greenhill has arranged for Georg Kåhre's book about my Father's remarkable career as an owner of sailing ships to be translated and has edited it for publication in the English language. The translation by Louis Mackay is excellent and the editing prepares the book for a wider audience.

This publication is one of the mutually helpful results of co-operation between the Ålands Sjöfartsmuseum, of which I am happy to be Chairman, and the great National Maritime Museum in Britain. This kind of international collaboration is most appropriate between museums which deal with the history of merchant shipping, perhaps the most important single element in the development of modern industry and world trade.

Chairman,
Ålands Sjöfartsmuseum.
Mariehamn, September 1977.

''The secret sweetness of the sheltered place
lies not in its tranquility
but in the fjärd running white and green
in the storm, far off like a memory—''

''Läornas ljuvhets hemlighet
är inte stillheten härinne
men fjärden som går vit och grön
i stormen, fjärran som ett minne—''

Georg Kåhre

Contents

Note on the pronunciation of Swedish words in Åland

å is pronounced like the *a* in *small* (thus Åland is Awland)
ä is pronounced like the *e* in *nest*
ö is pronounced like the *ea* in *heard*
j is pronounced like *y*
w at the beginning of a word is pronounced like *v*
v at the beginning of a word is sometimes pronounced like *w*
g is often silent but at the beginning of a word is *y* as in *yeast*
sk is pronounced as *sh*

Thus the name of the parish of Vårdö, frequently referred to in this book, is sometimes pronounced approximately *Warder* with the accent on the first syllable and sometimes a slight rolling of the middle 'r'. The final 'r' is silent. In Sweden, and often in Åland, it is pronounced *Vorder*.

The word fjärd (*fyerd*) means 'an expanse of water enclosed by islands and groups of skerries (skärgård - *Sharegord*) or by arms of land'. As the photograph at the beginning of the book shows these fjärds bear no resemblance to what is understood by the anglicised Norwegian word *fjord* and I have therefore kept the local term. A *vik* (*veek* or *week*) is a deep bay.

List of Illustrations

Introduction

by HRH The Duke of Edinburgh

From the moment the first primitive steam engine hissed and spluttered into action the days of ships driven by wind and sail were numbered. In the end it took well over a hundred years before engines replaced sail throughout the world in all but the smallest cargo carrying ships, the Arab Dhow probably outlasting all the others. In Europe it was the builders and owners of merchant ships in the little known, and otherwise not particularly significant, Finnish Åland Islands, who have the distinction of operating ocean-going merchant ships under sail longer than anyone else. The whole idea that this little community of sea-going farmers in the Baltic should be engaged in international maritime trade at all seems wildly improbable and why they should have succeeded with sailing ships for so long, where others failed, is even more surprising.

This book gives the whole remarkable and romantic history of this aberration and it also provides a fascinating record of what was, and to certain extent still is, an astonishing social and economic success story.

There have been several other instances of relatively small communities becoming exceptionally successful and prosperous as trading and business enterprises. Each had their own key to success, but what they all seem to have had in common, apart from the human qualities of honest hard work, shrewd common sense and the willingness to cooperate, was an economic system which gave full play to these qualities and actively encouraged the natural enterprise and will to adventure of their people.

I was fortunate enough to visit Mariehamn during the State Visit to Finland in 1976. The great figure of the barque *Pommern* dwarfs in height the much larger modern ships which now use the modest harbour; it only needs a little imagination to picture the scene as it must have been barely 50 years ago. I wish this book had been available before that visit.

Philip

Buckingham Palace

S I G Y N

What This Book Is About

The three-masted wooden square-rigged sailing ship was probably the most important vehicle in human history. Its invention in the shadows of the fifteenth century opened up the world to the economic and political domination of northern Europe. By its use particularly by Captain James Cook, RN, in the eighteenth century the final limits of the habitable world were determined and the first outlines of the world trade patterns of the Industrial Revolution were laid down.

Although the square-rigged vessel's monopoly was under very gradually increasing threat from the developing schooner rigs from the middle of the eighteenth century onwards, the three-masted square-rigged sailing vessel was an important factor of the industrial expansion of the nineteenth century. This dominance lasted until about 1870, when the capabilities of the wooden three-masted square-rigged vessel were outrun by the industrial conditions it had played such a part in creating. Smaller square-rigged sailing ships were increasingly replaced by schooners. Increasingly important economies of scale demanded larger vessels than the ordinary medium-sized and big wooden three-master, and although many wooden vessels remained at sea until the present century, steamships and iron and steel square-rigged sailing ships, latterly rigged with four masts, rapidly took over their work on the world's trade routes.

Left, plate 1 The barque *Sigyn* being rerigged in the harbour at Åbo in 1977 (Basil Greenhill)

Between 1880 and 1909, on the east coast of North America big four-masted wooden schooners were built by the score. These vessels up to a certain size and in certain trades, were perhaps the most efficient merchant sailing ships ever built. Later, five and six masters were also constructed in considerable numbers.

But steamships developed and by 1885, the compound-engined steel screw steamer had reached such a degree of efficiency and economy that it was steadily and with increasing rapidity replacing the big sailing ships in general world trades which were demanding larger ships than the largest practical sailing vessels. At the beginning of the present century, with the *Pommern* of 1903 - now magnificently preserved at Mariehamn - to which many references appear in this text, and the *Kurt*, later *Moshulu*, and the *Mozart* and *Beethoven* of 1904, the *Archibald Russell* of 1905, and the *Sunlight* and the *Rendova* of 1906, the building of large steel merchant sailing vessels ceased in Britain. The three-masted *P T Harris*, launched at Appledore in 1912 for the home trade, and the three-masted *Gestiana*, built at Porthmadog in 1913 for the salt fish trade with Newfoundland and the slate trade with Germany marked the end of the launching of wooden merchant schooners in the United Kingdom.

The building of wooden square-rigged vessels of the classic pattern had ended long before. Today there is only one cargo vessel left, the barque *Sigyn*, built in Gothenburg in 1887 and owned and registered for many years at Vårdö in the Åland Islands. Today she lies in the harbour at Åbo in mainland Finland, her masts and rigging restored, preserved intact as a merchant ship. Owned by the Åbo Academi she is of great historical importance as the last surviving example of one of mankind's longest lived and most significant inventions.

But the later years of the First World War and the three following years saw a sailing ship building boom on both coasts of North America and in Scandinavia, Finland, Germany, the Netherlands and Italy which was almost unparalleled in history. More than six hundred big wooden schooners and barquentines, some of them very big, some steel schooners, four wooden barques which were little different from eighteenth century vessels, a wooden full-rigged ship, and many smaller schooners and ketches were launched for American, Canadian and European owners between 1916 and 1923. Small wooden schooners with auxiliary oil motors continued to be built on both sides of the Atlantic for another twenty years. None of these vessels were

Above, plate 2 The four-masted schooners *Frances L Tausig* and *Bradford E Jones* under construction at Boothbay Harbour, Maine, in 1918. (W J Lewis Parker)

Left, plate 3 Deck view of the four-masted schooner *Sam C Mengel* before launching at Bath, Maine, 1917. (Maine Maritime Museum)

Right, plate 4 The four-masted schooner *Laura Annie Barnes* built at Phippsburg, Maine, 1921 and lost on Nantucket Shoals, 1939. Like many twentieth century four-masters this vessel was extraordinarily economical. She was sailed by a crew of only six. (W J Lewis Parker)

Above, right plate 5 The three-masted schooner *Victory Chimes* under construction at Cardigan, Prince Edward Island, Canada in 1918. (Public Archives of Prince Edward Island.)

built in the United Kingdom, which took no part in this Indian Summer of the merchant sailing ship.

It is a fair enough statement that this post-war boom period marked the real end of the merchant sailing ship and that she died in the industrial depression which immediately followed. This is the period described in Chapter 5 of this book as 'The Worldwide Abandonment of Sail'. In fact her disappearance took another twenty years or so and was a very complicated process. The last big steel square-rigged merchant sailing ship at sea registered at a home port in the United Kingdom was the full-rigged ship *William Mitchell*, which made her last voyage in 1928. The last square-rigged merchant sailing ship registered at a home port in the United Kingdom to earn her keep carrying cargoes was a vessel of classic pattern, the wooden barquentine *Waterwitch* owned by the Stephens family of Fowey and she made her last voyage with cargo in 1936. Two other wooden barquentines, the Åland-built *Ingrid*, referred to several times in this book, also

owned by the Stephens and formerly owned by Gustaf Erikson, and the *Frances and Jane* owned by Albert Westcott of Plymouth had sailed into the 1930s, and the latter, laid up, survived into the Second World War to be the very last British square-rigged merchant sailing ship registered at a home port in the United Kingdom. The schooners *Katie* and *Mary Miller* were the last of all sailing vessels without engines, other than London River barges, registered at ports in the United Kingdom, to work around the coasts of Britain. They ceased to sail during the Second World War but the Slade family of Appledore operated a fleet of motor schooners, vessels comparable with Erikson's *Vellamo* and *Sirius*, until well into the Second World War; and a vessel fitted with a powerful engine, the fore-and-aft schooner *Kathleen & May*, now restored somewhat to her appearance as a sailing vessel and preserved by the Maritime Trust, worked on the west coast of Britain until the beginning of the 1960s.

It is more difficult to name the last merchant sailing vessels in North America. An American built steel three-masted barque, the *Kaiulani*, made a passage under the Panamanian flag from Aberdeen, State of Washington, to Durban, South Africa, with a cargo of lumber as late as 1941-42. The *Kaiulani* then took a part cargo to Tasmania, where she was requisitioned as a coal hulk. The last big Canadian steel square-rigged sailing ship was the four-masted barque *Garthpool* of Montreal, operated from Britain and lost in 1929. A traditional wooden three-master, the barquentine *Maid of England* launched at Grosses Coques, Nova Scotia, in 1919 and the last square-rigged vessel built in eastern Canada, had been abandoned at sea only a year before. The last steel square-rigged vessel to carry cargoes under the flag of the United States was the British built full-rigged ship *Tusitala* which arrived

Above left, plate 6 The five-masted barquentine *Forest Friend* of Seattle, built at Aberdeen, State of Washington, in 1919. (National Maritime Museum)
Middle left, plate 7 The German five-masted steel motor schooner *Carl Vinnen* built at Kiel in 1922 photographed in the Baltic in 1937. (Basil Greenhill)
Left, plate 8 The steel full rigged ship *William Mitchell* built at Londonderry in 1892, the last big steel square-rigged merchant sailing ship registered at a home port in the United Kingdom. (National Maritime Museum)
Above right, plate 9 The three-masted barquentine *Waterwitch* built at Poole in 1871, the last square-rigged sailing ship registered at a home port in the United Kingdom to work as a merchant vessel. (Basil Greenhill)
Right, plate 10 The three-masted barquentine *Frances & Jane*, built at Harwich in 1878, laid up in Chichester Harbour in 1939. She was the last square-rigged merchant sailing vessel to be registered at a home port in the United Kingdom. (Basil Greenhill)

in New York from Hawaii with a cargo of sugar in 1932. She never again went to sea as a merchant ship. A five-masted wooden barquentine, the *Marsala*, may have carried cargo after the *Tusitala* was laid up. She continued to sail as a training vessel until 1938.

Big schooners lasted in North America longer than they did in Europe. In 1939 there were thirty to forty of them trading between Canada and the United States on the East Coast, down to the West Indies and sometimes across the Atlantic to Britain. As with sailing ships in Europe, the Second World War brought their end, but a few survived

Above, plate 11 The three masted schooner *Mary Miller.* One of the last two merchant schooners working without engines registered at a home port in the United Kingdom. (Graham Gullick)
Below, plate 12 The three masted fore-and-aft schooner *Haldon,* built at Plymouth in 1893 and owned by W J Slade, one of the most successful latter-day British motor schooners, outward bound from Appledore. (National Maritime Museum)
Right, plate 13 The last square-rigged merchant sailing vessel to be built in eastern Canada, the barquentine *Maid of England,* launched in 1919. (Nova Scotia Museum)

Left, plate 14 The American steel full-rigged ship *Tusitala,* built in 1883, the last big steel square-rigged merchant sailing ship at sea registered at a home port in the United States. (National Maritime Museum)

Above, plate 15 The *Theoline,* one of the last three American four-masted schooners at sea, under cargo grabs against a mid-twentieth century skyline. (W J Lewis Parker)

Below, plate 16 The four-masted schooner *Annie C Ross* photographed at Queens, New York City, 1954. (Basil Greenhill)

much longer. The three-masted Canadian auxiliary *City of New York* sailed with cargo until 1952. The Maine-built *Lucy Evelyn* lasted in trade until 1948 without an engine and the Newfoundland auxiliary *Bessie Marie,* like the British *Kathleen & May*, was still earning her living in 1959. The last active five-masted schooner was the *Edna Hoyt* which lasted until 1937 and the last four-masters were the *Theoline,* the *Constellation*, both lost in 1943, and the *Herbert L Rawding.* The four-master *Annie C Ross* was laid up at Queens, New York City, in 1940. She, the last surviving United States four-masted merchant schooner afloat, was still there in 1954 when I took the photograph reproduced here. She sank at her moorings a year later, but another four-master, the *Luther Little* still lies on the shore at Wiscasset, Maine. She has been there since 1932, but when I photographed her in 1976 she was still an impressive sight.

On the West Coast, the last active four-masted schooner was the *Commodore*, which took a lumber cargo to Durban in 1942, where she was sold locally and operated until 1946. The last five-master, the *City of Alberni*, reached Valparaiso in distress under the Canadian flag in 1944, and in 1946 was lost off Brazil as the Chilean *Condor*. Two hulls, originally British-built four-masted barques, were re-rigged as six-masted schooners in 1941. The *Star of Scotland* carried a cargo of lumber to Cape Town but was sunk by a German U-Boat while crossing in ballast to Paranagua, Brazil, in November 1942. *Tango* also carried lumber to Cape Town in 1942, was sold to Portuguese owners, and was scrapped in 1948 at Lisbon. The three-master *C A Thayer*, now being preserved at San Francisco, made annual voyages north in the Bering Sea cod fishery through 1950, while the *Wawona*, being preserved on Puget Sound, last went north in 1947.

In the early 1990s a small fleet of wooden two-masted sailing vessels without engines, some of them restored merchant schooners, earn their livings carrying vacationing passengers by the week from Camden and other small ports in Maine.

There were still one or two big steel square-rigged sailing ships carrying cargo on the west coast of South America in the 1950s, and scores of wooden schooners and ketches with auxiliary engines were then still at work in the Baltic. As late as 1954 I saw fully rigged schooners and ketches without engines trading in the Aegean. Wooden sailing vessels lingered in the Indian Ocean for even longer, and it seems likely that the last engineless square-rigged merchant sailing ship ever to carry cargoes was an Indian brigantine with the hull shape and sails and rigging of a vessel of the early 1800s, the very name of which is not recorded.

During this prolonged process of the final abandonment of sailing ships as a means of commercial transport between 1921 and 1939, a remarkable phenomenon occurred in the shipping world. A ship owner whose vessels sailed under the Finnish flag succeeded in the face of experience everywhere else in making a growing and profitable business out of the operation of sailing vessels, both of the classic kind, wooden square-rigged three-masters, and of the newer types, three- and four-masted schooners and big steel square-rigged vessels. Starting out with very little capital he made a fortune with which he was able to lay the foundations of a great steamship line which, now equipped with motor vessels, is still owned by his descendants. He lived and belonged in the Åland Islands in the mouth of the Gulf of Bothnia between Sweden

Left, plate 17 The four-masted schooner *Luther Little*, built at Somerset, Massachusetts, in 1917, photographed at Wiscasset, Maine, in 1976. (Basil Greenhill)
Above, plate 18 The Indian brigantine which may have been the world's last engineless square-rigged merchant sailing ship at sea, entering Colombo Harbour in 1952. (Basil Greenhill)

and mainland Finland. The name of this remarkable man was Gustaf Erikson. Behind the story of his achievement there is, of course, a complex story of social and economic development in the Åland Islands in the nineteenth and twentieth centuries which is itself fascinating. As merchant sailing ships became rarer and rarer so Gustaf Erikson's vessels aroused more and more interest wherever they went. They attracted the attention of a brilliant Australian journalist, Alan Villiers, who had begun life as a professional sailing ship seaman and had sailed in an early Erikson ship as a young man when such vessels were still commonplace. He made two more passages in Erikson ships and wrote a very successful book about each of them, one of which, *Falmouth for Orders* (London, 1929), is still in print at the time of writing, sixty years later. He then entered into partnership with a number of Ålanders in the purchase of the four-masted barque *Parma* which was very successfully operated for a number of years. His writing made these last big sailing ships world famous and for many years they became the newspaperman's dream, the perpetual story wherever they were seen.

Alan Villiers had many imitators in writing about the Erikson ships, but three books in the English language which came out of the widespread popular interest were outstanding. They were each, in different ways, written from inside. Two, *Mother Sea* and *Pulley Haul* (London, 1964, and 1966) were the work of an Ålander, Elis Karlsson from Vårdö parish, a professional seaman with a great gift for the English language, who wrote at first hand from his experiences, boy and man, in Åland ships. *Mother Sea* is particularly notable for its description of a childhood spent on the main island of Vårdö, where Elis Karlsson grew up with his elder brother Karl V Karlsson, later to command the four-masted schooner *Atlas* and the four-masted barque *Parma*, who is mentioned several times in this book. The particular value of Karlsson's work is that it shows so clearly that the Åland ships operated against a social and economic background of which they were a normal part. Manning, maintenance and management of merchant sailing vessels were all part of everyday life in Åland and the appropriate business

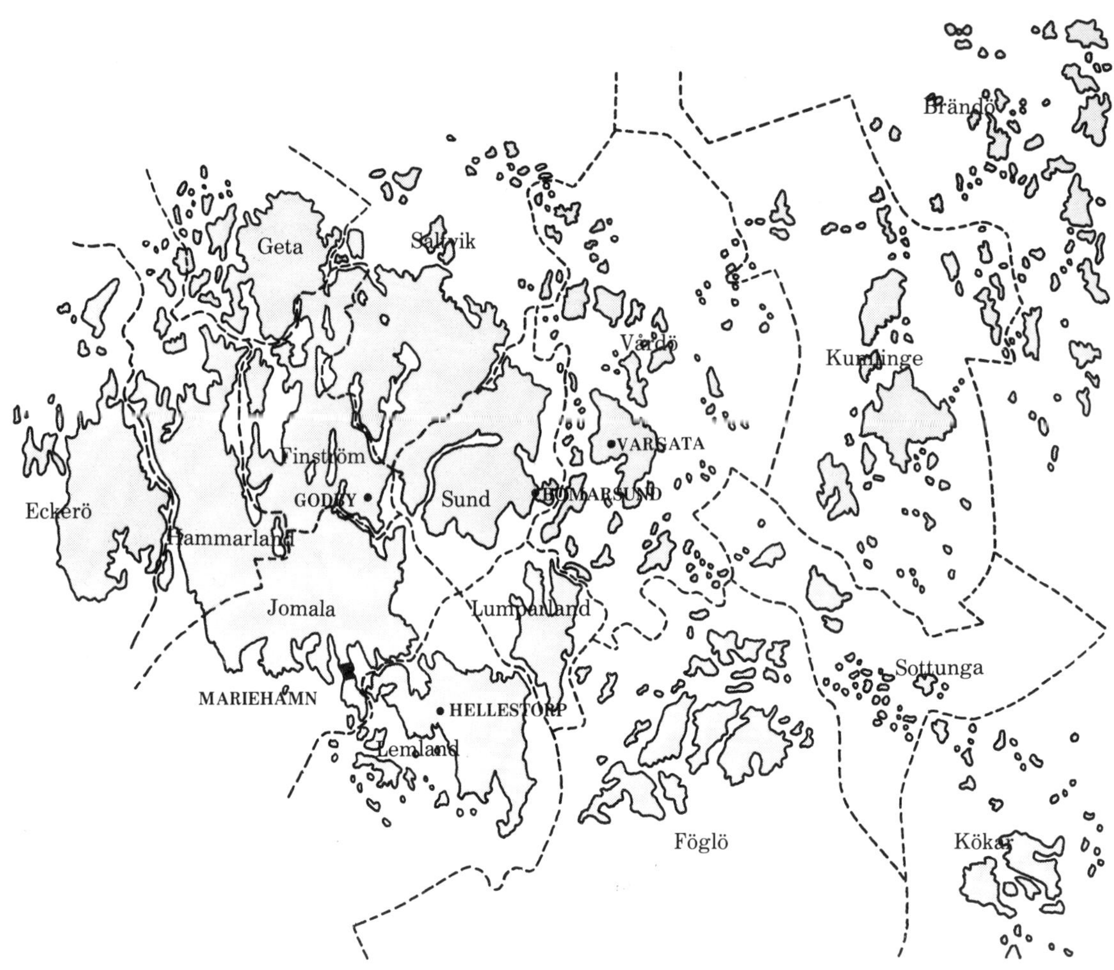

structures still existed in the trades in which the vessels worked. Such ships could only be operated under these conditions. Once the conditions changed the ships ceased to exist. You cannot conserve, preserve, or restore a whole society, and you cannot keep a small part of it alive in isolation from the rest of the body.

The third book was very different. Called *The Tall Ships Pass* (2nd edition, Newton Abbot, 1970) it was written by a very successful British underwriting member of Lloyds, Bill Derby, whose interest in the vessels, extending into voyaging in them to the Baltic, stemmed from a business concern with some aspects of their operation, management, and especially insurance. The book is a brilliant study of its kind and, inter alia, deals in depth with the construction and career of the steel four-masted barque *Herzogin Cecilie*, Gustaf Erikson's flagship for many years.

It is fifty or more years since the Erikson barque *Eläköön* ended the five hundred years of the history of the wooden three-masted square-rigged merchant sailing ship with her round voyage from Veitsluoto to Esbjerg and back to Mariehamn in July and August 1939; thirty odd years since the *Passat* and the *Pamir*, owned then by the Erikson Company, made the last two roundings of Cape Horn in July 1949; and more than a generation since Gustaf Erikson's son Edgar and his daughter Eva presented the last of the Erikson sailing vessels, the British-built four-masted steel barque *Pommern*, to Mariehamn to lie in the western harbour alongside the Åland Maritime Museum, preserved unchanged as she was when she came in from her last voyage; and the company are now the operators of a large fleet of modern ships in world trade. However, interest in Gustaf Erikson's astonishing achievement in successfully operating merchant sailing ships until the Second World War is still strong. The present day popular enthusiasm for sail-training vessels of various kinds, the 'Tall Ships' which every year congregate somewhere in the world and race each other stems, at least in part, from the interest those very, very different merchant vessels aroused fifty years ago, and from what was written about them by those who knew them at first hand.

Yet, surprisingly no comprehensive study of the story of the Erikson fleet as a most successful business enterprise against the peculiar social and economic background of the Åland Islands has yet appeared in English. Georg Kåhre, an Ålander, intimately involved with the business and its personalities, wrote such a study in Swedish in the last years of Gustaf Erikson's life, working from the voluminous company records, which still exist in the basement of the firm's modern offices in Mariehamn. His book, in Swedish entitled *'Under Gustaf Erikson's Flagga'*, was intended as a salute to Gustaf Erikson on his 75th birthday on 21 October 1947. Because he died two months before, the tribute became a memorial. The book is highly readable and we at the National Maritime Museum in Britain felt it to be an important piece of maritime economic and social history, well worthy of translation and publication to make it available to the English speaking world. In 1978 we therefore had it translated.

The Last Tall Ships is Georg Kåhre's book most ably translated by Louis Mackay, published with the cooperation of Edgar Erikson, Gustaf Erikson's surviving son and at the time of writing the Chairman of the Company, and of Captain Karl Kåhre, one of Georg Kåhre's several brothers. Karl Kåhre was formerly a seaman in the *Archibald Russell* and the *Mozart* and is now Director of the Åland Maritime Museum, which published the original Swedish edition of the book. I have edited as little as possible, adding the notes when they seemed likely to be useful to the reader, adding a few paragraphs and brief statements in italics, and making small changes, principally of phraseology, to bring the book up-to-date in a few references. I have also compiled the list of sailing vessels of the Erikson Fleet which appears as Appendix 1. The only substantial change I have made has been to omit some material on the general history of sailing ships from the first chapter and in consequence of this to fuse the first two chapters into one. I have also collected, selected and captioned the illustrations, a number of which, with the help of Edgar Erikson and Karl Kåhre, I have made especially for this book. All the photographs taken on board at sea except my own and the ones by Lars Grönstrand were made by professional seamen employed in the vessel illustrated, and not by passengers.

The Åland Islands are far from the industrial centres of middle Europe. Half way between Stockholm and Helsingfors, they lie like dust upon the Åland Sea at the mouth of the Gulf of Bothnia, roughly 6,500 of them with a population of about 22,000 people. They are mostly granite with a

Left, plate 19 Map of the Åland Islands (National Maritime Museum)

Below, plate 20 The Åland Islands lie like dust upon the sea. (Basil Greenhill)

reddish tinge, clothed in dark softwoods, with deep *fjärds* stretching in between them. Even the biggest islands are so broken up that one is almost always near an arm of the sea. The general appearance is very like parts of the coast of Maine. The capital, Mariehamn, the only large settlement, has broad tree-lined streets laid out in grid fashion so that it is altogether very like a small town in New England. But the climate is more rigorous than that of Maine, with short warm summers and long winters when the sea is frozen - Prince Edward Island and Cape Breton in Canada provide a close parallel, though the Åland winter is longer and its days are shorter than the Canadian. The Åland winters played their part in conditioning a society which could successfully develop a merchant shipping industry through the operation of sailing vessels in their last days.

The population has always been, and is today, dependent on farming and seafaring. Georg Kåhre describes the historical background to the remarkable merchant shipping expansion of the later nineteenth and early twentieth centuries in some detail in this book, and in greater detail in his major work of maritime history, *Den Åländska Segelsjöfartens Historia* (Mariehamn, 1988). David Papp has described the economics of small ship sailing in his study *Ålandsk allmogeseglation 1800 - 1900*, (Stockholm, 1971) Lars Grönstrand has written a number of detailed studies of Åland shipping, notably in the *Meddelanden Fran Sjöhistoriska Museet vid Åbo Akademi*. The social realities which lay behind the capital development which made possible the merchant shipping industry are powerfully if not objectively described in the novel *Katrina* (in English, London, 1937) written by Sally Salminen, an Ålander who became world famous as a novelist in the middle of the present century. Her characters were based on shipowners, masters and seamen of the generation before Gustaf Erikson, and of the same generation, whom she herself had known in her childhood and youth in Vårdö. Today Åland society at all levels has a flavour all of its own, arising in part perhaps from the fact that the islands, unlike most of the rest of Europe, have known neither feudalism nor industrialisation.

Left, plate 21 Woods in Vårdö. (Basil Greenhill)
Below, plate 22 Österviken, the east bay, Grundsunda, Vårdö, a typical *vik*. (Basil Greenhill)
Above right, plate 23 Street in Mariehamn. (Basil Greenhill)
Right, plate 24 Västergård Ytternäs, the farm, built around a central gård or yard, which was the home of Captain John Andersson, owner of the four-masted schooner *Gunn*. (Basil Greenhill)

At the ultimate end of the sailing ship era in 1939, in the summer before the outbreak of the Second World War, the Åland fleet consisted of 11 steel sailing vessels, 37 wooden sailing vessels, 10 auxiliary sailing ships and, already, 44 steamers. At the end of the war the fleet was effectively reduced to 19 steamers, 3 steel sailing ships and a few wooden auxiliaries. Thirty years later, in 1975, with 17 tankers, 12 refrigerator vessels, 27 other cargo vessels and 15 car ferries totalling over three quarters of a million tons of modern shipping, ten joint stock companies in Mariehamn owned more than a third of the whole foreign-going merchant fleet of Finland. These companies operate from offices in the quiet streets of Mariehamn, controlling their vessels, which the daily position charts show to be all over the world, by radio and teleprinter. The shares are owned almost entirely by some 2,000 - 3,000 Ålanders (except in the case of the Gustaf Erikson Company, which is a family affair), while the earnings from over 2,700 jobs at sea substantially exceed the earnings from agriculture, forestry and

Below, plate 25 The great barn of Captain Andersson's farm, solid granite blocks for the basement, vertical boards above. The traditional tarred roof has been replaced by tiles. Here, as in similar structures in New England and Canada, the cattle spend the long frozen months of winter. (Basil Greenhill)

Above, plate 26 The parish church of Vårdö, built in 1786 and incorporating a much older chapel. Here are buried the successive generations of the great shipowning families of the parish and the master mariners and the seamen and their families. (Basil Greenhill)

fishing put together. Almost half Åland's national income at the time of writing comes from merchant shipping. Certainly the Ålanders have remained a people of the sea.[1]

Åland is an autonomous province of Finland, but its people speak Swedish and the unilingual status of Åland in bilingual Finland is protected by law: Swedish is the only official language. Ålanders govern themselves to a great extent. The islands are a demilitarised, neutral zone of Scandinavia and Ålanders are not liable for Finnish military service. Many of the functions performed elsewhere in Finland by the central government are performed in Åland by the Provincial Administration: Police, Health, Education, Museums and Ancient Monuments, Communications, Commerce and Industry, are governed largely by the Provincial Parliament. Åland functions in many ways as if independent, and has been descibed as 'a state within a state'. The islands even have their own flag, which consists of a yellow and red cross on a blue ground.

I never met him, but I would like to add to the picture of Gustaf Erikson, 'Papa Gusta' to his family, which emerges from Georg Kåhre's narrative a few additional notes, based on the recollections of Åland friends and on what I heard when I travelled as a boy in one of his sailing vessels from western Britain to the Baltic in the middle 1930s when he was at the height of his powers.

He spoke little of himself, but was very good at making others talk to him about themselves. He

1 For a detailed study of Åland's shipping history to the mid 1980s see Greenhill and Hackman, *The Grain Races*, Conway, 1986.

had a very remarkable memory and seemed to retain in his head every detail of the operations of his complex enterprises. He knew all his young crews by name and remembered those names when he met them after they had returned from a year's voyaging. When the *Archibald Russell* sailed straight out from the quay in the western harbour at Mariehamn without the use of a tug, Gustaf Erikson standing on the shore, did not only cry out 'Good Luck' to the Master, but also 'Captain, Captain, don't forget about the economy!'

He rode a bicycle, holding his silverheaded cane across the handlebars when he, for instance, went from his office to the harbour to inspect his vessels in port. The family Lincoln was driven by his eldest son or by any of his friends. That was simply because he had no driver's licence himself and never bothered to get one. He was a very sociable man. He loved a good party and especially to give parties for his friends on board the ships laid up in the harbour. In a restaurant, even when visiting abroad, he was known to take a violin in the orchestra and break out into his favourite *The Wide World Waltz*. He enjoyed the society of women and he liked to tease them. A tall woman was always 'A Royal Rigged Ship!' He did not like to be regarded as an old man. He liked young family friends to address him in the familiar name of 'Gustaf'. Like many successful men he himself expected to be a hundred but he died suddenly in his beautiful summer house, Styrsö, at 74.

As for the author of this book, Georg Kåhre (1899 - 1969), he was a man of considerable and varied talents. He was by profession a schoolmaster, teaching Swedish at the Åland Nautical School and both Swedish and Latin at the Åland Lyceum in Mariehamn. He loved the sea and liked to sing a shanty among his sailor-friends. Besides his two books of merchant shipping history he was a poet of wide reputation and connected with seafaring both through his teaching and through his family - one brother was master of the *Mozart* and later headmaster of the Nautical School, another, Hilding Kåhre, was one of the men behind the success of the Erikson fleet, while recently Karl Kåhre directed the admirable Ålands Sjöfartsmuseum, Maritime Museum, one of the best institutions of its kind in the world. Georg Kåhre was therefore very specially qualified to write the history of the world's last big fleet of merchant sailing vessels.

I am greatly indebted to Captain Karl Kåhre, and to Mr Lars Grönstrand and Mr John Hackman, both of the Åbo Akademi, for their assistance with matters of fact and detail in editing this translation. I would also like to thank Eva Wilson and her husband, David, Director of the British Museum, for their help, and the late John Lyman and Captain W J L Parker U S C G for their help with information about the last sailing vessels of the United States and Ann Giffard for proof reading and her index.

Basil Greenhill
Boetheric, 1989

TECHNICAL NOTES

The unqualified term 'schooner' in this translation always means a two-, three- or four-masted vessel all the masts of which were in two parts, a long lower mast and a relatively short topmast, setting standing square sails from her foretopmast. There may also be a squaresail, usually furling to the mast, set from the fore yard on the forelowermast, but all the other sails, gaff sails and topsails, were fore and aft. The term 'fore-and-aft schooner' is used for vessels with not more than one yard. Some fore-and-aft schooners were pole-masted without separate topmasts.

This usage follows British practice. In the days of the sailing vessels in Britain the schooner with yards and squaresails on her foretopmast was so common that she, the 'topsail schooner', was the norm and so designated simply 'schooner' by people connected with merchant shipping. The schooner without yards was the exception and was so distinguished as the 'fore-and-aft schooner'. In the United States and Canada in the late nineteenth and twentieth centuries the reverse was true, and the word 'schooner', used unqualified, meant a vessel without yards. The exceptional vessel with yards on her foretopmast was distinguished as a 'topsail (or square topsail) schooner'.

In consultation with Louis Mackay and Karl Kåhre, I have followed British practice because it was nearest to the Åland terminology. Georg Kåhre's nomenclature follows Åland practice. In Åland in the present century a two-masted schooner without yards was called a *galeas*, a two-masted topsail schooner or a brigantine was a *skonert*, three or more masts made her, not a three-masted topsail schooner or a barquentine, but a *skonertskepp* without distinction - see footnote on page 35. The three-masted fore-and-aft schooner was a *slättoppare*, or, more rarely, a three-mast *galeas*. If her masts were of the same height, like those of a Canadian or American 'tern schooner', then she was a one hundred and eleven. A four-masted *slättoppare* was also a one thousand, one hundred and eleven. The identical terminology was not necessarily used in Swedish speaking areas other than Åland.

Author's note to the First Edition

Authors who have not succeeded in what they had planned have a custom of pointing out modestly the shortcomings of their work in an introductory chapter. I find this method of meeting criticism at the door, disarmingly and smilingly, very attractive, since the greater part of the manuscript has been completed and the result can be surveyed. It was my original intention to give a fairly complete picture of the life and times of the last deep-water sailers, set against a background of earlier seafaring under sail. The book was to be called *The Last Sailing Fleet.* Lack of time and nautical experience, difficulties in obtaining literature and in printing and other circumstances summarily modified this rather pretentious ambition. If by chance anyone remarks that this book concerns itself more with the business of shipping than with sailing and seamen, the observation is right. It would doubtless have drawn more attention if the pages had had a stronger salt-water content, if adventures at sea and in harbour had predominated. But those who have not themselves sailed the oceans have good reason to preserve a certain modesty. Alan Villiers complains in one of his books about the hordes of landlubbers who busy themselves with writing about ships and sailing. He has perhaps some justification.

The matter can also be seen from another viewpoint, more agreeable to the author. Gustaf Erikson spent many years at sea, both before and abaft the mast, but his real achievement was as a shipowner. His experience at sea was only a prelude, though a necessary prelude for the sequel to become what it did. Seamen have an easily understandable inclination to regard the shipowner as a necessary evil, if necessary even. He sits at home, sheltered from all storms, drawing dividends, living well and wasting his time calculating how long it ought to take to make passages and to load and to discharge cargoes. But the figures in the office ledger books are probably not without their own risks and adventures. All those -shire, -bank, -glen, Loch-, Cambrian, and P- Lines which once started, grew, flourished and disappeared, lived their eventful lives not only at sea but also in the shipping office.

The mizzenmast flies the ship's good name,
The foremast the pilot's flag when she seeks a port.
The nation salutes from the end of the gaff,
From the mainmast the owner's pennant.

It is a result of the more or less enforced pruning of this book's format that the skippers of the fleet receive such short mention, that many smaller vessels appear only briefly in the text though they are in the illustrations, and that the account concentrates on the period when the fleet was being built up.

The most important source has been the duplicate books in which Gustaf Erikson kept copies of all his correspondence, especially those from his years as master of *Albania* and *Lochee* and from his first ten years as a shipowner in Mariehamn when he nursed his extensive enterprise virtually alone. The collection, which comprises several thousand closely-written pages, paints a lively picture of his nautical experiences, and his financial calculations (often hurriedly improvised), his restless energy, his boldly speculative spirit, his great affection for his family and the unrestrained originality of his temperament. A shipowner perhaps needs copies of his notes, but a young skipper who kept a copy of every word he wrote, not only to his shipowner but even to personal friends, must have been very unusual.

I am very grateful to the gentlemen in the office on Norra Esplanadgatan for the help which their work with position-lists and the like gave me, and I have made much use of the notes made by my brother, economist Hilding Kåhre, and Captain K A Frederiksson, who have sat together in the office for almost twenty years.

Left, plate 27 Georg Kåhre, 1899-1969 (Ålands Sjöfartsmuseum)

CHAPTER 1

Åland's Seafaring Tradition

In a shallow and enclosed inlet of the Atlantic with a low salt-concentration, far from the limitless expanses of the great oceans and the thousand mile long trade routes, on a high northerly latitude, about the same as that of Cape Farewell, the southernmost point of Greenland, the world's last sailing-fleet found its home. By an esplanade of lime trees uniting two harbours, one to the west for Australia-sailers and one to the east for local skerry boats, in an idyllic little town which hibernates for the winter and hides its buildings in sighing masses of leaves for the short but beautiful summer, a very young capital in a district with ancient cultural traditions, the last fleet's headquarters was set up - not in London, Liverpool or Rotterdam, Bordeaux or Boston, nor any other great city with a celebrated name in the annals of deep-water sail. Mariehamn was founded in 1861. Forest, cloudberry marshes and a few meagre plots of cultivated land belonging to Övernäs, one of Åland's poorest townships, were all that existed on the present site when America's clipper-ships surprised the world with their fast passages.

But Åland's countryside had what Mariehamn lacked: traditions of seamanship dating back centuries, not an outstanding tradition on the high seas, not even on the Baltic, as was the case in Gottland for example, but strong and deep-seated traditions nevertheless, however local and unassuming. The Ålander has the sea in his blood; it is no surprise to him that he became the last exponent of deep-water sail. On the contrary, it seems entirely natural to him. In case this book falls into the hands of others than Ålanders, it would be well to devote a few pages to Aland and its seafaring.

The stranger contemplating a sufficiently large-scale map of Åland finds it easy to believe that fishing is the main life-blood of the archipelago. Someone once entertained himself by adding up the exact number of 6,654 islands, holms and skerries, islets and rocks. It is true that *Fasta Åland* (mainland Åland), as the principal island is known, is about 50 kilometres in length from Geta Rock in the north to Herröskatan, the southernmost point of Lemland, and about 40 kilometres in breadth; but the map does not really give an impression of a mainland. From south to north and north to south, the land is broken up by deeply penetrating inlets which in places widen out into inland bays. Åland's maritime tradition is thus readily explicable in terms of the intimate interaction with the sea which is part of a fishing people's daily life. But such a conclusion would be mistaken. Åland is an agricultural community and has been for a thousand years. Seafaring went hand in hand with agriculture, not as a secondary activity, but as late as the mid-nineteenth century as an integral and necessary part of it. Fishing is the mainstay of life for many Ålanders today. The farther back in time one looks, the more significant it was. But in historical times the soil's harvest has always weighed more than the sea's.

Whether Åland's farming population took part in the Vikings' epic voyages to Russia and to the Greek capital is not known. The countless Arabian silver coins which turn up in Åland soil could have been brought home as booty, but could also have constituted payment for pilotage and provisions. One thing can be said with certainty, that Viking fleets passed Åland's skerries. Known accounts of sailing routes from the thirteenth century mention Lemböte in the parish of Lemland (two or three kilometres from Mariehamn) and Kökar as anchorages. Mariners of the period sailed along the coasts as much as possible and put into a harbour for the night. Today passenger traffic between Åbo and Stockholm via Degerby in Föglö (another name appearing in the itinerary mentioned above) follows part of the ancient course which over the centuries has seen the passage of countless sails and royal pennants.

Historical documentation loves to preserve the strange and the unusual for posterity; obscurity is good enough for the commonplace. Original documents have very little to say about Åland seafaring during the centuries when Hanseatic and Dutch merchantmen sailed the Baltic.[1] Century after century, the Åland peasant loaded his boat with his produce, butter, meat, wool, tallow, livestock, salted, dried and fresh fish and so on, and above all else firewood, and sailed to his market - Stockholm, and also Åbo to some extent, according to royal decrees governing provincial trade. He returned with iron, salt, grain if the harvest had been poor, cloth and miscellaneous articles for his household. More prosperous farms owned their own sailing boat, others made do with a half or quarter share. The boat, or a share in a boat, was as necessary for the farmer's housekeeping as his farm implements. Firewood gradually became the most important commodity and this had significant consequences. Wood is a bulky material, demanding a lot of cargo space. It was also found in sufficient quantities for more than one trip across the Åland sea during the course of a summer. When, in the eighteenth century, both the secular and the ecclesiastical authorities complained that the Ålanders 'abounded' with too much sailing and neglected the land, it was doubtless the export of firewood that they had most in mind. In one respect the complaint hit the nail on the head; the Åland sea was more alluring than the plot of land at home.

The larger timber-carrying boat was two-masted and carried a squaresail on the foremast which was also the mainmast. In time the two masts became equal in height and both gaff-rigged but the vessel kept the name *galeas*[2]. The smaller single-masted smack, yacht or well-boat (*skuta, jakt* or *sump*) was fore-and-aft rigged. As recently as a hundred years ago, both galeases and smacks were undecked and clinker-built.

In 1809 Åland, together with Finland, was incorporated into the Russian Empire, but it was not until a couple of decades later that there was any recession in the time-honoured Stockholm sailings. After the separation from Sweden, things had continued much as before thanks to special customs tariffs. When these went out of force in the 1830s, the Åland Sea ceased to be the main trade route for Åland shipping. In more recent years[3] the Åland log boats moored along Strandväg in Stockholm have generally taken their cargoes from the Finnish coast.

As the Stockholm sailings declined, one after another of the larger galeases went over to carrying freight on the Baltic. The first schooners are mentioned about this time. The most common cargo was timber from one of the towns in the Swedish province of West Bothnia to one of the German Baltic ports, most often Lübeck, though Copenhagen was also a

Below, plate 28 Many different kinds of boat have been used in Åland. This model in the Maritime Museum at Åbo of a shallop rigged boat from Kökar represents a general type which occurred widely and was in use at least from the seventeenth century to the mid-twentieth. (Basil Greenhill)

1 But traces remain in names like Kuggholm, near Degerby, where the cogs used to shelter and Kuggsund north of Styrsö where they used to pass. There is a fine medieval wall painting of a cog in Finström Church.

2 Which normally applies to a ketch-rigged vessel in Scandinavia.

3 That is until the 1930s.

Below, plate 29 The galeas *Svea*, built in Finström in 1890. (Ålands Sjöfartsmuseum)
Above, plate 30 Åland galeaser discharging firewood in Stockholm in 1930s. (Ålands Sjöfartsmuseum)

frequent destination. In 1854, when the first ripples of the Crimean War reached Åland and the citadel of Bomarsund capitulated after bombardment, Åland already had a Baltic fleet of schooners and galeases, and a corps of professional skippers who, while they had admittedly not the benefit of schooling in navigation which captains from bigger seaports might have had, were nevertheless thoroughly tested in nautical practice. Until this time the sailing privileges of skippers without formal qualifications had been restricted to the Baltic.

They were extended to the North Sea by a Russian imperial edict of 1856. Two years later, the first Åland vessels sailed through Öresund. By 1860 more than thirty voyages had been made to

Above, plate 31 The ruins of part of the fortress of Bomarsund as they stand today, lost in the forest of spruce and birch. (Basil Greenhill)

England with freight. During the following decade and a half Åland sail experienced its golden age. The construction of ships went over from clinker to carvel[1] and from galeases and schooners to larger vessels, brigs, larger schooners and barques. The largest of Åland's home-built sailing vessels, the barque *Flora*, measured 619 tons net. Since ship's timbers were in short supply in the forests of Åland, a number of vessels were supplied by the parishes of East Bothnia, known since ancient times for their skilful carpenters. Between 1860 and 1875 the fleet grew from 11,000 to 42,000 tons net. Eckerö and Hammarland were pioneer parishes, Finström and Geta stood foremost in building their own vessels, while Lemland and Vårdö vied with each other for the greatest total tonnage and developed into the dominant shipping parishes. The skerry parishes of eastern Åland took very little part in North Sea sailing; Föglö was an exception. Shipping became an independent activity, but it was still closely bound to the soil of Åland. Most of the skippers and the major part-owners were farmers; their homes provisioned the vessels each spring. Farmhands, crofters' lads and sons of the soil manned the fleet. Since 1856, Åland had had a savings bank, but during these splendid years for shipping it lived a singularly ailing life. Both those with property and those without put their savings into the part-ownership of vessels - usually 100th or 80th part-shares. In 1875 the mainland parishes of Åland, including Eckerö, had about 15,000 inhabitants and between two and three tons net per capita. The inhabitants of Vårdö were ahead with 6.8 tons per capita, most closely followed by the Lemlanders with 5.8 tons. Marie-

1 That is, in the terms of the archaeology of boats, to skeleton-built non-edge-joined construction.

Above, plate 32 The ' rogbrödkaker', here seen drying on poles in the roof of the kitchen, were a staple provision for the crews of Åland wooden sailing vessels. By the end of the sailing season they could be as hard as the timber of the vessel. Taken in one of the houses in the Luostarinmäki Museum in Åbo this photograph nevertheless conveys a good general impression of the interior of a small Åland farmhouse of the period of the farmer-shipowner-shipmasters. (Basil Greenhill)

Below, plate 33 Norrgårds, the home in Geta of the Söderströms, farmer-shipbuilders, and their ancestors since the 1600s; Eric Söderström built many vessels including the schooner *Ingrid* (Plate 74) in 1906. She was later owned by Gustaf Erikson. (Basil Greenhill)

Above, plate 34 The schooner *Ingrid* was built at Knutnäs, Geta, in 1906 by twenty farmers working under the direction of master shipbuilder Söderström in the style of their fathers in the great days of the farmer-shipmasters of the 1870s. Shares in the vessel were issued in return for labour, timber and materials. (Ålands Sjöfartsmuseum)

Below, plate 35 Another late example of Åland local wood shipbuilding (other than the vessels built in the First World War period) was the three-masted fore-and-aft schooner *Lyckan,* shown under construction at Kvarnbo, Saltvik, in 1902. (Ålands Sjöfartsmuseum)

hamn got its navigation school at the beginning of the 1870s, but, as a rule, the North Sea skipper was still self-taught - a farmer on his own homestead and skipper of a vessel of which he himself owned part[1]

It was a busy and festive period. Launchings were celebrated with joy and merriment and at the feasts following the annual settlement of accounts each winter, the tables groaned with food and drink. The parishes had their shipping magnates, powerful tycoons who directed and dictated. 'You fellows go on chatting, I'm going into my room to write the minutes, I am,' one of them is reputed to have had a habit of saying when he opened meetings. The fleet was young and stately: 40 barques, the same number

Above, right plate 36 In the summer while the men were away at sea, the women worked the small family farms and were employed by the bigger farmers — as here on Lundqvist property at Vargata, Vårdö. (Hilding Lundqvist)
Right, plate 37 The big houses of the farmer-shipowners gave employment to many local women. In the middle and early nineteenth century even the flax for sails was spun in the farmhouses. This is the kitchen of the Lundqvist home at Vargata when Åland was still part of Russia. (Hilding Lundqvist)
Below, plate 38 The shop on the Lundqvist property at Vargata which served all the families and the local vessels at fitting out in the spring. (Hilding Lundqvist)

of larger schooners and barquentines, 50 smaller schooners, 16 brigs and 25 larger Baltic galeases, as well as one full-rigged ship, in the year 1876 [2]

But by then storm-clouds were already beginning to gather on the horizons of Åland navigation. Bad years with low rates had been experienced earlier. But in the years around 1880, Åland shipping went through a major crisis. It was no longer a commercial proposition to build vessels. Tramp steamers had brought down freights for the Baltic and the North Sea as elsewhere, and the medium-sized, square-rigged wooden vessel had its work cut out in the hardening competition with the propeller and the big steel sailing ship. The ringing of hammers died away in the shipyards of Åland and East Bothnia, and the happy launching celebrations suddenly became a thing of the past. But sailing had become a necessity. The golden years had fostered a multitude of professional skippers and seamen who were dependent on the sea for their livelihood.

The crisis was overcome with a great deal of agony, and Åland shipping entered a new era, the era of secondhand tonnage which later became the era of deep-water sail. Old, cheap vessels, mostly barques, were bought from the four corners of the globe, sometimes at scrap value. They originated from the seaports of Finland, Scandinavia, England, France, and many of the largest from Nova Scotia and other parts of the eastern seaboard of North America. Among their numbers there were strong, oak-built and copper-rivetted vessels; many sailed under Åland command for decades. But there were also tragicomic hog-backed old hulks, commemorated in the saying 'God save the officers and let the men in the boat first.' Iron vessels were too expensive, as were steamers; the acquisitions were limited to wooden ships. It was not to be the turn of the iron barques until around the turn of the century.

But as explained later in this chapter, by 1914 Åland already had a significant sailing-fleet in iron and steel. The formerly common practice of vessels being manned by Åland crofters slowly but inexorably came to an end between 1880 and 1914. Shipping became commercialized and Mariehamn

1 The master also frequently retained 5 per cent of the freight money. This was known as the 'kaplake' and often represented the greater part of his income. It was this 5 per cent which built up family fortunes, built the big farmhouses, the 'skeppargårder', and encouraged the vigorous pursuit of profitable cargoes. At this time shipmasters' qualifications were governed by an 'order concerning what has to be observed in relation to the command of Finnish city — or peasant vessels. Given Helsingfors, 15 April, 1874', in the name of Tzar Alexander II. Under this order sailing vessels engaged in trade with Stockholm and northern Sweden, or to Russian ports in the Gulf of Finland, could be in charge of masters without certificates. Sailing vessels engaged in trade to ports in the Baltic Sea, the Kattegat, the North Sea and the English Channel and to ports in Great Britain and Ireland could be in charge of masters with a qualification known as 'kofferdiskeppare' roughly equivalent to that of deep-water mate. Sailing vessels sailing beyond these limits had to have a master with a full general certificate. In Britain in the late nineteenth century a distinction was made between masters qualified for fore-and-aft and those qualified for square-rig. A master with a certificate of competence to take charge of a fore-and-aft rigged vessel could command a three-masted schooner with square topsails on her foremast on an ocean voyage, but not a barquentine, with her fully square-rigged foremast in three parts. For a barquentine an 'ordinary' certificate was required. The distinction between a schooner and a barquentine therefore became important in Britain. Russian, and later Finnish, regulation and practice did not make this distinction, which was therefore of little importance, a fact which is reflected in terminology. In the Åland Islands, the same term, 'skonertskepp' was used for both barquentines and three- and four-masted schooners with square topsails, the term 'slättoppare' being used for such a vessel without square topsails. Only by examining a painting or photograph of the vessel is it possible to determine whether a skonertskepp had a fully square-rigged foremast or not.

2 Among their masters and mates were men who used the traverse board to plot their course. Still employing it in the early twentieth century they probably were the last people in Europe to use this sixteenth century navigational device. For an explanation of how it was used by Åland seamen in the present century I quote a translation of an account by Captain Karl Kåhre:

The Traverse Board was used in the nineteenth century and the beginning of this century. It is a 'memory board', with the aid of which it was possible to calculate the average course and distance sailed after a four-hour watch.

On the board are radii corresponding to the points of the compass, with eight holes per radius, making one hole per half-hour, covering a four-hour watch.

The pegs hanging by it were inserted one at a time per half-hour according to the course sailed, beginning from the centre.

When the watch was over and all the eight holes were filled, the pegs were 'connected', being brought in towards one another the same number of holes from each side until they were collected in one and the same radius, showing the average course sailed during the watch. Naturally the course could also be plotted direct on the chart, showing the result per half-hour or whole hour.

The lower part of the board consists of a distance indicator with four horizontal rows, one for each of the watch divided up into 12 peg-holes, each corresponding to as many knots in speed. With the hand log, the speed was logged once an hour, a peg being inserted into the hole of the row corresponding to the speed in knots.

Since speed in knots is equal to distance sailed per hour, at the end of the watch the four values in knots marked by the pegs were added together to give the distance sailed during the watch.

This was at a period when there were no chart-rooms on the poop-deck, charts and logbooks being kept in the captain's cabin.

At the end of the watch the Mate took the traverse board below to the Captain, whereupon the latter marked the position in the chart and ship's logbook.

Above, plate 39 The barque *Rock City* built in Quebec in 1868 hove down in the West Harbour, Mariehamn, for repairs to her bottom about 1900. It is evidently March, before the Gulf of Bothnia is free of ice. Over forty vessels used to lie in Mariehamn during the closed season, from November to April. Heaving down was effected with the aid of huge heeling blocks, making up an enormous tackle. Examples are preserved in the Ålands Sjöfartsmuseum. (Ålands Sjöfartsmuseum)

Below, plate 40 The barquentine *Wilhelmina,* built at Stavanger in 1874 and owned in Vårdö from 1907 to 1914. (Ålands Sjöfartsmuseum)

became its headquarters. Skippers became qualified sea captains. The farmer returned to his soil after a century of going to sea. Land-use was intensified and dairy farming was encouraged. Apart from the easily understandable disaffection with the new, and, as veteran seamen saw it, regressive order of things, the process was economically arduous. Between 1895 and 1905, about 2,800 emigrated from Åland, the great majority to the USA. This was more than 10 per cent of the population. According to parish records, Åland had 29,000 inhabitants in the mid 1940s, but several thousand of them were in America.

As elsewhere, navigation under sail became a matter of deep-water sailing. As early as the 1860s, the little barque *Preciosa* had taken a cargo of coal to Havana and returned with sugar. But even in the '70s, North Sea routes were still absolutely predominant, together with trade in the Baltic. A few White Sea and Mediterranean voyages, the occasional Atlantic crossing and the barque *Per Brahe*'s passage from Kronstadt to Vladivostock in 1878-9, were exceptions to the rule. But in the 1880s, the bigger secondhand -purchased vessels began winter sailings, as did many of the home-built barques.

Above, plate 41 *Roxane* was built as the barque *Pontiac* at Quebec in 1860. Rerigged as a barquentine in 1896 she was owned in Åland by Robert Mattsson and later by G Jansson of Lemland and commanded by Severus Gustafsson. She is here shown towing up the Bristol Avon under the Clifton suspension bridge. (Ålands Sjöfartsmuseum)

Summer sailings in the North Sea were combined with an Atlantic passage during the winter. The harbours in the Gulf of Mexico where pitchpine was loaded for Europe - Pensacola, Mobile, Pascagoula, Apalachicola and others - became for the sea-captains of the 1890s (especially for those sailing big Nova Scotiamen) what Grimsby, Hull and London had been for the crofter-skippers of the '70s, apart from the fact that shipbrokers, chandlers and runners seem to have been considerably more hard-boiled on the other side of the Atlantic than in Old England. One common outward cargo was timber from the Baltic to South Africa.

In his book *The Tall Ships Pass*, writing of the world at large, W L A Derby refers to the period 1870-90, as the 'glorious era' in the history of sail. Increasingly bigger sailing vessels were built and fitted out for all the world's shipping routes, whereever a cargo could be sought. The clipper's lines were preserved as far as possible, but the demand

Above, plate 42 Captain Mathias Alexanderson and the crew of the barque *Hera*, built at Bremen in 1875 and bought by Robert Mattsson of Mariehamn in 1898. (Ålands Sjöfartsmuseum)
Right, plate 43 An Åland barque, probably the *Robertsfors* built at Sikea in 1883 and owned in Lemland, Åland, by Captain Severus Gustafsson, hauled out on I L Snow's marine railway at Rockland, Maine. The schooner is the *Robert W*. (Peabody Museum of Salem)
Inset, plate 44 Captain Severus Gustafsson and his wife Sigrid with the crew of the *Robertsfors*. Captain Gustafsson later became managing owner of the vessel. (Ålands Sjöfartsmuseum)

for increased deadweight tonnage was strong and it necessitated compromises in hull construction. The main thing was to sail profitably, not to break records. Crews could be reduced thanks to the rationalisation of rigging and mechanical aids to sail-handling. Studdingsails, skysails and anything else that could be considered mere trimmings were mercilessly dispensed with. Full-riggers became increasingly rare; the barque-rig was less of a workload. The battle against the tramp steamers allowed no extravagances. When iron plating began to replace planking in the 1870s the capacity of sailing vessels became greater. During the following decades steel took over. An iron vessel weighs about three quarters the weight of a wooden vessel of the same size, and steel reduces the weight by a further 15 per cent or so. Moreover, dimensions could now be increased far beyond the maximum possible with wooden ships. In the rigging too, wood and cordage was gradually partly replaced by steel.

But even though shipbuilders and shipowners did their utmost to maintain the economic viability of the sailing vessel, it was to no avail. The world's sail-tonnage reached its peak in the 1870s but it was really another couple of decades before definitive decline and stagnation began on the high seas. The years around 1890 saw hundreds of big steel barques launched from the shipyards of the Clyde, but by the turn of the century the construction of sailing vessels was already virtually at an end. A number of large sailing vessels continued to leave the slipways of German and American yards, but they were swallows that did not make a summer. Experiments with a gigantic format were also to no avail. The five-masted full-rigger *Preussen*, built in Geestemünde in 1902, measuring 5,081 tons gross, combined deadweight with speed in an extraordinary way, broke all records in the saltpetre trade, but left no successors in her class when she ran aground off Dover in 1910. Attempts to fit auxiliary engines to ocean-going sailing vessels led nowhere. The five-masted barques *R C Rickmers*, measuring 5,548 tons gross

1 Some vessels were built in Åland, Sweden and mainland Finland in imitation of these big United States schooners. Others, like the magnificent four-master *Atlas* ex *Bertha L Downs,* built at Bath, Maine in 1908, were bought when disposed of by American owners and operated profitably from Mariehamn in the Baltic and North Sea trades.

2 This subject is examined in *The Bounty Ships of France* by Alan Villiers and Henri Picard, London 1972.

and built in Bremerhaven in 1906 at a cost of £75,000 and *France*, built in Bordeaux in 1912 and about the same size, had no success with their engines. Despite everything these proved too weak to make the vessels independent of costly towage. The installment of engines and the paying of wages to personnel increased costs too much.

At the outbreak of the First World War there was still a significant fleet of sailing vessels on the high seas, but it had no heirs in any shipyard in the world. It was no longer the property of the great maritime nations. These rapidly withdrew from the game as soon as the final decline began. A locally-centred deep-water sailing tradition with a strong predeliction for the fore-and-aft schooner rig had long been in existence on the east coast of North America.[1] The gaffsail is more easily handled than the squaresail, and more effective when sailing close to the wind. There too there were experiments with giants: *Thomas W Lawson,* built of steel in 1902 at Quincey, Massachusetts, had seven masts and measured 5,550 tons gross. In Europe it was the Scandinavians, the French, the Germans and last but not least the Ålanders who continued the traditions of deep-water sail-navigation in proud barques which the shipyards of Clydeside had once sent out on the ocean under Britain's red duster.

At the turn of the century, the French were supported their sailing-fleets with increasingly generous state subsidies. The consequences were doubtful; subsidies brought freight rates down.[2] But the large Bordeaux shipowners Bordes et Fils still had a sizeable fleet in the saltpetre trade in 1914. The German ports, Bremen and above all

Inset, plate 45 The five-masted full-rigged ship *Preussen* (National Maritime Museum)

Below, plate 46 The four-masted schooner *Bertha L Downs,* later to sail from Åland as the *Atlas,* ready for launching from the old New England Company yard at Bath, Maine, in 1908. (Maine Maritime Museum)

Below right, plate 47 The *Bertha L Downs,* later *Atlas,* almost becalmed when owned in Newhaven, Connecticut. Note the careless way in which the topsails have been left set, though they are bearing against the jump or triatic stays. Captain Karl V Karlsson, her master when she was owned in Åland, commented when he saw this photograph that Ålanders could not afford to mistreat sails in this way. (W J Lewis Parker)

Hamburg, also had large fleets in the same trade. The P-Line of Hamburg was the most renowned of the world's sailing ship lines when the First World War broke out and put an end to its glory. The five-master *Preussen* had been one of its ships. The firm had been founded in the 1870s by Ferdinand Laeisz who gradually built up his saltpetre trade from Chile until his sailings resembled regular line-traffic. Throughout the quarter century before the First War, P-vessels reckoned on completing three return trips to Chile every two years. Several of them were bought up by Gustaf Erikson between the Wars.

The process of commercialisation of shipping centred on Mariehamn, which went on in the Åland Islands between 1880 and 1914, meant that although a large part of the population of the archipelago still held shares in ships and actively participated in running them, there were now for the first time several individuals who dominated the management of the business. Among them were four who towered above the rest. Two of them were sons of two of the very first large scale operators of merchant ships in Åland, Matts Mattsson of Vårdö and Mathias Lundqvist, Snr. of Lemland.

The first of the four was Nikolai Sittkoff of Mariehamn, who began his career as a shipowner in 1870. Over the years he became the foremost person involved with shipping in Åland. He managed in all 16 vessels of which the largest was the 800 ton barque 'Svea'. His vessels included the barque 'Mariehamn' built at Dundee in 1866 which on 30 July 1882 when on passage from Malden Island, north east of Samoa, to Kastrup in Denmark under

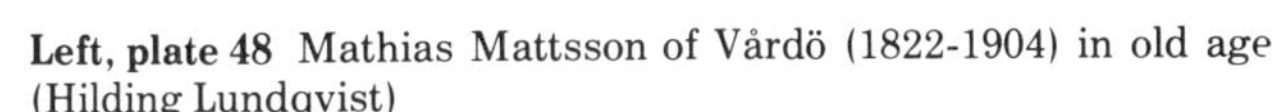

Left, plate 48 Mathias Mattsson of Vårdö (1822-1904) in old age (Hilding Lundqvist)

Above, plate 49 Matts Mattsson's house in Vargata, Vårdö, as it stands today. (Basil Greenhill)

Above right, plate 50 Mathias Lundqvist Senior (left)and Anders Nylund, both from Flaka in Lemland, photographed in Hull in the 1870s when in command of their own vessels. (Ålands Sjöfarts-museum)

Right, plate 51 The steel barque *Prompt,* built in 1887, owned by Mathias Lundqvist Jnr, under tow in the Thames in 1934. (National Maritime Museum)

Captain August Lauren from Jomala with a cargo of grain became the first Åland vessel to round Cape Horn, and the schooner 'Adéle', later the first vessel to be commanded by the young Gustaf Erikson.

When Nikolai Sittkoff died at the early age of 59 in 1887, Robert Mattsson [1851-1935] assumed his role as the biggest Åland shipowner. Behind him, at the beginnings of large scale capital generation in Åland shipping, is the somewhat mysterious figure of his father, Matts Mattsson of Vårdö, known as 'Varg Matti', 'Wolf Mattsson' [born in Vargata, Vårdö in 1822, died 1904]. It is said that he was employed as a provision master at the great Russian fort at Bomarsund on the part of the mainland of

Åland nearest to the principal island of Vårdö and that after the fall of the fort to the combined British and French Baltic Fleets during the Crimean War he suddenly became rich and began investing heavily in shipping. Certainly he built a very fine house in the Imperial Russian style which was partly a residence, partly a ship chandlery and store. It still stands, little changed, in the possession of one of his descendants. His barque the 'Olga' has a special place in the history of Åland. Built in Prästö, opposite Bomarsund in 1874, she was owned in Vårdö from her launch until 1920 when she was sold to Norwegian owners. She was commanded in turn by Robert Mattson, Matts' son, and by his two sons-in-law, August Troberg and Mathias Lundqvist Junior [1853-1926]. Robert Mattsson moved to Mariehamn from Vårdö and between 1883 and the First World War, when he transferred his business to Helsingfors, he owned or was the principal owner of 31 vessels, including 11 large iron and steel sailing ships. One of his two brothers-in-law, August Troberg of Mariehamn, managed a fleet almost as large as Mattsson's. He sold his vessels during the First World War. Among his donations to his town is the church of Mariehamn

The other son-in-law of Wolf Mattsson, Mathias Lundqvist Junior represented the old maritime traditions of Åland to a greater extend than did the others. His father, Mathias Lundqvist Snr, [1829-1897] had been one of the foremost

skippers and shipowners of Lemland in the old days of the farmer/skippers. Like Varg Matti himself he represented the earliest days of large scale capital generation in shipping in the era before the rise of Mariehamn. Although like Troberg, and in due course Gustaf Erikson and his son Edgar, Mathias Lundqvist Junior received the title of 'Sjöfartsråd', Maritime Counsellor [an esteemed honorific, conferred by the Government], he remained at his home in Vårdö [to which parish he had moved from Lemland] working as a farmer/shipowner in the style of the flourishing days of the '60s and '70s. Amongst his vessels were the four-masted barque 'Frieda', the full-rigged ships 'Pera' and 'Parchim' and the barque 'Prompt'. His son Hugo, 1878-1936, moved to Mariehamn and added the British-built four-masted barquentine 'Mozart', the barque 'Plus' and the four-masted barque 'Ponape' to the fleet. Arthur Lundqvist, 1877-1942 [another son] owned the wooden barque 'Sigyn', now lying in Åbo preserved as the last survivor of her type in the world, and the barque 'Sverre', built as the steamer 'Aalto' in 1872 at Nystad in mainland Finland and not lost until 1941. She was the last composite three-masted square-rigged sailing vessel at sea.

Hugo Lundqvist gradually disposed of the

Left, plate 52 The iron barque *Plus*, built in Hamburg in 1885 lying in Rochester in 1927. She was tragically lost with most of her crew in the entrance to Mariehamn in December 1933, when homeward bound from Lourenco Marques. (National Maritime Museum)

Below, plate 53 The patriarchal farmer-shipowner-shipmaster and his family in the snow. From left to right, Arthur Lundqvist (*Sverre, Sigyn*, Master of *Parchim*) Bertrel and his wife Jenny and in front of her Mrs Mathias Lundqvist, Mathias Lundqvist Junior in the centre, by his left shoulder Jacob (master of *Pera*) and his wife Ann and son Sven, then Hugo (*Prompt, Ponape*, and *Mozart*) and his wife Anni. The other three women have not been identified. (Hilding Lundqvist)

sailing ships and in 1927 founded the joint stock company which became the first Åland shipping company to change over successfully to powered vessels. Gustaf Erikson was associated with the Lundqvist business in several ways and was involved with their early steamship investments. In the 1990's the Lundqvist family is still deeply involved in large scale shipping operations.

In 1914 the shipowners of Åland, foremost among them Robert Mattsson and August Troberg and Mathias Lundqvist Jnr, who owned four-fifths of the fleet between them, possessed 27 iron and steel sailing ships whose combined tonnage was close to 45,000 tons net.

3-Master Iron Barques
Montrosa, Borrowdale, Hermes, Asia, Isabel Browne, Axel, Sivah, Vidylia

3-Masted Steel Barques
Prompt, Professor Koch, August

Steel Full-Riggers
Pera, Parchim

Iron Full-Riggers
Endymion, Thomasina, Tasmania, Imberhorne

4-Masted Iron Barques
Dundee, Mariechen, Lucipara, Marlborough Hill, Frieda, Åland

4-Masted Steel Barques
Margareta, Garnet Hill, Lawhill, Lynton

The chaotic economic conditions during and after the First War gave deep-water sailing vessels their last opportunity to make their owners happy with good dividends. Many were sunk. Then followed the large scale and world-wide demise of sailing tonnage. The only major prospective buyer was to be Gustaf Erikson. His fleet became the last true fleet of ocean-going sailing vessels afloat.

1 These paragraphs in *italics* do not appear in the original text of *Under Gustaf Erikson's Flag*. In order to complete the story of Åland's seafaring tradition for a wider readership they have been condensed from passages in Georg Kåhre's general history of the Åland shipping industry under sail *Den Åländska Segelsjöfartens Historia* and from notes of the Editor's discussions with descendants of the people concerned.

CHAPTER 2

To Sea

On 21 October 1872, a boy child was born on Hansa's farmstead in the township of Hellestorp in Lemland, and was baptised with the name Gustaf Adolf Mauritz, Gustaf's son.[1] This boy was to live for 75 years, a mere handful of years in the long history of sail, but eventful years, magnificent and tragic; the flowering and decline of the thousand-year-old commercial sailing tradition within the narrow boundaries of one human life.

In 1872 the world's sailing-fleet was greater than it had ever been. The zenith would be reached a couple of years later. Iron had begun to replace wood as the building material. *Mermerus,* later known as a fast ship in the Åland fleet, left the stocks and made her maiden voyage for the famous Golden Fleece Line. Forests of square-rigged masts towered against the murky smoke-filled skies of the great seaports, a hundred sails could be seen at one time in the busiest shipping lanes, and the lonely father of the west winds had his faithful clients. There was no shortage of grounds for anxiety. The Suez Canal had been opened, and steam-driven tonnage had recently been growing at a considerably faster rate than sail tonnage. There were prophets of doom to be found, but also optimists who believed sail to be unconquerable, at least on deep-water.

At home in Åland townships, the mood was one of unclouded optimism. Between 1871 and 1875 the crofters built 11 barques, 12 large schooners and barquentines, 4 smaller schooners and galeases on Åland slipways, and 7 barques, 10 large schooners and barquentines, 12 schooners and galeases and a brig in East Bothnian yards. The newly-built barques had an average tonnage of 425 tons net, and the larger schooners and barquentines, 270 tons net.

The fleet sailed at full capacity. About 150 cargoes of timber, a total of 22,000 standards, were carried to Britain in 1872, 120 from Swedish ports, 30 from Finnish. 60 or so cargoes of coal for German, Danish or Swedish destinations were taken in return. A further 130 shiploads of timber, totalling over 11,000 standards, were taken to Baltic ports in Denmark and Germany. Five vessels sailed on the White Sea, the barque *Ulrika* made a Mediterranean trip and the full-rigged ship *Harmoni* crossed the Atlantic. Hull, Skellefteå, Lübeck, Gävle, Copenhagen, Piteå, Grimsby, Kiel and Sundsvall were, in that order, the most frequently visited ports that year. About 60 Åland barques, brigs and schooners, big and small, discharged timber at Hull during the course of the summer and autumn. According to the shipowners' annual reports to the Crown Commissioners, the year's net yield came to half a million marks.

The year was good but it had its dark side — the loss of ships. The Jomala barque *Maria,* one of the North Sea pioneers of 1858, was wrecked off Ystad. The *Jenny Lind,* Saltvikarna's finest barque, built in 1869 at Karvik in the home parish, ran aground on the Goodwin Sands on 13 December 'as a result of storm, Scotch mist and current'. Six men died. The remainder were saved after spending 15 hours in the mizzen top. The Eckerö barque *Dagmar,* newly built and the fourth biggest of the Åland barques, went down in the North Sea, and one of Lemland's largest barques, *Eugenia,* ran aground on Gottland on 12 December, on her way home from Grimsby in ballast.

Since Lemland's fleet was manned by about 340 seamen, and since there were in the parish, with its 1600 inhabitants, about '350 persons, male,

1 Above the word 'Gustafsson' in the Parish Record is written in faded pencil the word 'Eriksson'. Gustaf Erikson signed himself Gustaf Adolf Mauritz Eriksson for many years. The assumption is that the clergyman in the old-fashioned way named him after his father, Gustafsson.

Above, plate 54 Hansa's farmstead in 1976. The buildings have been almost completely changed since Gustaf Erikson's day but the great barn retains some of its old atmosphere. (Basil Greenhill)

between the ages of 15 and 50, it is clear that if seamen from elsewhere were not resorted to sometimes, we would have 10 men at our disposal to work the land, apart from old men, women and children', so it says in a letter written by a Lemlander in May 1874. Seamen, skippers and shipowners were to be found in every township. Gustaf Adolf Erikson, master of Hansa's homestead in Hellestorp, was a partner in the ownership of several vessels, and over the years skipper of the barques *Amalia* and *Ljuba* and the schooners *Ax* and *Adéle*. He is described as a strict and order-loving father of the house. That strictness was a useful quality where Gustaf and his younger brother Axel were concerned and was something which they themselves were in hearty agreement upon as mature men. As a boy, Gustaf Erikson was a wild lad who, in the words he used himself at our last meeting, never climbed over fences like a human being, but leapt over them like a dog. His father taught him manners and orderliness, and saw to it that he became *folk av honom,* — 'people of his', as they say in Åland, teaching him never to mollycoddle his hands with gloves. His mother was an industrious lady of the house who looked after both farming and shipping matters when necessary, when the master of Hansa's farm was away at sea.

Hellestorp harbour and Söderby Sjö, further into the same Lemland inlet, were among the most popular winter quarters for Åland ships. The guests arrived in late autumn, a barque or two, two or three large schooners or barquentines, a brig perhaps, and a few smaller schooners. On rare occasions, some storm-lashed North Sea vessel might not appear until the bells were ringing in the New Year. For those at home, the late autumn was a time of waiting. No one knew how the winds were blowing in the North Sea and off the Skaw, in the Kattegat, and on the Baltic. Every cold spell awakened misgivings. The old interpreted the signs and fancied they could remember autumns when the bays and inlets froze in November.

Freeze-up closed the anchorage. If an expected guest failed to turn up, there was nothing for it but to wait and see. Mariehamn did not have telegraphic connection with the rest of the world until 1876, and the post was slow. It could happen that the missing vessel lay ice-bound in some safe harbour, perhaps in ballast, perhaps with a cargo of coal for Stockholm or Kronstadt in her hold; but it could also happen that she had joined the ranks of those which never returned.

Economically, it meant a great deal to part-owners if their vessel fulfilled her itinerary and managed to make it home for the winter. There, according to well-established custom, she would be provisioned the following spring, and the majority of her crew had their homes in the townships nearby. There were others, too, who appreciated the sight of the vessels lying in the frozen inlets, the lads of the local townships who paid their respects on sleds and homemade skates. They would be going to sea themselves after confirmation, if not before. The tarred hulls, bleached by North Sea swells and chafed by quays in foreign ports, the fo'c'sles with their rank, left-over smells, the rigging, with its magically ringing names for spars and tackle, were all enchantingly representative of the great wide world, waiting to be seen and experienced.

On 16 November 1882, *Neptun*, a barque of 422 tons net, anchored in Söderby harbour. *Neptun* had been built in Vasa in 1862, and had been purchased a few months earlier by A J Eriksson in Söderby, and his shipowning partners. Under the command of K J Eriksson, she had made one passage from Uleåborg to London with timber, when she was bedded down in her first Åland winter quarters.

When *Neptun* weighed anchor the following spring, fitted out, provisioned and manned for the summer and autumn's sailing in the North Sea, a cheerful and, according to what is told, pretty self-assured ten-year-old waved goodbye to the womenfolk on the home shore. The future shipping magnate began his nautical career as a cabin boy. His duties on board were to look after the skipper and to help the cook. In addition to this, he had a more unusual obligation: to read Biblical history. K J Eriksson was an implacable commander, not least in the matter of religious instruction. Every day had its lesson; if the cabin boy was negligent, the punishing hand was never far away.

After spending the year 1884 at home, the cabin boy was promoted. He sailed as cook in *Neptun* in 1885 and 1886 and during the following years, as seaman, boatswain and steward in *Adéle*, a 'skonertskepp' of 225 tons net built in Sideby in 1878,[1] *Ansgar*, a barque of 393 tons built in Germany in 1849 and purchased into Lemland in 1889, *Fennia*, a schooner of 249 tons built in Sideby in 1874 for the Lemlanders, and the barque *Southern Belle* built at Church Point, Digby, Nova Scotia, in 1871. All these sailed with timber to ports in Germany, Denmark, Britain or France, and came home for the winter whenever possible.

In 1893, Gustaf Erikson, at the age of 20, took command of the 'skonertskepp' *Adéle*. Since he lacked the formal qualifications for command, he sailed with a flag captain.[2] *Adéle* had been built 15 years earlier for Nikolai Sittkoff, young Mariehamn's first major shipowner. When he died in 1887 his fleet was sold and *Adéle* was bought for Lemland.

The young skipper's 'sailings' accounts book' still survives. It was the first of a long life's shipping accounts, kept first on shipboard and later at home in Mariehamn. Seeing that the sequel was so brilliant, I am quoting the first two pages — not because the content is in any way remarkable. It is, on the contrary, mundane and typical of the time.

Örnskôldsvik No 1
June 1893

DEBIT		
Towage in from sea	Kr 16.70	
Discharge of ballast	19.00	
Ship chandler's account	83.42	
Ship broker's account	194.02	
Galley firewood and sundry hardware	38.25	
Towage to sail	8.00	
Outgoing pilot's dues	21.30	
1 Hold man, 2⅓ days @ 2	4.50	
Dr Wallmark	5.15	
1 water cask & 2 lamps	5.50	
Journeys to Örnsköldsvik	3.25	
3 churns milk	0.60	
Brandy for Drogden	4.75	
Petty cash on board	40.00	444.44
To the crew according to portage bill		82.90
Balance to me for cargo		40.91
		568.25
CREDIT		
Received advance on freight		568.25

Morlaix No 2
July 1893

DEBIT		
Ship broker's account	Francs 901.30	
Ship chandler's account	161.75	
Ditto	83.15	
Painter's account	49.70	
Meat	10.00	
Vegetables & potatoes	16.70	
Bread	6.25	
Ironmongery & sundry hardware	15.20	
Steering chain and rudder chock	23.90	
Coffee grinder, mugs, tea	5.90	
A mirror and a ceiling lamp	13.70	
Chairs, paintbrushes	5.50	
1 ballast trimmer	3.00	1,296.05
To the crew according to portage bill		106.75
Remittance to Axel Erikson		3,000.00
Me for cargo		12.55
		4,415 35
CREDIT		
Received freight for 125,765 stands		
Full freight @ Fr 42.00 per stand		5,282.20
Advance on freight	811.00	
2% Assurance Deruti	16.20	
1½ % discount	39.65	866.85
		4,415.35

The ship brokers' accounts, which included incoming and outgoing clearance, harbour dues and other unavoidable expenses, represented the major items of expenditure. It paid to keep ship chandlers' accounts buttoned up. It was traditional that a little business would be transacted at sea while passing through Drogden (a channel off Copenhagen). The remittance home did not constitute any net profit. The principal shipowner paid for the spring provisioning on behalf of the joint-owners; likewise the 'keel money' which was levied when necessary during the winter for the vessel's fitting out and repairs at home. Part of a skipper's salary, the commission, was generally kept back until the statement of accounts for the year's sailing.

Adéle made two voyages to Morlaix with freight; the second became lengthy with severe gales and headwinds in the Channel. On account of this she was late returning home and in December she was obliged to put into Karlshamn to sit out the winter. The following year she made two trips, from Sundsvall to St Servan, and from Hörnefors to Apenrade. On 3 October 1894, Gustaf Erikson signed his last account as skipper of the vessel.

Two years of his own command had had the attraction of novelty for the twenty-year-old. But in one respect his experiences were scarcely encouraging. Sailing on the North Sea and the Baltic in small, elderly sailing vessels had no future. [3] Tramp steamers had pushed freight-rates down to a level at which sailing vessels were only viable if they could sail with good luck and no setbacks. There was no margin for any extra expenses. Vessels had to sail uninsured. The Åland Maritime Insurance Association, which had flourished during the 1870s, ceased to exist in 1887. The 1890s had begun with an improvement in the freight market; three new barques had even been built in Åland. But in the middle of the decade lathwood freights to England sank as low as 28 Shillings a cord, while pit-props fell to 22/-, considerably less than half the rates of the 1870s.

But on deep-water there were still routes remaining for bigger square-rigged vessels. It was there that the future lay, but only for those with a master's ticket in their pockets. A programme was planned: schooling and practical experience on deep-water sailing vessels. Gustaf Erikson took his master's certificate at the navigation school in Vasa, then named Nicolaistad, a coast town in western Finland, in the spring of 1900, the intervening time between periods of study being spent gaining practical experience on the barques *Mathilda* (ex *Hercules*), *Finland* and *Mariehamn*, all measuring about 500 tons net and principally engaged in carrying pitchpine to Europe from the Gulf ports. Among others, he had as his skippers Captain Lindström, an Ålander whc later became a ship-

1 *Adéle* is almost the only vessel closely connected with Gustaf Erikson of which neither a painting nor a photograph has been found. It is not possible, therefore, to say whether she was a schooner or a barquentine.

2 The qualifications required of masters under Russian law for different kinds of sailing have already been explained (Note 1, Page 41). When the man appointed by the owners as master did not have the requisite paper qualifications he was covered by a qualified master who actually served in a subordinate capacity but appeared on the vessel's papers as master and signed as master. The same practices were adopted in British vessels in similar circumstances, see, for example *The Last Log of the Schooner 'Isabella'*, National Maritime Museum Monograph No 24, 1976.

3 Or rather, more precisely, seemed to have no future at that time for an ambitious young master anxious to build up capital. The trade itself was to continue in wooden sailing vessels until 1939 and to pass through spells of prosperity when new ships were built for it. Gustaf Erikson himself was later to be a major owner of Baltic and North Sea sailing vessels and to do very well out of the trade, even in the 1930s. These vessels were an essential complement to his larger steel world trading vessels and masters and mates moved between the two different types of tonnage. Throughout this book the word 'splitved' is used in the Swedish text to describe the wood carried by the Åland sailing ships. This word has been translated uniformly as 'lathwood'. In fact, however, a number of different classes of timber were carried, lathwood proper, staves, battens, cargoes of big timber of various kinds. The word 'splitved' should properly be applied to timber off-cuts from the mills on the Swedish coast of the Gulf of Bothnia loaded at places like Sundsvall, Uleåborg, Luleå and Skellefteå. Captain Karl V Karlsson of Vårdö, master of a number of vessels in this trade, including the barquentine *Nils*, the American-built four-masted schooner *Atlas* ex *Bertha L Downs* and the Erikson four-masted fore-and-aft schooner *Odine*, and later of the four-masted barque *Parma* in the Australian trade, in 1977 described the splitved trade proper to me in the following terms:

"So called splitved was of 1'6" to 6' in length, boards and battens, mostly pine, used in Britain for several purposes, the best for furniture making, which we called Swedish mahogany; poor stuff was sold for firewood. In-between qualities were used for making fish crates, boxes, etc. Up to forty women used to come on board to stow the cargo, with the crew of the 'Atlas' working the winches from her primitive American oil donkey engine but never touching the cargo. Stowing was very difficult because the timber came alongside unsorted in lighters. Nevertheless the women sorted it and stowed it very quickly."

Mr Viktor Anderson of Föglö, who also served in vessels in the trade, remembered cargoes which were used for making the wooden blocks with which the roads of the dock areas of many British ports used to be paved when most of the heavy cartage was done by horses.

Many splitved cargoes came into Regent's Canal Dock in London. According to Captain Karlsson a principal importer into Britain was the firm of Ronaasen and Son, which was of Norwegian origin.

broker in West Hartlepool, and Gustaf Lundberg, a well-known veteran in his time, who saw to it personally that no time was wasted in idleness on shipboard, either at sea or in port.

In *Finland,* Gustaf Erikson's sea-going career nearly came to an abrupt end. He fell from the foretop in Pensacola while carrying out repair work on rigging which had been damaged in a storm on the trip to the Gulf. Lying on the deck with a broken thigh, the first thing he did was to order up a few buckets of water to refresh himself with after the shock of his trip through the air (possibly remembering the wonderfully warming and health-giving wet compresses his mother had given him in his youth). Then he gave the order to rig up a tackle from the mainyard-arm, with which he was lowered ashore.

After six weeks in hospital, the local horse-doctor declared that he was recovered, regulations prohibited anyone from staying in hospital any longer; it was of no importance that the leg was unusable. After a further spell in Pensacola, he managed to get himself signed on as mate of *Mariehamn,* with a crutch under each arm — a singularly unsuitable outfit for the mate of a barque carrying a deck-cargo of pitchpine. The leg continued to trouble him after he returned home. Finally he visited a junior doctor in Finström, and when he next went home, he 'left his crutches behind him', as he once related.

At the end of August 1900, Gustaf Erikson went, with seven men, to Stockholm, where the barque *Southern Belle* lay, awaiting a skipper. The vessel, popularly known as *'Sjutton Pelle'* (literally 'Seventeen Pelle', Pelle being a boy's name and 'sjutton!' being a common, mild expletive), was built in Nova Scotia in 1871, measured 462 tons net, and joined the Åland fleet in 1891. As her steward, her new skipper had learned to know and respect her. In her younger years she had carried freight on the Atlantic. Now she had been reduced to a North Sea trader, but she could sail and she was strongly built. She was to survive the Great War.

During the years 1900-1905, *Southern Belle* made the following passages:

1900 Kemi/London. 29 days, 8 Oct — 6 Nov.
London/Mariehamn, in ballast. 11 days. Passed Copenhagen on 16 Dec.

1901 Sundsvall/Southampton. 28 days, 3 June — 1 July.

Left, plate 55 The barque *Southern Belle* in her old age, badly hogged. Note the windmill pump with sails set. It was in this vessel that Gustaf Erikson really began his career as a shipmaster and by purchasing one eighth of the shares in her he also began his shipowning career. (Ålands Sjöfartsmuseum)

Southampton/Uleåborg in ballast. 18 days, 20 July — 7 Aug.
Uleåborg/Hull. 14 days. 26 Aug — 9 Sept. Passed Copenhagen 4 Sept.
Hull/Söderhamn. 32 days. 5 Oct — 6 Nov. With coal.
1902 Söderhamn/London. 24 days, 3 June — 27 June
London/Uleåborg in ballast, 26 days, 16 July — 11 Aug.
Left Uleåborg on 29 Aug, entered Mariehamn leaking on 6 Sept.
Cargo of timber discharged. Vessel repaired winter 1903.
1903 Hudiksvall/Newport, Mon. 22 days, 31 May — 22 June.
Swansea/Gävle with coal. 16 days, 26 July — 11 Aug.
Gävle/Londonderry. 22 days, 15 Sept — 7 Oct.
Londonderry/Mariehamn in ballast. 12 days, 27 Oct — 8 Nov. Passed Copenhagen on 5 Nov.
1904 Hernösand/Cardiff. 27 days, 3 June — 30 June
Swansea/Luleå with coal. 24 days, 26 July — 19 Aug
Luleå/Hull. 33 days, 22 Sept — 25 Oct.
Hull/Stockholm with coke. 6 days, 17 Nov — 23 Nov. Copenhagen 21 Nov.
1905 Gävle/Newport. 33 days, 30 May — 2 July.
Swansea/Luleå with coal. 23 days, 27 July — 19 Aug
Båtskärnäs/Whitehaven. 23 Sept —?

The passage from Hull to Stockholm in six days was a fine achievement. The main topgallant rigging was lost in the North Sea with the upper topsail yard.

The skipper's wages on *Southern Belle* were paid partly in the form of a 5 per cent commission on the gross freight, partly in a monthly salary. In 1904 the commission on a cargo of floorings and pit-props, together with one cargo of coal and one of coke, amounted to £47 and a few shillings, about 1,200 Finnish Marks, added to which there was 50 Marks in monthly salary, that is 353Mk 32p from 2 May to 4 December — about 1,550 Marks in total.[1]

Gustaf Erikson's position in *Southern Belle* left nothing to be desired in the way of freedom and independence. He made his own negotiations concerning charters and chose his own brokers. But deep-water was beckoning with its greater opportunities for earnings and experience. Besides, he now had an important personal reason to consider his future and to look to wider waters; he had become engaged to sixteen-year-old Hilda Bergman, one of the daughters on Södergård's farmstead on the island of Bergö in Finström parish.[2]

But before we follow him any further in his travels, *Southern Belle* deserves a few lines. Gustaf Erikson was succeeded as skipper by his brother Axel, who commanded the vessel for many years. Gustaf became one of the vessel's joint owners, initially with 5/40th parts and later with the major part.[3] He became her ship's husband[4] in 1917. In the spring of 1919, Captain Axmar Erikson took over the command and went to Lovisa, where she had been laid-up since 1914, to get her ready for new sailings. It seems, judging by his correspondence, that Gustaf Erikson was glad to have a vessel close to home on which to spend his excess energies. His letters to Lovisa deal with a thousand things: tarring, caulking, the drawing up of inventories, replacement spars and replacement crewmen, the discharging of ballast, trimming, towage, instructions to the cook concerning the preparation of yeast from potatoes, hops and sugar, the delivery of half a ton of herrings and 50 kilograms of peas from Mariehamn, and so on. A certain fondness for *Southern Belle* comes through. He and his brother had sailed her for many years, and their father had been involved in the purchase of the vessel 28 years earlier. But now she was nearly 50 years old and she was suffering the aches and pains of old age. Her leaks worsened after grounding while being towed to Mariehamn from Strömfors, where she had taken on a cargo of timber for Denmark. This was discharged in Alborg. After an examination by divers, it was established that there was no point in thinking of docking and repairs. *Southern Belle* sailed home and was sold to Granboda shipyard, where the new barque *Carmen,* later to be owned by Gustaf Erikson, inherited part of her rigging.

On an autumn day in 1905, the full-rigged ship *Albania* dropped anchor in Mariehamn roads

1 About £60 and his keep and some perquisites for seven months' work. This was not an unreasonable sum for a farmer-seaman at the time, but not the way to found a fortune.

2 The couple had met in Mariehamn where Hilda Bergman had come to study to prepare for confirmation.

3 This investment in this traditional wooden three-masted square-rigged sailing vessel thus began Gustaf Erikson's shipowning career.

4 That is, the vessel's manager and (usually) biggest shareholder.

after a splendid 48 hour passage from Copenhagen. Captain Petter Troberg gave up the command. When she sailed the following spring, in ballast to West Bay, Bay of Fundy, Gustaf Erikson stood on her poop as skipper. The first mate was Kalle Karlson from Vårdö, known to his friends as *Runda Kalle* (chubby Kalle), and the second mate was Conrad Palmer from Eckerö, later a teacher at Åland's nautical training school. Both were still with the vessel to the end of her career in Rio in 1908.

Albania was visiting her home waters. She had been built in St John, New Brunswick, in 1884 and had joined Mariehamn's fleet in 1903. She measured 1,428 tons net and was Finland's biggest wooden sailing vessel before *Avonia*, which was bought for Mariehamn in 1907. Otto Tamelander was her ship's husband. Earlier in the spring, Gustaf Erikson had bought a 1/10th share in the vessel for 6,540 Finnish Marks.[1]

The passage to West Bay went well in 44 days. On the way out they put into Copenhagen to settle a number of business matters with Schierbecks, the Ålanders' general factotum on Öresund. A cargo of timber was taken on in West Bay: 338 standards whitewood at 37/-, 227 standards birch planks at 38/- and 30 standards stowage at 25/-. The birchwood in particular was difficult to load on account of its varied dimensions. Of the freight, which amounted to £1,191, £175 was collected in advance. The skipper's £47 commission corresponded to about 1,200 Finnish Marks. The vessel was uninsured, though the freight and liabilities for earlier fitting-out were covered. The Bay of Fundy was not exactly a quiet anchorage for *Albania.* Twice she found herself 'drifting before gales and tides' as Gustaf Erikson said in a letter to Tamelander.

On 16 July, *Albania* was towed to sea, at a cost of 70 Dollars. After a fine passage of 27 days, she put into Swansea on 12 August.

Here there were busy days for her skipper. The owners, who had no charter ready, immediately received a cabled exhortation to make haste, echoed in a lengthy letter. *Albania* was in a difficult position, it said; she needed sizeable cargoes but her draught (24½ feet heavily laden) was a hindrance. It was too late in the year for another load of timber from Canada, and it would not pay to go to the Baltic for timber. The only alternative seemed to be to take coal to Port Nolloth or, preferably Pernambuco, and to sail from there to the Gulf for pitchpine — the water at Mobile was deep enough. A subsequent letter expressed a strong discontent that a Pernambuco cargo had been lost through delay; the skipper should have been fully empowered by the owners to arrange charters himself. He was better able to walk the tightrope between ship brokers competing for freighting commissions. Two London firms were involved in this case: H Clarkson & Co, and Andorsen & Becker, as well as Broderson & Vaughan in Liverpool, who had arranged the charter from West Bay. Clarksons are mentioned many times in this context, and this firm later became the preferred brokers among major foreign shipowners. Gustaf Erikson put a high value on his friendship with one of its directors, the East Bothnian M Ingman.[2]

Albania had an old debt of £400 to Andorsen & Becker, probably for fitting-out. Immediately after arriving in Swansea, there was a diplomatic exchange of notes with this firm, who wanted payment. A letter of 20 August reads: 'I find to my great astonishment that you bid me welcome by threatening to take steps to clear up the vessel's debt. However, take it easy, it is always best. I should almost have expected a firm such as Andorsen & Becker to proceed with more sense and consideration, especially as they are represented by a countryman of mine'. The debt was paid when the freight from West Bay was drawn, with the exception of £22 which the owners refused to approve. In September, when *Albania* was already under charter for Port Nolloth through Clarksons, Andorsen and Becker indicated that they might eventually consider writing off the disputed sum, if the next charter was arranged through them. Gustaf Erikson objected. 'I will not agree to such conditions' he wrote to Mariehamn on 28 September,

Right, plate 56 The barque *Carmen,* launched at Granboda, Lemland, in 1921. Her masts and spars came from the condemned *Southern Belle* and it was their availability which determined that *Carmen* should be a barque rather than a schooner. Note the old fashioned rigging with deadeyes and lanyards even to the topgallants shrouds. (National Maritime Museum)

Inset, plate 57 The *Albania* Gustaf Erikson's first deep water command. Note the unusual fidded fore and main royal masts. (Ålands Sjöfartsmuseum)

1 About £260 which must have represented quite a large part of his total resources at the time.

2 The firm of H Clarkson and Company, London, is now, at the time of publication, more than 125 years old. Intimately linked with the development of Åland shipping, both Edgar Erikson and Hilding Kåhre of the Erikson office served as 'Foreign Clerks' that is, as trainees, in the London office, as did also Fraenk Lundqvist, now Head of the Lundqvist Rederierna. Today the firm, considerably larger than at the period covered by this book, specialises in insurance of all kinds and in this field has maintained its close links with Åland.

Above, plate 58 Gustaf Erikson at his desk in *Albania,* note the fiddle on the table. Canadian-built, she had a very high standard of accommodation aft. (Ålands Sjöfartsmuseum)

and in a letter to Andorsen & Becker dated the same day: 'If the owners are able to pay the major proportion, they are, no doubt, also capable of paying the other, and would do so if it were right and proper. However, it seems to me that in order to avoid making matters any worse, Messrs A B should not harass the owners any further, but should let the whole matter drop and make peace so that everything can be well again and new business may again be conducted with the owners in the future'.

As a skipper the future shipowner carried on a lively and often strongly-spiced correspondence with ship chandlers and brokers. He seems to have derived a deep and unclouded satisfaction from being able to play competing firms against one another, and when, on one occasion as captain of *Lochee,* he saluted free enterprise in a letter, his enthusiasm was intense and sincere.

After unloading, *Albania* went into dry-dock for copper sheathing. After appropriate negotiations, the copper plates (2,850 standards) were supplied by the Hamburg firm of Ernst Levers, who also bought the old copper. The weather was fine while she was in dry-dock, 'it was worth a hundred pounds', not a single raindrop fell. The recoppering was the last item in the Bureau Veritas classification begun in Mariehamn. 'A pity we do not have the means to keep the vessel insured, now she is so fine', he says in a letter to Tamelander.

It has been mentioned that *Albania* was chartered to Port Nolloth in South Africa. The freight went up to £1,461 for 615 tons coal at 13/- and 1,179 tons coke at 18/-. Half was paid in advance. The copper suppliers in Hamburg received a six month draught for 8,122.20 Reichsmarks (about £400) and the dry-dock was paid in cash with about £250. Fitting out was done by ship chandler Charles H Huss in Cardiff, whose bill for £424 was payable after one year reckoned from 18 October, when *Albania* was ready for sea.

It is difficult to assess the results of the freight from West Bay. The old debt to Andorsen & Becker was settled and the dry-docking paid for. The copper was bought on credit but the new sheathing was an asset which would last for several years to come. The fitting-out would take care of two, perhaps three, freight trips outside Europe. Most of the advance on the freight to South Africa was used for the settlement of debts. Schierbecks were sent £141, a firm in Mariehamn received £180 and so on. The ship's husband had to make do with £144 for expenses at home. Clarksons retained £125 on their own behalf for chartering and consignment commissions, including a £4 premium for harbour risk insurance at Port Nolloth, where the anchorage had a rather bad reputation.

In Swansea, Gustaf Erikson was given the authority he had wanted to negotiate his own charters, and a couple of days before sailing he could report that the next freight was ready. 'As *Albania* is difficult to place and freights are not on the increase, I accepted charter yesterday through Clarksons for Mobile or Ship Island free of $2 clause to Port Natal for orders at 100/-, or if ordered Delgoa Bay, 102/6d, per standard.'

Albania's skipper seems to have had his hands full in Swansea; but he was well satisfied with his work and in Swansea he had a special reason to be content with his life. Immediately upon his arrival he had written to his fiancée and asked her to come to Britain. When he sailed, he had a young and beautiful wife at his side.

It was not an idyllic pleasure cruise with sweet honeymoon breezes. One gets the impression the mood of the ocean must have seemed somewhat surly to the captain's wife on shipboard. *Albania* confirmed the doubtful reputation of ageing Canadian-built vessels; she was sea-soft and thought badly of coal cargoes. A letter to her ship's husband remarks that it was impossible to keep her gunwale seams watertight. The 'windmill pump' or mylla (also called the pumpmill or windpump) was going every watch.[1]

The roads at Port Nolloth lived up to their own notoriety too. 'An anchor stock and a considerable length of cable have been lost' as a result of the constant heavy lurching caused by the endless rolling swell. At times they were hit by 'severe gales, when we had to stand ready, expecting the cables and windlass to give way at any moment, with the risk of being driven onto submerged reefs where a certain death would have awaited us', Ingman, Gustaf Erikson's friend at Clarksons, read in a letter of 31 January.

Unloading went slowly. It was a laborious business, since it meant discharging into lighters in the open roads, and since the company receiving the cargo refused to discharge more than the 40 tons per day stipulated in the charter party. However, it proved possible to double the quantity by using two gangs.

Expenses at Port Nolloth were small. The rigging was in need of minor repairs, but these could wait until Mobile. More than half of the sum remaining from the freight could be used to settle Levers' account in Hamburg. £250 went on the crew's wages, ship chandlers' accounts and ballast. Port Nolloth was not a gay harbour, especially not for a young captain's wife who hardly found it alluring to be rowed into a port without friends or amusements, and who therefore chose to stay on board. Social life of any sort was extremely scarce. 'No vessel for three weeks,' Gustaf Erikson wrote to Ingman on 25 February as the unloading entered its final stages, 'no company except for *Shetfield*, a steamer under timecharter.' In the same letter he asked for credit of at least £800 to be forwarded to Mobile for provisioning, an anchor stock, spars for a new main topmast and mainyard, and other things.

1 The windmill pump (the name is self-explanatory) was a feature of the larger Russian, Finnish and Scandinavian wooden sailing vessels. It was the effective device for dealing with the perpetual leaking of elderly wooden ships (and some new ones). Although it was a British invention and the ironwork was sometimes marked as British made, dependence on a windmill pump does not appear to have been countenanced in the administration of the British Merchant Shipping Acts (though dependence on very frequent manual pumping was). As far as is known the device was not widely used in United States vessels, though in the late nineteenth and early twentieth centuries the steam pump was absolutely essential to the operation of some of the big schooners. The wooden barque *Sigyn*, preserved at Åbo, is equipped with an excellent example of the windmill pump. All old wooden vessels leaked. The more cheaply they had been built and the harder they had been worked the sooner they leaked more. Captain Gerhard Sjögren, Honorary President of the Åland Cape Horners and master of three of the Erikson four-masted barques and the wooden four-masted schooner *Madare* had extensive experience of wooden vessels in the Baltic timber trade before he became master. He told me in 1977 that even with the windmill pump going hand pumping was sometimes almost continuous. He felt he had pumped all the North Sea and the Baltic through the vessels he sailed in as a boy and young man. Captain Einar Palmqvist had the same experience, though not in the *Sigyn*, of which he was master for some years.

Above, plate 59 Gustaf Erikson and friend in South Africa. (Ålands Sjöfartsmuseum)

Most of the passage to Mobile, in ballast, was with the tradewinds in sail's most agreeable waters. *Albania* reached her destination on 23 April 1907 after 50 days at sea. On 4 May the discharging of ballast was completed and after another 12 days loading could begin. During this time the rigging was renewed on the foremast as well as the mainmast. Loading went according to plan, but from a crew of sixteen, seven men jumped ship, which was nothing unusual in the Gulf ports. Sometimes Ålanders went to sea in the secret hope that sooner or later they would reach the emigrant's promised land by this inexpensive means. Keeping a sharp watch was no great help, and had little more overall effect than the occasional success the authorities ashore had in laying their hands on some unlucky runaway. It was not always easy for skippers to find new crewmen, and bills for seamen's wages increased.

Since the conclusion of the charter in Swansea, pitchpine freights had risen. The owners were discontented and had set up a chartering committee which decided to give preference to Andorsen & Becker over Clarksons. Gustaf Erikson was himself displeased and Clarksons were informed that they had shown themselves to be badly oriented in relation to trends in the freight market. But what angered him more than anything was that he had himself been deprived of his authority to make charters. In a letter to the ship's husband, there was no shortage of caustic comments regarding the new chartering system. He did not expect any good to come from the committee.

The passage back to South Africa was against the tradewinds and it was slow. *Albania* arrived at

Port Natal on 18 October after 115 days at sea. Part of the deck cargo, about 15 standards, had to be jettisoned overboard 'in the Gulf of Mexico in a storm with 19 nautical miles to a lee shore'. The mizzen topmast had been broken.

The total freight was drawn in Port Natal. This amounted to £2,632 for 519 standards at 100/- and 10 standards stowage at 66/-. The credit Clarksons had advanced to Mobile could be paid off. Huss in Cardiff received payment for fitting out in Swansea and £440 was remitted to the owners. The chartering committee then concluded a new charter through Clarksons: pitchpine from the Gulf to Rio de Janeiro at $13 per 1,000 superficial feet (ie calculated to the nearest complete foot). On 5 December, *Albania* sailed for Barbados for orders, arriving there after 40 days. She weighed anchor a couple of days later and put into Gulfport on 3 February 1908. Barbados was frequently used as an order port.

In South Africa *Albania's* skipper had said goodbye to his wife, who returned home by way of London. The steward who now attended to the chores under the poop proved a poor substitute and had to be forbidden entry, since he could not go anywhere without leaving his well-known black marks on the bulkheads, as Gustaf Erikson wrote to Tamelander from Barbados, asking for a new steward to be sent from home — preferably a married man who knew how to run things in an orderly fashion. In Gulfport, an incompetent steward expected £8 a month, while a first rate man could be found at home for half that wage or perhaps a trifle more. The journey from home might prove costly but it always paid to have a reliable and capable steward, with whose help 'many unpleasant occurrences between the men and the officers could be avoided, for it is as if there is no food to be had if it cannot be made edible, even though there are sufficient provisions on board and of the best quality.' In later years, as a shipowner, Gustaf Erikson was known to take a lively interest in the pea soup on his Australia-sailers, and to sample it as an expert when his ships visited Mariehamn. In the letter from Barbados he specified exactly whom he wanted. Heading the list was 'tailor Karlsson's brother from Finströms Kulla, and next Axel Lindqvist from Kuggsholma in Lemland'. A steward from Ytternäs or 'a Jansson from Ören in Lumparland' also had good qualifications. Both the former had sailed with him in *Southern Belle.*

That the solitude abaft the mast made itself felt is evident in a letter to Ingman, also from Barbados, asking him to send freight lists and the newspapers *Åbo Underrättelser* and *Nya Pressen,* together with 'some pages from the Viborg shipping journal'. The same request was repeated in Gulfport 'which was the right place to read newspapers' — a doubtful recommendation for the town.

In Gulfport, Gustaf Erikson was able to point out that his misgivings concerning the effectiveness of the chartering committee had been justified. Other vessels, *Endymion* for example, had had higher freight-rates to Rio. The charter party stipulated 1 March as the first loading day, which meant several weeks waiting for cargo. The depth of water of Gulfport was only 20 feet, so the last quarter of the cargo had to be taken on from lighters at Ship Island, and the vessel would have to bear the cost of the lighterage. A letter to the ship's husband speaks of 'foolish points in the charter party'. If the owners would not dismiss the chartering committee, or at least one named member of it, they had best look for a new skipper. Clarksons too were treated to caustic observations concerning other vessels with better charters. *Albania's* skipper did not intend to 'sail himself down into bad books' for the sake of any committee or ship broker, and Ingman should have been a priest, he was so good at talking and writing and reasoning away all objections to the charter party.

Loading was able to begin a couple of days before 1 March and went according to programme. After taking on 380 standards in Gulfport, *Albania* was towed to Ship Island, where the rest was loaded from lighters 'extremely cheaply, thanks to kindly treatment and persuasive talking'. The total taken on was 542 standards. Difficulty finding new men to replace deserters delayed sailing for several days. On 10 April 1908, *Albania* weighed anchor.

In Gulfport, the old full-rigger had shown a disquieting tendency to increased leakage, which greatly dampened any joy over the safe arrival of the new steward from home. The 93 day passage to Rio became troublesome with the wheel pump and the 'windmill' in continuous operation. After arriving, the pumps were kept going day and night 'with a six man sea watch', and Gustaf Erikson hoped that none of the men would get 'sick from drink, sick from bruises, or otherwise sick', as he wrote to Clarksons. On 28 July he could report that the ship was half empty but the leakage had not diminished. He was himself scarcely able to sleep

1 An iron barque built at Glasgow in 1873 and owned in Åland by August Troberg.

for the music of the pumps, and he was having trouble with the crew. Happily, he had the company of Captain Emanuel Eriksson of *Ocean.*[1] The same day he wrote to the ship's husband, demanding that the vessel be sold. A week earlier, he had hinted that this might prove necessary, at the same time coming up with an interesting suggestion. In Rio there were a number of old unrigged iron hulls, dismasted vessels which had once put into a port of refuge and remained there ever since. It might be worth moving *Albania*'s rig over to one of them; they could be bought for a song. On 3 August he wrote that he had offered £1,200 for the four-masted steel barque *Galgate*, built in Whitehaven in 1888 and measuring 2,200 tons net. Nothing came of this proposal. *Galgate* had come into Rio 'dismasted'; she must have been reconditioned however, as, according to Lubbock, she was sunk by a U-boat in 1916.

At the end of August, *Albania* was finally empty and ready for sale. The leakage was unchanged. An attempt to seal the vessel had little result; an entry for 11 sacks of sawdust at 1 Milreis per standard appears in the accounts. The leak was presumed to be in the keel but it could not be located. Since the crew had been paid off, the pumps were being tended by the mates and a gang from ashore. Prospective buyers showed no enthusiasm but in the end *Albania* was sold. As for her later fortunes, I have no information.

Her selling price was £800. The account from Rio lists in addition an entry for £85 for the sale of fittings and fixtures. The freight, less consignment commission, amounted to £2,851. When all debts had been settled, including Clarksons' £1,000 credit to Gulfport and tickets home for the skipper and mates, £1,400 could be remitted to the ship's husband. *Albania* proved to be anything but good business.

Three years later, one of her topsails and a spanker still haunted Gustaf Erikson's correspondence copy books. The sails had been sold on credit to *Queen of Scots,* whose captain had jumped overboard after sailing from Rio. His successor had refused to pay.

In Frederikstad in the summer of 1909, Gustaf Erikson took command of the three-masted barque and former full-rigger *Lochee.* She measured 1,654 tons net and was built of iron in Dundee in 1874. She was registered in Nystad, where the vessel had been bought in the mid 1890s. Her ship's husband was John Rivell. Sailing under the British flag, *Lochee* had made a good name for herself, and she became one of the first iron sailing vessels in the Finnish fleet. Conrad Palmer was her first mate. *Lochee* took on timber for Melbourne. She made the following passages under Gustaf Erikson's command:

1909 Frederikshald/Melbourne 103 days, arrived 31 Oct. Freight £1,400.
1910 Williamstown (nr Melbourne)/Plymouth for orders 118 days, arrived 21 May. Long wait for orders.
Plymouth/Glasgow 4½ days, arrived 8 June. Wheat, 2,509 tons @ 22/-. Freight £2,739. Empty and in dry-dock 23 June. No 2 Surrey, minor repairs. Ready for cargo 30 June.
Glasgow/Montevideo 47 days, arrived 25 Aug. Coal, 2,472 tons @ 14/-. Freight £1,731. Empty 10 Oct. 800 tons ballast taken on 15 Oct.
Montevideo/Pensacola in ballast. Arrived 11 Dec.
1911 Pensacola/Rio 70 days, arrived 21 April. Pitch-pine @ $14 per 1,000 superficial ft. Freight £3,284.
Rio/Matane in the Gulf of St Lawrence in ballast 56 days.
1912 Matane/Buenos Aires 68 days, arrived 2 Jan. Planks. Freight about £2,300.
Buenos Aires/Melbourne in ballast for orders, though destination Sydney.
Melbourne/Newcastle NSW 3 days.
Newcastle/Valparaiso 40 days, arrived 16 Sept. Discharged 1,913 tons coal @ 23/6. Freight £2,248.
Valparaiso/Antofagasta 4½ days, arrived 5 Nov. Discharged remainder of coal cargo, 562 tons, £660. A coastal cargo: 1,400 cases beer, 420 sacks corn, about 4,500 bales hay from Valparaiso, brought in £243.
1913 Antofagasta/Falmouth for orders, 122 days, arrived 15 April.
Falmouth/Dunkirk. Gustaf Erikson leaves command.

Rivell in Nystad received:

From Melbourne 1909	£ 42
From Glasgow 1910	1,150
From Montevideo 1910	400
From Rio 1911	200
From Buenos Aires 1912	360
From Valparaiso 1912	1,200
TOTAL	**£3,352**

In addition to this there was the balance from the cargo of nitrate to Dunkirk, which I have no information about. Even if the ship's husband had a number of expenses at home for premiums and

Below, plate 60 The iron full-rigged ship *Lochee,* later barque-rigged, photographed at Gravesend on 17 September 1896, shortly after her purchase by owners in Nystad. (National Maritime Museum)
Left, plate 61 The British four masted full-rigged ship *Wendur* built in 1884. (National Maritime Museum)

suchlike, these results from four years' sailings showed that it was possible to sail at a profit on deep-water.

On the outward passage to Melbourne from Norway one man and the port lifeboat were lost in a hurricane. In the damage reports the ship's husband received from Australia, the cost was estimated at £116. In Glasgow Gustaf Erikson was joined on board by his wife. She returned home from Buenos Aires. In December 1913, Gustaf Erikson sent 675 Finnish Marks to Rivell for her upkeep on board, 18 months at 1.25Mk[1] per day.

Gustaf Erikson writes that the passage from Pensacola to Rio was one of the most unpleasant in his experience, with headwinds, storms and calms in the North Atlantic. Captain Palmer tells how a brand new main-course was blown to ribbons in a squall that lasted no more than ten minutes. Several other vessels had similar difficulties at the same time. *Endymion,*[2] commanded by Bruno Donner, made a passage of 80 days, and the barque *Dora* of Kotka, 87 days. When *Lochee* departed for Australia in 1912, Sydney was her intended destination, but because of damaged rigging she put into Melbourne, where she went into dock for repairs. Among other damage, the fore lower topsail parral had sheared. The total damage was estimated at £479. It was a good thing *Lochee* had put into Melbourne, Gustaf Erikson wrote to Rivell; in Sydney, where she was destined for dry-docking, no claim for compensation could have been maintained.

The passages from Newcastle to Valparaiso and from Glasgow to Montevideo were Gustaf Erikson's fastest in *Lochee.* 'Beaten *King Edward*'s time by three days, even if that passage had so much written about it in the newspapers', he wrote in a letter to Rivell from Valparaiso. According to Lubbock, *King Edward* once sailed from Newcastle to Valparaiso in 31 days — the year is not mentioned. The vessel's fame was probably based on this fine achievement and not on her passage of 1912 which must have taken 43 days. It was not often that that passage was made in less than 40 days, but on 26 October, ie before *Lochee* had sailed on to Antofagasta, the four-masted barque *Grenada* ran into the roads off Valparaiso after a passage of only 36 days — certainly no nice surprise for *Lochee*'s skipper, who, according to what he wrote to Rivell, could have made it in 33 days if a long-lasting calm had not spoiled the end of the passage. The previous year, *Grace Harwar*, under the command of Captain Fearon had made 39 days from Newcastle to Coquimbo. A race, which was famous in its time, took place in 1896 between *Loch Torridon* and *Wendur*, which left Newcastle on 1 January. After 29 days, *Wendur* anchored in Valparaiso, her rival coming in seven hours later; record achievements on that route. [3]

Rio, Pensacola, Buenos Aires, Melbourne, Newcastle NSW, Valparaiso and Antofagasta were still ports where the skippers of sailing vessels met one another, and where skippers met a skipper was at one with his vessel, something which added spice to the social life of these ports. *Lochee* looked like a yacht, best of all in the harbour, despite her 36 years, says a letter to Rivell from Pensacola. It is not known whether other skippers shared this opinion. In Rio the ship lay 'fine and free of rust, which is not the case with other vessels here.' Rust was a deadly enemy; to paint over rust was almost a mortal sin. It was not worth buying anything but the highest quality sail cloth, the same letter continues; topsails are made with No 1, royals and staysails with No 2, no new sails are made with No 3.

Newcastle was visited by several vessels from Mariehamn in 1912. Among the Finns, Gustaf Erikson mentions *Woodburn,* which was later to enter his own fleet, and *Favell,* whose skipper Captain Södermann, had his wife and daughter aboard. There were therefore some possibilities for social life in the ports, and Gustaf Erikson was not one to forfeit any opportunity. In Rio, the captains of four Finnish vessels were invited to dinner with their wives, by the Russian Consul. The evening was rich in topics for conversation; among other things, unexpected extra harbour dues for dock construction had drawn protest from the port's Skippers' Association. Lighterage was another fertile ground for discussion. Gustaf Erikson, together with the masters of *Triton* and *Endymion,* was attempting to break 'the powerful stevedore Generoso's monopoly', a task which was very much to his taste. They united to form a new company with 25% lower tarrifs. But an essential prerequisite for the attack to have any lasting success was that future charter-parties should never stipulate free lighterage.

Captains must have a free hand to chose stevedores, Gustaf Erikson wrote to Andorsen & Becker from Matane. If cargo consignees were to decide matters of lighterage where discharging timber was concerned, Generoso would soon elbow the new firm out of the market. After the gay life of Rio, the stormy roads off Matane were far from pleasant, particularly as loading could only be carried out in calm weather, and then only at a snail's pace. But it was a good enough place to write letters. He had heard that a steamship company was being planned in Kristiansand. During his time in *Southern Belle* he had met the man who was to be marine superintendent, Captain Snellman, in Cardiff. He now wrote to him offering to invest in the enterprise if he could rely on being given a command.

Desertions were a matter of course in every port. That even the 59-year-old sailmaker should jump ship in Pensacola was, however, noted with a certain surprise. It was never worth signing on a new seaman before the day of sailing, it says in a letter from Montevideo; even then agents stole men back again.

A lawsuit with a shipper in New Orleans over a matter of £50 was another experience in *Lochee.* It was begun in Pensacola. In Matane a hearing is mentioned at which the skipper and the mate appeared before a Notary Public. In Melbourne Gustaf Erikson was happy to hear that he had won the action. In Valparaiso, where cargoes of coal were discharged into lighters out in the roads, he refers to the harbourmaster as 'a paid tool of the cargo consignees'. As soon as the wind blew from the north, there were 'surfdays' which were not reckoned as unloading days, even if unloading could quite easily have been carried out. The harbourmaster had absolute authority in deciding where a day was to be considered a 'surfday' or not.

1 Just over 1 Shilling, or 5 Pence, or 9 Cents, a day.

2 An iron full-rigged ship built at Sunderland in 1875 and owned by Robert Mattsson and Erik Nylund in Åland.

3 A fine rigged model of the four-masted full-rigged ship *Wendur,* together with her builder's half model, are in the stores in the National Maritime Museum at Greenwich.

For the future shipowner, these years of command in *Albania* and *Lochee* were a valuable education. The close personal contact with ship brokers, chandlers, stevedores, shippers and consignees, and the insight into their business practises, together with his personal familiarity with a great number of those ports and trade routes that were still open to deep-water sailing vessels, he was able to make use of as a shipowner when calculating the changes for sailing vessels in their difficult eleventh hour. Luck and misfortune were ruled by no one, but vessels, routes, harbours and charters were factors he could deal with in his estimates.

He set his mind on the idea of establishing himself as a shipowner. 'It seems hard to sail merely for a skipper's salary,' he wrote to Ingman from Pensacola. Discussing his remittances home from Glasgow and Montevideo, he noted that *Lochee*'s market value was not so very much greater. He longed for a vessel of his own, 16 to 18 years old and with a cargo capacity of 2,500 to 3,000 tons. Ideally he would have Ingman as ship's husband and joint-owner, while her skipper, naturally, would be himself. He possessed £1,200 or perhaps £1,300. If Clarksons were to lend him the remainder he required, about £2,000 at 6 per cent interest, everything could be arranged. The vessel would in any case be insured and the policy would be security. There was also another possibility that Clarksons lent him £1,000 and he enlisted joint owners in Mariehamn to provide the other thousand. In Melbourne he had looked at several vessels; *Carmanion* among others. 'Besides, I own my father's estate in Lemland, worth at least £400 — £500, as something to fall back on in my old age, should the sea take back what it has hitherto provided,' he says in a letter which ends with a request for freight — and shipping-lists in which he might study rates and ship prices. He also asked for freight- and shipping-lists for various ports from Andorsen &Becker, through whom *Lochee*'s ship's husband seems as a rule to have arranged charters.

He did not forget the family farm in Hellestorp. He wrote lengthy letters home from Rio and Pensacola, for example, concerning such things as the sale or possible storage of the hay crop, the clearing of woodland and rents to tenant farmers, all as detailed as the stipulations in a charter party.

Freight-rates rose sharply in 1912. While *Lochee* was loading in Antofagasta for 17/- nitrate rates came close to 30/- per ton. This must certainly have strengthened Gustaf Erikson's resolution, since he left his command in Dunkirk without having any new post within reach. 'Nice to come home for the summer after not seeing a summer at home for 13 years,' he wrote to J E Erikson in Söderby from Antofagasta. He seems to have hesitated at the last moment though. On 5 May he wrote to Rivell from Dunkirk, saying that *Lochee's* charter to Buenos Aires tempted him to make one more trip in command. If a new skipper had already been selected, he committed himself to the owners' goodwill for the future. In case a new vessel should be purchased, he would gladly be a joint-owner and skipper.

For the time being the parting from *Lochee* did not signify what it would eventually prove to be — retirement from a life at sea.

The twenty years between 1893, when Gustaf Erikson took command of *Adéle*, and 1913, when he stepped ashore from *Lochee,* were eventful years in the history of sail. The end of the last chapter was inexorably drawing near. An impressive fleet of iron and steel barques still sailed the oceans, but one could search shipyards anywhere in the world for one under construction, without success.

The Åland fleet had undergone a radical transformation:

	1893	1913
Iron or steel sailing vessels		24
Wooden barques	61	22
Large schooners & barquentines	37	18
Brigs	13	2
Smaller schooners	22	5
Fore-and-aft schooners over 100 tons	18	8

In fact the change was greater than is indicated by this table. Crofter-sailings had virtually come to an end. Lemland was no longer of any significance as a seafaring parish. Vårdö was an exception thanks to Mathias Lundqvist Jnr. Mariehamn with its big shipowners Robert Mattson and August Troberg had become the headquarters of Åland navigation.

One cannot say that the prospects for a sailing vessel shipping concern were conspicuously good in 1913, as all the signs pointed to the fact that sail would inevitably wither away and disappear from the oceans. That it would have such an illustrious final fling could not have been suspected, even by *Lochee*'s optimistic, 40-year-old skipper, as he travelled home from Dunkirk to enjoy the Åland summer.

CHAPTER 3

Tjerimai

Some of the famous British tea clippers of the 1860s like the *Cutty Sark* were built with hardwood planking over iron frames.[1] Wooden planking had one advantage over iron plating: it could be sheathed in copper and nothing was so effective as copper plating against barnacles and other parasites which love to attach themselves to vessels in tropical waters. The Dutch, too, with their flourishing seaborne trade to and from their colonies in the East Indies, used this composite construction, as it was called, to a great extent.

In their later years, four of these Dutchmen belonged to the Åland fleet: *Slamat, Christiani, Louis* (ex *Thorbecke*) and *Tjerimai,* all built in Amsterdam. However, at least two of these vessels, *Christiani* and *Tjerimai,* had not only iron ribs, stringers and deck beams like the British tea clippers, but complete iron plating in addition. Outside this, *Tjerimai* had copper-sheathed wooden planking, which extended up to the load-line amidships according to one authority. The planking was between 4 and 4½ inches thick, 6 inches according to another account. The stem and sternpost were also of wood.

In September 1913, some months after his arrival home from Dunkirk, Gustaf Erikson established himself as a ship's husband by entering into partnership with several friends (captains Severus Gustafsson[2] and Erik Nylund in Mariehamn, Victor Johans in Lumparland, Erik Bamberg, Erik Sjölund and S G Jansson in Lemland), purchasing *Tjerimai* and personally retaining the major part in the ownership of the vessel, which cost 42,500 Finnish Marks (about £1,800). The seller was N Tarasoff of Lovisa and partners. A citizen of Åbo, K Löhnström, became the second greatest part-owner with 20/100ths. Gustaf Erikson increased his share of 40/100ths to 65/100ths at the turn of the year 1914-15, by buying up the shares of other partners, and ultimately to 87/100ths according to the last list of dividends in 1924.[3]

Tjerimai (the name is that of an Indonesian softwood tree) was built by J F Meursing in Amsterdam in 1883 and measured 827 tons net, 976 tons gross and 1,550 tons deadweight. Her dimensions were 188ft 3in by 36ft 7in by 21ft 1in.[4] She loaded about 450 cords of lathwood, and 420 to 430 standards of pitchpine in the Gulf ports. Timber cargoes from Canada varied between 495 and 500 standards, depending on dimensions and the season. If one adds 1,150 tons of logwood from the West Indies, there is little left to be said concerning her

1 The *Cutty Sark* is now preserved at Greenwich, London, adjacent to the National Maritime Museum. The last tea clipper to earn her living at sea, which was the Åland-owned *Frideborg*, formerly the British *Cleta*, built at Sunderland in 1866 and lost in the Gulf of Bothnia in 1937, was also composite. In her youth she made a number of passages with tea from China to the United States. In 1977 her entire poop accommodation was still preserved in use as a summerhouse near Luleå at the northern end of the Gulf of Bothnia.

2 Captain Severus Gustafsson (Plate 44) from Lemland was master of the *Roxane* (Plate 41) from 1905 to 1907 and was also a shareholder. Later he married Sigrid, the beautiful daughter of the ship's husband of the barque *Robertsfors,* W Holmberg, and was given command of the vessel. At the time the photograph in Plate 64 was taken he was still master of the *Robertsfors* but a year later he settled in Mariehamn as a shipowner. He prospered during the first World War with *Robertsfors,* the barque *Diaz,* his investment in *Tjerimai* and other vessels, and built a fine house in Mariehamn. In 1919 he joined with others in financing the construction of the four-masted barquentine *Dione* (Plates 88 & 89) later owned by Gustaf Erikson. Tragically he lost his fortune playing poker with his fellow shipowner/shipmasters and committed suicide shortly after the war.

3 British legislation required a vessel property to be divided into 64ths. In Åland 100ths or 200ths were customary.

4 She was thus a little smaller than the *Cutty Sark* but larger than the *Sigyn* and considerably larger than the wooden whaling barque *Charles W Morgan,* preserved at Mystic, Connecticut, their respective lengths being *Cutty Sark,* 212ft, *Sigyn* 45.5 metres, and the *Morgan* 105ft.

Right, plate 62 The decks of the *Cutty Sark* when she was laid up at Falmouth in 1935. She is now preserved in drydock near the National Maritime Museum at Greenwich. (Basil Greenhill)
Below, plate 63 *Christiani* with a well stowed deck cargo of timber in a heavy sea. (Ålands Sjöfartsmuseum)
Opposite top, plate 64 This photograph shows from left to right, Samuel Jansson the farmer-shipmaster-shipowner, who was ships husband of the *Roxane* (Plate 41) and a primary shareholder in *Tjerimai*, and his wife; Captain Severus Gustafsson, also a primary shareholder in *Tjerimai*, and his wife Sigrid (see also Plates 43, 44 and 65) and Gustaf Erikson and his wife Hilda. The photograph was taken in Vastra Jakos, Söderby, Lemland, in the summer of 1913. All three men were Lemlanders and the Gustafssons and the Eriksons were on a visit to the Janssons. The photograph was almost certainly made to celebrate the purchase of *Tjerimai*. Gustaf Erikson, at 41 years of age, still only on the threshold of his career, radiates confidence. (Ålands Sjöfartsmuseum)
Opposite bottom, plate 65 Captain Severus Gustafsson, third from right, and his wife Sigrid with friends standing on a partly stowed cargo of 'splitved', on board the barque *Robertsfors* off a Swedish Bothnian port. Note the windmill pump. (Ruben Jansson)

cargo capacity and the routes she sailed in her old age. As for the voyages of her younger years, I have no information; but in all probability she sailed in the East Indies trade during her Dutch period.

By comparison with the 15 iron and steel vessels Åland acquired between 1911 and 1914 (mostly bought by 'the great Maritime Counsellors Robert Mattson, August Troberg and M Lundqvist', to quote Gustaf Erikson in a letter of the time), *Tjerimai* was a very unexceptional vessel whose classification, moreover, was due to expire at the end of the year, and whose 5-year-old copper-sheathing was already considerably battered. When, somewhat later the same autumn, Gustaf Erikson succeeded in setting up a company to purchase *Renee Rickmers*, rechristened *Åland*, and, with his 15/100ths, became ship's husband for this magnificent and renowned deep-water sailer, *Tjerimai*, with her uncertain prospects, was completely overshadowed by the new acquisition. But the story of Cinderella was borne out. That the old composite-built barque gives her name to this chapter is in recognition of the fact that she, as opposed to *Åland*, not only came up to her expectations but greatly surpassed them, helping to finance the rapid expansion of Gustaf Erikson's shipping concern during the First World War.

She was bought empty in St Petersburg with a favourable charter: lathwood from Koivusaari to London at 48/- a cord; 1913 was a good year for shipping. Captain J A Westerberg from Hitis, himself a joint-owner with 5/100ths in the vessel, moved from St Petersburg to the port where she was to load without informing his new ship's husband of the fact and immediately received his first directive: always to telegraph arrivals and departures.

She had taken on a good cargo. The way it turned out it was, alas, too good: 480 cords. *Tjerimai* sailed on 13 October: insured for half her hull value at 9% with the *Sjöassuransforening* in Åbo, and arrived in London after a passage of four weeks. Here Captain Westerberg found himself in a dispute with the cargo consignee, who could point to the fact that three years earlier the vessel had held no more than 434 cords. He refused to accept the 480 cords and demanded a remeasurement, a time-consuming

Below, plate 66 *Tjerimai* loading timber at Pensacola, Florida during the First World War. (Ålands Sjöfartsmuseum)

and costly procedure. After the departure from Koivusaari Gustaf Erikson seems to have smelt a rat. Possibly he had found particulars of *Tjerimai's* earlier cargoes. Westerberg was kept informed about the situation by several letters, some addressed to the Sound[1] and some to London, and he learned among other things that the vessel had been enrolled in the *Norsk Frakt & Liggedagsklubb* (The Norwegian Freight and Lay-days Club) who had a particularly sharp-witted lawyer in Fenchurch Street. 'Make protests at every opportunity, to keep the matter open whether there are grounds or not!' The dispute seems to have been resolved amicably in a compromise, after the above mentioned lawyer got his hands on the matter. The 480 cords were reduced to 450. The gross freight was also reduced, admittedly, but an uncertain remeasurement was avoided.

The question of a new charter was worrying. The freight market had deteriorated. In November Clarksons offered 34/- for lathwood for the summer of 1914. It was difficult to find a cargo in Canada for an unclassed vessel. Gustaf Erikson preferred to wait and see. He succeeded in getting a cargo of coke for Copenhagen, where *Tjerimai* arrived on 15 December. There, in accordance with her contract, she did service as a coke bunker until 31 March 1914. The yield from the lathwood and coke freights allowed a handsome dividend; 16,000 Marks (about £650) were paid out.

During this time Gustaf Erikson succeeded, after all, in securing a charter from Canada, at 42/6d per standard. *Tjerimai* sailed in ballast in the middle of April, arriving at Matane on 30 May, and weighed anchor again on 11 July, bound for Liverpool. As she headed for her destination across the pleasant expanses of the Atlantic in the height of summer, the First World War broke out. Sailing vessels were suddenly swept from the coastal waters of Northern and Western Europe; many of Åland's North Sea and Baltic vessels fell into German hands, others were laid-up until the end of the war. *Tjerimai* found herself relatively safe on deeper water. If she had stayed in the lathwood trade many things could have turned out differently for her and her owner.

On 2 August Gustaf Erikson wrote to Westerberg, who was expected in Liverpool at any time, giving him full powers to conclude the most favourable charters from Canada himself, should communications with the home country be broken off. During the first days of August, rumours buzzed like swarms of bees in shipping offices around the world; the first sinkings were reported, large scale naval engagements were expected in the North Sea, and a powerful German cruiser squadron was lurking in the Pacific. German marauders could appear anywhere, and the German U-boat fleet was an ominous question mark. On 8 August, *Tjerimai* arrived in Liverpool. Gustaf Erikson at once telegraphed the glad news to Captain Westerberg's mother. 'Have no fear about the Germans troubling sailing ships off the west coast of England. No, the waters there can be considered safe enough', he wrote, somewhat optimistically, to Westerberg on 12 August. In the same letter he writes that a foreign-going service had successfully been opened on the Raumo-Gävle line. But as the unloading proceeded, optimism waned. On 19 September the telegram came with the news of the loss of *Åland*. The freight market was paralysed, everything was uncertain, nothing could be anticipated. Not until the late autumn did prospects improve; the atmosphere of panic abated and freights slowly began to pick up. At the beginning of December 50/- was offered for spring loading in Canada; Gustaf Erikson did not accept. The Gulf was tempting, but as she was unclassed and her copper was in poor condition, (and would therefore provide little protection against the marine borers in the warm waters of the Gulf), *Tjerimai* was thought obliged to look for a new freight from Canada, which meant she would have to postpone her departure until the spring. In such circumstances there was no need to hurry a charter.

In order to avoid expensive harbour dues, *Tjerimai* moved to Bangor, Menai Straits. Captain Westerberg shipped on a tramp steamer. The mate, Stenroos, received instructions in a letter sprinkled with question marks. Was the anchorage considered safe? How many feet of water were there under the keel at the lowest tides? Was the bottom sand or mud? Was the vessel swinging to both anchors? How many fathoms of cable were there? Were the cables securely fastened to a 'mooring swivel' so that turns could be kept out of the cable when the vessel swung round? Was there a reserve anchor? Had the royal and topgallant yards been sent down to the deck to reduce wind resistance? Were her riding lights burning safely? A letter every fortnight was requested. The steward, Förbom, the son of one of Gustaf Erikson's friends, also received a letter

1 That is, to Copenhagen or Elsinore, to be conveyed to the vessel as she passed through the narrow international channel out of the Baltic.

containing greetings and pious hopes that industry on board would flourish, with rust-chipping, painting and sail-sewing, 'so that in the spring the vessel will look like a yacht, free from everything in the way of rust, both internally and externally.' Time would drag for the idle. If the days were short, then there were lanterns. Förbom should devote his Sundays to his nautical studies; the mate would certainly be ready to provide advice and information.

Freights rose steadily, charterers' pretensions sank, and on 20 February *Tjerimai* put to sea, still unclassed, bound (despite the state of her copper) for Pensacola under the command of Captain M Nordberg, formerly skipper of *Åland*, who had come to England from Australia. The Gulf ports, Pensacola particularly, were frequently visited by Åland ships during the war. *Margareta* sailed from Liverpool on the same day as *Tjerimai*, followed a few days later by *Parchim* and *Asia*, which was lost with all hands on another passage later that year from Pensacola to the Clyde. In Pensacola, *Tjerimai* took on 419 standards of sleepers at 135/- for Bowling near Glasgow.

Up to September 1917, *Tjerimai* made the following passages:

Bangor/Pensacola in ballast. 20 Feb — 27 April 1915
Pensacola/Bowling. 25 May - 13 July.
Bowling/St John, NB in ballast: 15 Aug - 20 Sept.
St John/Rochefort, timber. 15 Oct - 20 Nov.
Rochefort/Gulfport in ballast. 10 Jan - 1 March 1916.
Gulfport/Fleetwood, pitchpine. 4 April - 18 May.
Fleetwood/Matane in ballast. 17 June - 9 Aug.
Matane/Portishead, timber. 13 Sept - 17 Oct.
Portishead/Pensacola in ballast. 17 Nov. - 29 Dec.
Pensacola/Liverpool, pitchpine. 12 Feb-4 April 1917.
Liverpool/Black River, Jamaica, in ballast.
16 May - 27 June 1917.
Black River/Ponta Delgada.

In the middle of September 1917, *Tjerimai* put into Ponta Delgada, the port in the Azores, and was laid-up there for the rest of the war with her cargo of logwood. She had been bound for Fleetwood, but the German U-boat blockade, begun on 1 February, had transformed the waters around Britain, and especially to the west of Ireland, into a huge graveyard for ships. It is significant that whereas only two of Åland's deep-water sailers, *Hermes* and *Thomasina,* had been sunk beyond Britain in 1915, and none in 1916, nine of Åland's finest iron and steel vessels were lost between February and the end of May 1917: *Garnet Hill, Pera, Borrowdale, Endymion, August* (ex *Tropic*), *Lynton, Margareta* (ex *Craigerne*), *Imberhorne* and *Lucipara.*

Tjerimai seems to have come from Pensacola to Liverpool and sailed again during the worst months of the hunt. The day after her departure, *Margareta* was sunk on her way to Glasgow from the Gulf, having been bought by Gustaf Erikson a couple of months earlier. *Tjerimai's* arrival in Jamaica was awaited with considerable anxiety, and not without cause. She had got a new skipper in Liverpool, Captain K E Karlsson. A couple of weeks after his departure, Gustaf Erikson wrote to him in Jamaica, informing him that he had cabled Clarksons, asking them to try to get the logwood charter cancelled. If this succeeded, he should sail to Mobile and there have the vessel classed and re-coppered. The cargo consignees would not, however, agree to the cancellation, and seem to have had the law behind them in that the charter-party was dated 1 February, the day before the U-boat blockade had been proclaimed.

However, in Ponta Delgada the war was at an end so far as *Tjerimai* was concerned. She had done a good day's work. For one thing she had sailed well, and steadily, and sometimes fast. 'Magnificently fast passage', Gustaf Erikson wrote to Captain Nordberg about his 45 days from Gulfport to Fleetwood. It almost seemed as if the battered copper 'was not acting as a hindrance but rather as an advantage', he added jokingly. Another factor was that freights had risen above every limit a shipowner could have dreamt of in his most paradisical dreams. In 1914 *Tjerimai's* freight from Canada has been at 42/6d. For the passage from St John to Rochefort she had 146/-, and in the autumn of 1916 no less than 350/- from Matane to Portishead. There was of course a similar rise in Gulf freights, which before the war had exceeded 100/- only in good years: Pensacola/Bowling 135/-, Gulfport/Fleetwood 285/-, and Pensacola/Liverpool 476/-. In addition, the rate of exchange for sterling climbed at times to more than 30 Finnish Marks (it had been round about 24 before the war). In May 1916 Captain Nordberg received instructions to send his remittances in sterling through a bank in London to Nordiska Aktiebanken, who paid 25 Finnish Penni more per Pound than Kansallispankki. 'No more fitting out on credit!' the letter said at the same time — an order which before the war would have caused an Åland deep-water skipper to rub his eyes and polish his spectacles.

There was, naturally, an increase in expenses for wages, provisions, fitting-out and insurance. War risk premiums were relatively moderate during the quiet U-boat year of 1916, but in 1917 they shot up, and could swallow up to half the gross freights. 1916 seems generally to have been the war's best year for shipping even if freights reached their zenith somewhat later.

Shipping companies were deluged with remittances. After *Tjerimai*'s arrival in Rochefort in 1915, Gustaf Erikson wrote to his brother-in-law, Captain Ekblom of *Lynton:* 'This trip should yield about 50,000 Marks in net profit, which makes my future secure economically, at least for the present, seeing that I am still a businessman who can never stand having capital lying dead in a bank.' The following year he could issue receipts for no less than eight remittances totalling over £9,000 from *Tjerimai.* Dividends paid out on the year's sailings amounted to 235,000 Finnish Marks, corresponding to 550 per cent of the vessel's purchase price.

There is no doubt that it was nice to receive remittances. But on many occasions it was troubling to sit in Mariehamn as ship's husband during the war years. The mail was slow and uncertain. A letter from Captain Nordberg in Rochefort took 42 days to arrive, a telegram might take a week or more. Information concerning the often rapid fluctuations in the freight market was unreliable; no one could know whether instructions to skippers and characters would reach their destinations in time, or would be useless on their arrival. It was also not certain how long *Tjerimai* could sail 'on grace, unclassed, with worn-out copper sheathing and no load line!' — her description in a letter of 1916. And to squander time and money on classification at a time when an unparalleled economic situation offered generous opportunities was not an inviting prospect. On 10 May 1915 Nordberg telegraphed from Pensacola: 'Inspected loading commenced'. It was a pleasing message, but the wait was not pleasant when it was a matter of a telegram with news of safe arrival or readiness to load. The non-existent load-line and the battered copper are referred to again and again in letters to Clarksons and to Captain Nordberg, sometimes in connection with establishing the possibilities for new coppering, sometimes with a view to obtaining a postponement because of the unusual times.

Below, plate 67 *Åland,* built as the *Renee Rickmers* in 1887. (Ålands Sjöfartsmuseum)

But let us leave *Tjerimai* in Ponta Delgada for the time being. Her owner was, as has been said, a 'businessman' who would not allow her remittances to lie 'dead in a bank'. What he did with them will be seen later in the text.

But first a few words should be devoted to the barque *Åland.* On 27 September 1913 Gustaf Erikson wrote to a ship chandler saying that he intended to settle himself ashore as a shipowner for at least a year. He mentions the *Tjerimai* venture and reports that he is considering buying a larger vessel for Captain Nordberg who had recently returned to Mariehamn from Dunkirk, after inspecting a vessel that turned out to be 'rusted-up'

A trip to Moss which Nordberg undertook to look at a couple of Norwegian ships, one of which was *Cambrian Princess,* was also without result. At the same time, Gustaf Erikson was negotiating with the ship broker Robert Laesiner in Hamburg for *Renee Rickmers,* then on her way from Australia to Falmouth for orders, with wheat. He bid £6,000 pending a hull inspection. The transaction was settled when the offer was raised to £6,500. The vessel would be taken over after unloading and a favourable inspection of her bottom plating. On 26 October the vessel arrived at Falmouth and was towed to Cardiff (Captain Nordberg immediately set out to meet her there), where she went into dry-dock and was approved on condition that the owners covered the cost of some new plates. She was rechristened *Åland.* Captain Nordberg's report on the vessel was extremely favourable.

The purchase naturally exceeded Gustaf Erikson's own resources. *Tjerimai* had been cheap, owing to her bad condition and had consequently not drained his assets completely. However, he had to find partners to cover 85/100ths of the ownership of the new vessel, which incidentally seems to have caused him no problem. A vessel such as *Åland* represented the height of modernity in the Åland fleet of 1913. Iron and steel deep-water vessels had yielded good dividends, to which the prosperity of the three major shipowners bore witness. Gustaf Erikson's 15/100ths cost him 26,000 Finnish Marks (about £1,080). The remainder was shared among some 50 or so joint-owners, of whom most were content with 1/100th. It pleased him particularly that one of the big shipowners put himself down for 10/100ths, namely Mathias Lundqvist Jnr in Vargata, Vårdö. This strengthened self-confidence, prestige and credit.

Åland was a four-masted iron barque, built in 1887 by Russell & Co in Port Glasgow. Her deadweight was 3,300 tons, her gross tonnage 2,135 tons and her net tonnage 2,054 tons. Her dimensions were 283ft 0in by 40ft 5in by 24ft 6in. On 11 January 1914 she sailed from Cardiff with a cargo of coal, bound for Callao, where she arrived after a passage of 113 days. She continued in ballast on 1 July 1914 to New Caledonia to load nickel ore for Europe, but never reached port. *Åland* headed across the Pacific without a suspicion of the life and death trials of strength that had begun in Europe, and whose ripples were spreading out across the world. Captain Nordberg did not know that his lookout was watching for lights that had been extinguished because of the German cruiser squadrons which could appear anywhere in the world in the course of their secretive movements. One night, as the vessel approached her port of destination, she ran on to a reef and was wrecked. Apparently the pilot had already come aboard but had not warned the officers that the beacons had been put out. This occurred on 20 August. No one in Mariehamn had entertained any apprehensions; *Åland* was thousands of miles beyond the danger zone. On 16 September, Gustaf Erikson wrote to Clarksons in London, asking what they thought about the long passage. Three days later a telegram arrived from Melbourne: '*Åland* total wreck Amedee August twentieth crew safe consul refuses money send two hundred pounds Burroughs Mats Nordberg'. That same day Gustaf Erikson wrote to the Sjöassuransforening in Åbo, where the vessel was insured for 125,000 Marks: 'Have the painful duty hereby to give notice that the ship was lost...' His disappointment was great, but after a few days he was on the hunt for a new vessel, more attentive than ever to the freight and shipping lists from London, where his optimism was noted with a certain surprise at a time when the mood was typically one of uncertainty and war psychosis. It could have been worse he wrote to his friend Manne Eriksson in *Margareta,* expected in Falmouth; if the ship had been captured and taken as a prize, the insurers would not have paid anything. 15,000 Marks had been paid out from the coal freight to Callao. The loss to the owners was limited to 40,000 Marks.

Åland haunted Gustaf Erikson's correspondence for a long time. Fitting-out had been done on credit by ship chandler Charles Huss in Cardiff, and was insured with Salamandra, who refused to pay on the grounds that coverage did not include war risk. After endless correspondence and a legal action lasting several years which was taken through every level of the courts, the whole business came to nothing, as did plans to hold the French state responsible for the extinguished beacons. As late as August 1921, Gustaf Erikson was sending all relevant material relating to the question of damages to Clarksons. But space is limited; we shall leave the wreck of *Åland* on the reef in the Pacific, where, incidentally, she was sold with her fittings and provisions for 5,140 Francs.

Seamen have their portents — landlubbers have a certain inclination to call them superstitions. *Åland* should have been allowed to keep her original, honest, name. British nautical historians have noted, that after the loss off New Caledonia, Gustaf Erikson made it a principle to let his big ships, were they British or German in origin, sail under the names they had been given when they were launched.

The acquisition of one other vessel belongs to the time before the war. In March 1914 Gustaf Erikson bought 3/4ths in the old barque *Fredenborg,* built on Isaksö in Geta in 1881, and measuring 431 tons net, and loading 260 to 270 standards cut wood. The previous autumn, *Fredenborg* had been obliged to put into Gothenburg, in need of considerable

Below, plate 68 *Fredenborg* (Ålands Sjöfartsmuseum)

Above, plate 69 Accomodation in wooden vessels (1). The after deck house of the barque *Sigyn*. With its panels and decorated knees, the whole half buried in the low poop deck, the arrangement is typical of many Åland, Scandinavian and Canadian built wooden barques. Here the master, mates and steward lived. In the foreground is the base of the windmill pump with the deck casting including the outlet pipe. (Basil Greenhill)

Right, plate 70 Accommodation in wooden vessels (2). The mess room in the poop of the *Sigyn* where the masters and mates ate. Note the mizzen mast coming through. (Basil Greenhill)

repairs. The price was not high — 7,500 Finnish Marks (about £300) for the complete vessel. She arrived in Mariehamn in April 1914, bringing with her, among other things, two bottles of whisky, six bottles of cherry wine, eight tins of fruit and four jars of pickles for her new ship's husband. She sailed on to Kemi, took on timber, and sailed again for Rochester, near London, on 25 June, under the command of Captain Emil Mattson. So far she had cost her owners 16,800 Marks, and the intention was to try to sell her abroad at a profit after a couple of freight passages. She arrived on 1 August. Four days earlier Austria had declared the Serbian war; the German declaration of war against Russia was announced the same day. The avalanche had begun. Gustaf Erikson wrote to Captain Mattson on 2 August; he should try to get a cargo of coke to a neutral port, Danish or Norwegian. It was a matter

of following the events of the war carefully and acting in the interests of the company; it might prove necessary to lay-up. A few days later Mattson received the order to lay-up, pay off the crew, set a watch, and to try to convince the Russian Consul that the owners could not be expected to take the responsibility for getting the men home in time of war when all traffic was at a standstill. 'Sorry times at hand,' a letter reads, 'poverty and misery stand before the door'.

Captain Mattson succeeded in getting the crew signed on other vessels. This brightened the owner's spirits considerably. During the course of the autumn, he tried, unsuccessfully, to sell the old barque by various means. He asked Clarksons, for example, to offer her to the British government for £800. A plan to send her to the White Sea in the summer of 1915 went on the rocks; it was not possible to secure war risk insurance. In May 1916

Left, plate 71 Accommodation in wooden vessels (3). The forecastle house of the *Carmen* viewed from the poop. (National Maritime Museum)

Below, plate 72 Accommodation in wooden vessels (4). The inside of the forecastle of the barque *Helmi* as preserved in the Ålands Sjöfartsmuseum. She was built by Eric Söderström in Jomala Parish, Åland, in 1892 for the West Europe and West Indies trade and sold to owners in mainland Finland in 1910. (Basil Greenhill)

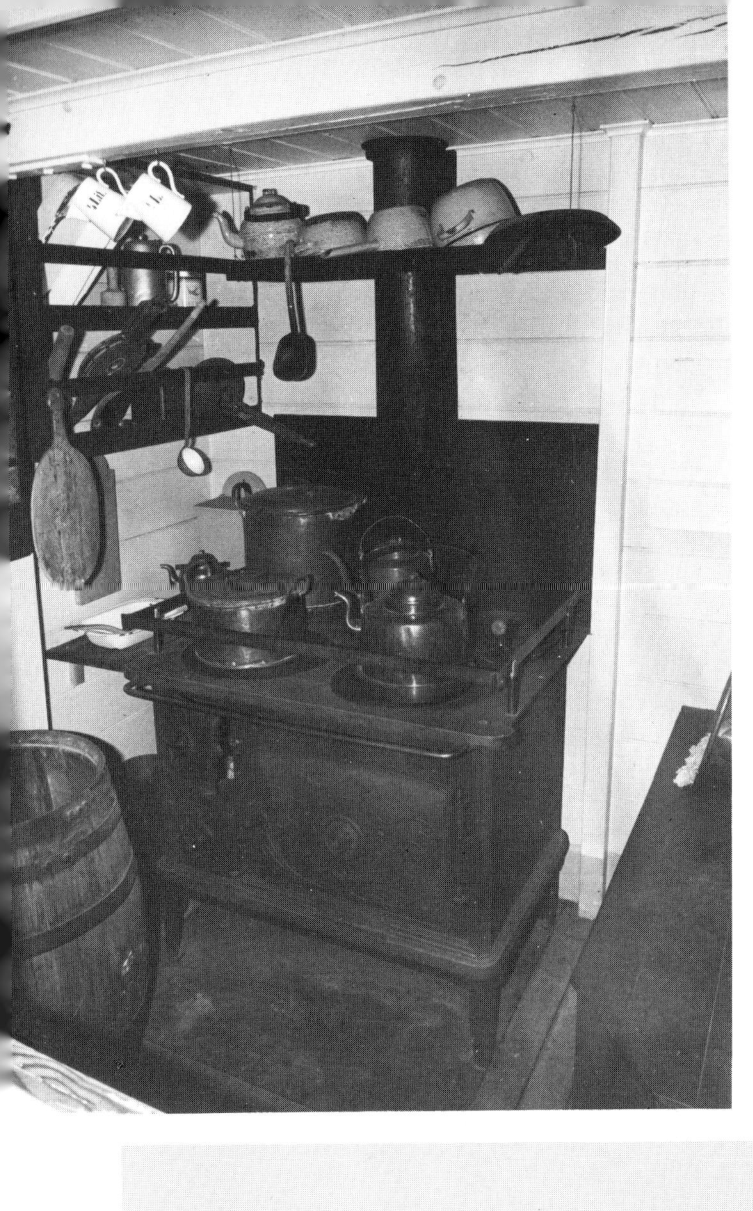

Fredenborg was finally sold to an Åboland company for 40,000 Marks. She is reported to have sailed on 1 July to load timber in Canada at 370/-, a fantastic freight — £4,000-£5,000 gross. But the venture was not successful. *Fredenborg* put into Cardiff, leaking and with a broken mainmast, which was about what could have been expected of a vessel of her age.

The ease with which a company had been created for the ownership of *Åland* in the autumn of 1913 was an encouragement to continued endeavour. In letters to the sea captains Emanuel Erikson of *Margareta,* N Törnqvist, who was on the point of giving up command of *Mariechen,* and his brother-in-law KA Ekblom of *Lynton,* Gustaf Erikson outlined his plans, exhorted them to be on the lookout for vessels, and himself approved a number of deep-water sailers as suitable for purchase. He names *Port Caledonian,* which was however 'snapped up' by Zachariassen in Nystad, *Brilliant,* one of the world's biggest sailing vessels, owned by

Left, plate 73 Accommodation in wooden vessels (5). The galley of *Helmi.* The cooked food was passed to the eight seamen and boys in the forecastle through the sliding hatch on the right hand side of the stove. (Basil Greenhill)

Below, plate 74 The schooner *Ingrid,* built by Eric Söderström at Knutnäs Geta, in 1906, entering Littlehampton in 1910. One of only three big vessels launched in Åland between 1892 and 1919 she was the last to be built and sailed as a joint venture by local farmers in the old style of Åland shipping (Ålands Sjöfartsmuseum)

Standard Oil, *Juteopolis* later to be re-named *Garthpool,* the full-rigger *Bay of Biscay,* bought by Norwegian shipowners in 1915 and torpedoed by a U-boat in 1917, *Glenholm,* which he had himself seen and been enchanted by in Antofagasta, *Crocodile, Hinemoa, Metropolis* and others. A company with Manne Eriksson and Törnqvist would be best, he wrote to the latter in March 1914. Credit should be obtainable for 50 per cent of the value, against security. Later the joint-owners could alternate with one another in command. 'But above all else, discretion!' the letter says. It would not do to let the big shipowners get wind of his plans.

At first the outbreak of war deadened Gustaf Erikson's taste for speculation, but the loss of *Åland* revived it. In October he heard a rumour that German sailing vessels seized in Britain were to be sold, and that only the 'allies' had the right to purchase; which meant that Norwegians and Swedes would be excluded. Great opportunities beckoned; the Germans had fine ships, fast sailers, and well-maintained. But any plans for new acquisitions abroad had to be shelved, mainly because of the difficulty of negotiating sterling in large amount. Neither Clarksons nor Andorsen & Becker had any desire to risk advance financing. When, in 1916, *Werner Vinnen* was sold by auction in London for £27,000, Clarksons had not even sent notice of the auction in time, which earned them a bitter reprimand. Why had they not even gone to the expense of sending him a telegram, seeing that they had sent one to August Troberg who had laid-up his vessels and sold them himself? It might be better to turn to someone who would 'risk more and venture more than R Mattson and Troberg put together'.

There remained one possibility, and that was exploited to the last farthing: to buy part-ownership in vessels at home as remittances came in from *Tjerimai.* 'I have spent over 300,000 on buying vessels in the last year and I have loaned and pledged everything I own as security, with the exception of little Edgar and my wife...I have risked prodigious sums of money — the greatest on a single keel — in *Borrowdale*', he wrote with grim humour to his brother-in-law Ekblom on 3 August 1916.

It is not possible here to give a detailed account of every part-purchase and all dividends, profits and losses. In 1915 he became a joint-owner in *Montrosa* and SS *Agnes,* Åland's first tramp steamer, bought shortly before the war and a highly profitable venture for those who invested in her. In 1916 he bought minor shares in a number of Åland vessels: *Norden, Asia, Ingrid, Frieda, Prompt, Pera, Parchim, Lucipara, Endymion, Concordia* and *Margareta.* Some of these ventures were successful, others were not. When, for example, *Prompt's* owner paid out 755,000 Finnish Marks (about £26,000 at the time) in dividends in 1917, he did very well with his 9/100ths. *Agnes* laid golden eggs. *Frieda* proved a bad investment, likewise *Ingrid.*

This three-masted schooner of 291 tons net was built in Geta in 1906, a late product of Åland shipbuilding, and was owned by a company in Geta. She had been laid-up in the same place as *Fredenborg* (Rochester) since the beginning of the war, but she was younger and had had better fortunes. Under the command of Captain Eric Hugo Mattsson of Geta, she made three freight passages across the Atlantic after New Year 1916: from Darien (Sapelo) to Brest, from Canada to Brest and from Jamaica to Bordeaux. Gustaf Erikson bought 15/100ths in her in the spring of 1916. The following year he became principal owner and ship's husband. But *Ingrid* was to remain in Bordeaux; the U-boat blockade had begun. Besides this her classification had expired and she was in need of quite fundamental repairs. During the uneasy autumn of 1917 and the spring of 1918 it proved impossible to obtain an exit permit from home for a new skipper. *Ingrid* was not ready to sail until 18 January 1919, after being recaulked throughout and fitted with a new foremast and mizzenmast. Bound for Martinique under the command of Captain K Lindblom, she was obliged to run into Falmouth for refuge, leaking and with all three topmasts overboard. She was condemned. In a letter to Clarksons in March, Gustaf Erikson estimated his losses as 60,000-80,000 Finnish Marks. He considered buying *Ingrid* back from the insurers for next to nothing and getting her repaired at home. Nothing came of that however. The vessel was bought by Allen Adams & Co Ltd in Southampton.[1]

1 Built by a group of farmers and their sons at Knutnäs the last successful example of the old style of Åland shipping of the nineteenth century, her ownership so fragmented that it was said that everyone in Geta had a share in the *Ingrid;* she had had a very successful career in the North Sea and Baltic trades before the war. After extensive repairs she was employed by her British owners in trade with the West Indies and subsequently, when owned by the Stephens family in Fowey in Cornwall, in the home trade, when she was the largest sailing vessel on the British coast. The only Åland-built vessel to pass under the British flag she was not broken up until 1938. She sailed both for the last large scale owner of sailing vessels in the world, Gustaf Erikson, and the last owners of square-rigged merchant sailing vessels in Britain, the Stephens family of Fowey. She was also one of the last three square-rigged merchant sailing vessels ever to operate from a home port in the United Kingdom. See the essay 'My Girlfriend *Ingrid*' in National Maritime Museum Monograph No 36.

Ingrid, and the other minor ventures of 1916, are however overshadowed by a few really big investments: the acquisition of 58/100ths in *Borrowdale,* 61/100ths in *Professor Koch,* and 69/100ths in *Grace Harwar.*

Borrowdale was a three-masted iron barque, originally fully-rigged, and built by W H Potter & Co in Liverpool in 1868. She measured 1,268 tons gross, 1,190 tons net and 1,850 tons deadweight. August Troberg and his partners had bought the vessel as early as 1899, and she was therefore a real veteran in the Åland fleet, not to mention on the great oceans. *Borrowdale*, which in 1899 had cost 105,000 Finnish Marks, had brought in constant if not spectacular dividends for her owners and by 1909 had 'sailed out of the book' — that is to say she had paid for herself with interest.

On 15 March 1916, she sailed under the command of Captain K Troberg from Pensacola, bound for Cardiff with pitchpine. A week later Gustaf Erikson bought 27/100ths in her according to a price of 300,000 Marks for the complete vessel. The freight from Pensacola was included in the purchase. It was a hazardous venture; *Borrowdale* was insured at 180,000 Marks for war risk, and only 25,000 Marks for sea risk. Besides this, her Bureau Veritas classification would expire upon her arrival in Cardiff — if she arrived. Her decks were worn out. If it proved necessary to reclass her, it would be a costly and time-consuming business. As *Borrowdale* headed from the peaceful reaches of the tradewinds into the dangerous waters around Britain, Gustaf Erikson was buying shares in her ownership. By the time she arrived on 28 April, after an unexpectedly fast passage, he owned 41/100ths in the vessel, and

Left, plate 75 Captain Eric Hugo Mattsson of Åkerlund, Geta, master of the *Ingrid*, photographed with his wife Selma in Dover in 1914 where the vessel was discharging lathwood. (Rakel Karlsson)

Below, plate 76 *Borrowdale* under tow in the Avon Gorge near Bristol. (National Maritime Museum)

he was still buying whatever he could come across. But it was without doubt easier, and cheaper, to buy while the vessel still lay out on the ocean.

From Cardiff, *Borrowdale* sailed with a lump sum freight of £8,800 to Port Nolloth, where she arrived on 21 August after a passage of 67 days. From there, she sailed in ballast to Sabine, Texas, where she arrived on 20 November and was chartered to Newport, Mon at 440/- per standard, arriving there on 22 February 1917 through the U-boat blockade. A few days before her arrival, Gustaf Erikson bought 11/100ths and increased his share in her to 70/100ths. For this trip *Borrowdale* was insured for £8,000 at a 12 per cent premium. But as she discharged her cargo bad news began to come in from the sea; premiums rose sharply. Her war risk insurance was raised to £18,000, then she was ready to sail under a new skipper, Captain A Björklund. She was outward bound when the skipper received the order to return from the British authorities; a U-boat had probably been reported in the shipping lanes. After waiting in the roads off Swansea for some time, *Borrowdale* was given permission to sail, but in the mouth of the Bristol Channel she was sunk. The telegram reached Mariehamn on 4 May 1917. The crew had managed to get ashore at Milford Haven in their own boats.

Borrowdale had been a profitable investment. In 1916, dividends totalling 250,000 Marks were paid out in three installments. Her insurance, as has been said, amounted to £18,000, and there was in addition part of the freight from Sabine to Newport to pay out.

On 14 August 1916, Gustaf Erikson signed a major new contract with August Troberg. It concerned 58/100ths in the three-masted steel barque *Professor Koch*, based on a price of 750,000 Marks for the complete vessel. From a couple of the other joint owners he acquired another 3/100ths. This vessel was bigger and, more important, younger than *Borrowdale*. This was followed a month later by the acquisition of the major part in the full-rigger *Grace Harwar*, according to a total price of 940,000 Marks. The shipping company A/B Delfin of Helsinki was the seller. These prices were generally considered to be fantastically high; one should remember that the Finnish Mark had not yet suffered any definitive weakening. Both vessels survived the war. Their sailings are described in the next chapter.

Plans flew higher. At the beginning of December 1916 Gustaf Erikson was in Helsinki. He visited August Troberg at his villa in Brunnsparken and discussed the remainder of Troberg's fleet. It had become clear that the great shipowner was considering winding up his company. For Gustaf Erikson it was a matter of striking while the iron was hot to secure his position as successor to the throne. After his return to

Below, plate 77 The barque *Professor Koch* built in 1891. (National Maritime Museum)

Above, plate 78 The steel full-rigged ship *Grace Harwar* built in 1889, discharging saltpetre from Tocopilla in the old City Docks, Bristol, in 1922. (National Maritime Museum)

Mariehamn, he wrote on 12 December, offering to take over Troberg's shares in vessels. He estimated the value of *Margareta* at 1.2 million Marks, *August* at the same amount, *Garnet Hill* at 1.6 million and *Lawhill* at 2.3 million. He was willing to buy any of the vessels if Troberg would sell all his shares — which would have involved a transaction of some five million Marks. He thought he could get Erik Nylund as a partner and had hopes of being able to pay cash with the help of a bank loan against the security of the vessels themselves. Negotiations continued, and by the end of January 1917 the transaction was as good as settled. On 29 January, Gustaf Erikson wrote to Clarksons that everything was ready for the purchase of Troberg's fleet, and that the bill of sale would be signed in Helsinki on 3 February. Captains Erik Nylund and Hugo Lundqvist would be partners, the former with 1/3 and the latter with 1/5 of the purchase price. Gustaf Erikson would himself be ship's husband for *Lawhill* and *Margareta,* Nylund for *August,* and Lundqvist for *Garnet Hill*, of which he had once been skipper.

But at the last moment the negotiations ran on to the rocks. The all-out U-boat campaign had begun on 1 February and had forced war-risk premiums up high. *Garnet Hill,* expected in England, found herself in the danger zone, and sure enough in February she was sunk. She was followed a couple of months later by *August.* In view of the menacing new omens, the purchasers called for an adjustment in the price, something which Troberg had no desire to discuss. Gustaf Erikson's partners withdrew. He carried on the discussion alone and on 6 March, bought *Margareta* (ex *Craigerne*), a four-masted steel barque built by Duncan & Co in Glasgow in 1889, with a deadweight of 3,100 tons, 1,873 tons gross, and 1,748 tons net. Her dimensions

Above, plate 79 The steel four-masted barque *Margareta* (National Maritime Museum)

were 270ft 2in by 40ft 0in by 23ft 6in. Troberg had bought the vessel in 1910. For Gustaf Erikson, she was to be a poor investment. Under the command of Captain Edvard Johnsson, *Margareta* was sunk on 17 May near her British port of destination. The crew came ashore on 20 May at Bantry, Castletown. Gustaf Erikson had paid for his 66/100ths of the 1.1 million Marks which was the vessel's price. He had bought 5/100ths the previous year. The British war insurance did not even represent 1/3 of the value, and an insurance at Salamandra for 373,000 Roubles (800,000 Marks) was rendered worthless because of the revolution and the depreciation of the Rouble, which left the company insolvent.

The sinking was a disappointment but hardly a surprise. He had written pessimistically to Clarksons a couple of weeks earlier, the same day he received the telegram about the loss of *Borrowdale*, '*Margareta* is expected in Liverpool in 10-14 days, even though she is probably heading for disaster.' He predicted the same fate for *Tjerimai* which should have been ready to sail from Liverpool — in fact she was already out in the waters from where a steady stream of lifeboats bearing shipwrecked seamen headed for land.

Margareta's story ends with a little mystery. Her mate, Captain J E Gustafsson (formerly skipper of *Thomasina*, until she was sunk in 1915), met Gustaf Erikson on a brief visit to Mariehamn in 1919 and related a strange story. Coming in to land after the torpedoing, he saw a sailing vessel being towed into Bantry Bay. He thought no more about the incident. He found work in the English woods and one day one of his comrades showed him a copy of the *Daily Sketch* in which there were a couple of photographs of a Russian four-masted barque and a cargo steamer which had been towed into Castletown as salvage. It had struck him that the barque resembled *Margareta*. Later, he began to ponder the matter, but by then he no longer had the newspaper. In February 1920, Gustaf Erikson wrote to Clarksons and asked them to make enquiries. In another letter some weeks later he complains about their lack of interest in the mystery, and with that it disappears from his correspondence.

Gustaf Erikson's biggest transaction during the war was made on 24 October 1917, when he bought *Lawhill* — but more of that in the next chapter.

Tjerimai's sojourn in Ponta Delgada became lengthy. The armistice on 11 November 1918 opened the way to England, but it was difficult to get a crew. Not until 16 December did she weigh anchor, still under the command of K E Karlsson. She finally arrived in Fleetwood with her cargo of logwood at the end of December. The demand for tonnage was as great as ever; it was a matter of making the most of opportunities as long as they continued to exist. The long-considered classification was postponed and sailings went ahead — first to Jamaica for a new cargo to Fleetwood, then to St John, New Brunswick, for a load of timber for London, where *Tjerimai* arrived on 6 December 1919 after a passage of 32 days. Captain Nordberg again took command. After yet another cargo of logwood, this time to Le Havre, and a timber cargo from Newfoundland to Hull, where she arrived on 7 January 1921 after a fast but difficult passage during which she suffered an assortment of injuries, deep-water had no further use for her. By the autumn of 1920, the world had all the tonnage it needed. Freights fell even more sharply than they had risen during the war years. It was now no longer worthwhile reclassing and fitting-out *Tjerimai* for Atlantic routes. Lathwood was her only chance and, like so many ageing Åland barques, she ended up in the North Sea traffic. According to one account, the battered copper nearest the waterline was removed in 1923, and the remainder went the same way a couple of years later when she went into dry dock in London, where the scrap served to pay for her docking. In 1921, Captain E Näsänen took over command, followed in 1924 by Captain Elis Mattson.

That year she paid out her last dividend. It might be of interest to see what the dividend lists have to report about the results of her sailings over the years. She paid out in Marks:

22 December 1913	16,000
30 September 1915	10,000
12 February 1916	60,000
23 June 1916	75,000
20 January 1917	100,000
10 May 1917	100,000
13 August 1917	120,000
31 August 1918	25,000
27 September 1919	200,000
31 December 1919	200,000
12 December 1923	75,000
31 December 1924	140,000

Especially significant were the dividends for 1916 and 1917, before the fall in value of Finnish currency. They were not nearly sufficient, of course, to finance the major vessel-purchases of these years, but their significance was not merely numerical. They strengthened self-confidence and optimism — good work for an old composite barque, unclassed and with her copper worn out.

After the stay in Ponta Delgada, *Tjerimai* played an increasingly modest role in Gustaf Erikson's fleet. *Professor Koch, Grace Harwar* and *Lawhill* had survived the war, *Woodburn* was bought in 1919, and *Herzogin Cecilie, Pommern, Penang* and others during the first half of the 1920s. When, on 22 August 1925, she went down in the North Sea after a collision with a Dutch trawler, and her last skipper, Captain S Sjölund, lost his life, some ten steel barques were still sailing on deep-water under Gustaf Erikson's flag — a stately fleet whose existence owed much to the good work done by the old barque on the World War's hazardous shipping lanes.

Below, plate 80 *Tjerimai* under sail in her old age. (National Maritime Museum)

CHAPTER 4

Ventures And Gains

'Instruct all skippers henceforth to send all remittances to you; they may be used to take care of freight advances or left over freights. If for some reason communications, telegraphic as well as postal, should be broken off, then look after the affairs of all vessels, charters etc, etc as if they were your own vessels' Gustaf Erikson wrote to Clarksons on 28 October 1917. If possible, the size of the remittances was to be telegraphed to him, and the money put in the bank. The accounts for different vessels should be kept strictly separate, and income from one vessel should not be used to defray any possible expenses for another.

The letter illustrates a Finnish shipowner's worries during the final phases of the First World War. The early years of the war were of course taxing for men at sea and for relatives at home, but sinkings were relatively few and sad news rare. Crews were given the chance to take to their boats. Shipowners too had their troubles, but these were more than compensated for by the fact that freights rose month by month, apparently with the certainty of a law of nature. Owners of sailing vessels who before the war had been directing ships valued at scrap price, were dictating conditions to charterers and paying cash for fitting-out.

But in 1917 a rapid succession of events complicated the problems of shipowners, and Finnish shipowners in particular: the all out U-boat campaign with its sinkings and astronomical war-risk premiums, the Russian Revolution with all its consequences, the Finnish civil war and the isolation from the rest of the world that collaboration with Germany occasioned, inflation and the fall of the Finnish Mark during the post-war years, and so on. The revolution made the Rouble gradually worthless, and equally worthless became the balance which Gustaf Erikson and many others with him had at the Salamandra insurance company. From the end of 1916 onwards, fears of a separate peace between Russia and Germany are glimpsed again and again in his correspondence. A separate peace while Finland still belonged to the Russian empire could have involved Finland in conflict between Russia and the Western powers, which would have meant Finnish vessels on the high seas running the risk of being taken as prizes. When the separate peace was finally concluded, Finland had already proclaimed her independence, but she found herself in a German harness, and had to put up with being treated accordingly. Finnish vessels were seized temporarily in the USA, among them *Grace Harwar* and *Professor Koch*, and lay idle for months of booming opportunities. Remittances from abroad could not get through; bank liabilities and other business matters at home had to be settled without them. 'No Åland shipowner has received a telegram for more than a month,' Gustaf Erikson wrote to his friend Viktor Sundman on 18 April 1918. He did not know whether 'The Professor' had sailed from New York, nor whether *Grace Harwar* had arrived in Boston. By 2 May there was still no sign of a telegram from England though it was later shown that Clarksons had cabled as early as 23 April about the American Board of Shipping's measures against these two vessels and the intention to time charter them on behalf of the US government. Enquiries and protests seem to have rung out into empty space; ships and skippers found themselves as remote as if they had sailed on to another planet. In the month before the armistice in November, Gustaf Erikson was still maintaining telegraphic contact with Clarksons through the shipowner F A Andersson in Stockholm, who forwarded telegrams by post or, if they were urgent, by cable.[1]

Under such conditions a shipping concern became a hazardous enterprise with high risks and unclear prospects. Of course the U-boats' decimation of the world's tonnage increased the value of the fleet which survived the war, and at the same time peace would bring with it a strong demand for cargo space — once it came and countries starved of foodstuffs, raw materials and industrial products had to be replenished. But there was no certainty as to how long the boom would last. It was later apparent that shipowners had generally under-estimated the capacity of British and American shipyards. There were not many who guessed that two years after armistice day the world would be full of cargo-hungry vessels.

Under pressure of the difficulties, Gustaf Erikson contemplated selling his fleet in the summer and autumn of 1918. Out in the world where freer conditions prevailed, vessel prices were higher than ever. In August, he offered his vessels for sale in *Norges Handels och Sjöfarts tidende* (the *Norwegian Trade and Shipping journal*); he had earlier taken steps to get a licence to sell abroad from the Senate. While the matter of the licence slowly dragged on without coming to any decisive conclusion, he replied to letters from prospective buyers in Sweden, Norway, Denmark and the Netherlands. On 27 August, he was asking 475 Kroner per ton deadweight for *Lawhill, Grace Harwar* and *Professor Koch*, 290 Kroner for *Tjerimai* and *Ingrid*, and 200 Kroner for *Southern Belle*, making a total of about 5.4 million Kroner. His quotations, incidentally, varied from one day to the next as prospects for the future became gloomier or more promising.

There was to be no sale. For one thing the matter of the licence was going sluggishly, and his correspondence with prospective buyers gives the impression that Gustaf Erikson was at heart more interested in finding out exactly what his fleet was worth than in disposing of it. Invariably the price he asked was a fraction higher than prospective purchasers were prepared to pay. One thing seems certain — he had no intention of giving up as a shipowner. If he was to sell, it was in order to invest in new vessels when peace eliminated the risks that Finland's pro-German policies carried with them.

In October his tone towards prospective buyers became chillier, and the armistice swept away all plans to sell. The matter of the licence lost its interest. 'We are not going to do any business this way, so far as buying a vessel is concerned. All's well that ends well. Yours faithfully, Gustaf Erikson,' he wrote laconically to a firm in Stockholm. On 12 December, he wrote to a broker in Amsterdam, saying in so many words that he was not selling a single one of his vessels; on the contrary he was buying vessels of 2,500-3,500 or 4,500 tons deadweight and was very interested in the German windjammers laid-up in Chile, *Kurt* for example. The same day, he wrote to Captain Anders Donner of *Grace Harwar*, painting a vivid picture of a shipowner's worries. *Professor Koch* had remained under seizure, fully loaded, in New York for five months, *Grace Harwar* had lain idle for seven months, *Tjerimai* had been lying in Ponta Delgada for a year and three months, *Ingrid* had been laid up since her purchase in 1917, and *Lawhill* had been lying in Brest for a year and two months. For easily understandable reasons a skipper was more inclined to take a retrospective view of things than to see the future with optimism; one result of the boom abroad and the expensive times at home was that the raising of skippers' salaries became a constant and topical bone of contention, all the more so as the vessels' crews sailed with their wages in Sterling or in Dollars.

The steel barque *Professor Koch* was built by Russell & Co in Glasgow in 1891 and measured during her Åland period 1,453 tons gross, 1,357 tons net and 2,350 tons deadweight. Her length was 236ft 2in, her beam 36ft 2in and her draught 21ft 7in. The vessel came into the Åland fleet in 1909, when she was bought by August Troberg and his partners. I have no information about her earlier history, except that during the 1890s she belonged to C H H Winters in Elsflet, and that *Professor Koch* was probably her original name. Lubbock mentions two steel barques of almost the same tonnage which were launched from Russell's slipway in 1891, namely *Collessie* for the Bank Line, and *Inveramsay* for the Inver Line, but he says nothing about the fate of these vessels.

1 Another of the difficulties was getting crews out from Åland to vessels in western European ports. Captain Karl V Karlsson of Vårdö recently described to me the route by which as a boy of 16 he was sent to join the Åland barque *Schwanden* in January-February 1915. He travelled by steamer from Vårdö to Mariehamn and then to Åbo, then by train to Tornio in Finland. Then they were taken in motor trucks to Karrungi and then walked across the ice over the Tornio River into Sweden. The next leg was by rail to Trondheim, then by steamer to Bergen, where they boarded another steamer for Newcastle. The final leg was by train for London and Gravesend. The whole journey took two weeks. There were eight of them from Vårdö, the master and mate were married men, the rest boys of 16 or 17. There were also 20 others from Åbo who were to join ships not from Åland. After 1916 it became increasingly difficult to get crews from Åland out to vessels in western Europe, or for crews to return home and some of them served in American vessels for the rest of the war.

On 14 August 1916, Gustaf Erikson bought the majority shareholding in *Professor Koch,* as has been mentioned in the previous chapter, according to a price of 750,000 Marks for the complete vessel, which lay in Portishead discharging a cargo from the Gulf. Her skipper was to be Captain K W Karlsson. Her first passage was with coke from Cardiff to Port Nolloth at 100/-, sailing on 25 September and arriving on 12 December. A possible charter with rice from Rangoon came to nothing as a result of the vessel being unclassed, similarly a cargo of wheat from Australia. On 13 December, *Professor Koch* sailed in ballast, bound for Pensacola, where she arrived on 10 March 1917 and underwent some of the repairs necessary for reclassification. She sailed again on 3 June for Buenos Aires with pitchpine at $40 per 1,000 superficial ft, and arrived, after a lengthy passage on 9 September. In Buenos Aires the classification was continued for a No 3 survey — altogether it seems to have cost between £3,500 and £4,000. On 26 November she sailed again with linseed at $13 per ton, for Boston. After arriving there on 14 February 1918, *Professor Koch* was chartered to South Africa, and she moved to New York to load. I have no definite information as to what her cargo consisted of.

So far everything had gone well on risk-free shipping lanes, even if passages had been lengthy and classification costly. But in New York unexpected difficulties arose. On 1 April the vessel was loaded and ready for sea when it was stopped by the American authorities, who considered themselves in need of all available freight tonnage in view of the decisive stage of the war. Although *Professor Koch* was never put to use, she was not released until July. She sailed on 12 August and put into Mossel Bay on 12 November, where part of her cargo was discharged. The major part went to Port Elizabeth, where the vessel arrived on 20 November 1918.

One often speaks of the capricious play of chance, a play well-known to sailing-vessel skippers in their daily interaction with the wind and the weather. Because of a misunderstanding or unclear orders, Captain Karlsson sailed to East London to load wool, very likely in accordance with the charter party's original stipulations. However, through Clarksons Gustaf Erikson had obtained permission to load at Port Elizabeth, but at the time the authorization was granted *Professor Koch* was already on her way to East London. There the crew jumped ship. Each deserter cost £50 and it was, besides, difficult to find new crew, as a result of which sailing was delayed. Finally — and here we see real finesse in the play of chance — she was ordered to Boston instead of New York, and off Boston the vessel sustained severe damage. Gustaf Erikson was already displeased before he heard of the damage and remarked, in a letter to Captain Karlsson, that the crew would have been kept on board if loading had been carried out in the open roads at Port Elizabeth instead of alongside the quay in East London.

Captain Karlsson had spoken earlier about resigning because of his salary being too low and while *Professor Koch* was on her way to Boston with 2,300 tons of wool, Gustaf Erikson decided to send a new skipper to America. On 23 May 1919 he sent his thanks to Captain Sundman in Helsinki who had succeeded in obtaining the necessary visas after two months of negotiations with the American Consulate, and the following day he wrote to Captain Karlsson that the new skipper, Captain Edvard Johnsson, was leaving immediately with a mate, Hellberg, and a steward, Häggblom.

The bad news of the damage had come three weeks earlier. *Professor Koch* had run aground 23 sea miles outside Boston and had been towed into port leaking. As has been said, it proved to be an expensive accident — about $96,000 in salvage and repairs. The insurance payment, 350,000 Finnish Marks, covered only a fraction of this at the current rate of exchange. Clarksons advanced over £15,000. In a letter to the firm, Gustaf Erikson thought he could cut this down 'to a minimum of a few thousand pounds again', thanks to the expected advance on the wheat freight in Buenos Aires.

Captain Johnsson took command on 23 June. On 30 September the vessel was ready for sea. She sailed for Norfolk, where she arrived on 7 October. Under Captain Johnsson's command, *Professor Koch* made the following passages:

1919 Norfolk/Buenos Aires. Coal @ $13 per ton. 3 Oct - 29 Dec.
1920 Buenos Aires/Falmouth for orders; ordered to Antwerp. Wheat @ 150/-.
Antwerp/Hampton Roads in ballast.
Hampton Roads/Copenhagen. Coal at 115 Danish Kroner per ton. Arrived 22 Oct.
Copenhagen/Frederikstad in ballast.
1921 Frederikstad/Melbourne. Timber @ 113/-. 665 standards below decks. 25 Jan - 20 Jun. Needing a cargo, wheat freights had fallen.
Melbourne/Newcastle NSW in ballast.
Newcastle/Iquique. Coal @ 35/-. 3 Sept - 1 Nov.

In Iquique, *Professor Koch* took on 2,317 tons of saltpetre at 40/- for Delgoa Bay and sailed on 29 January 1922, but met her destiny in Cape Horn's inhospitable waters. The vessel lost her rudder, bowsprit, fore-rigging and part of her main-rigging, as well as suffering other severe damage, in a collision with an iceberg, and subsequently drifted helplessly in the South Atlantic for a couple of months. On 17 April, her distress signals were spotted by a British cargo steamer which towed the disabled vessel into Montevideo on 20 April. By then the second mate, V Eriksson, had died. *Professor Koch* was sold by auction for 3,950 gold Dollars, and in September she was struck off the shipping register by the maritime court in Mariehamn. The time when it paid to recondition severely damaged sailing vessels was past by a couple of years.

Although *Professor Koch* was not a successful enterprise she was not a failure either, like *Margareta* for example. In October 1916, 160,000 Marks were paid out, her classification came in 1917, 100,000 Marks were paid out in February 1918, 400,000 Marks at the end of December the same year, and 200,000 Marks in 1924 in surplus from her insurance and sale. For Gustaf Erikson, the large remittance from Clarksons in December 1918 was especially welcome, as no ready money had come in that year. The repairs in Boston had swallowed up all income from the remaining freights of the boom years.

In the autumn of 1918, when there were plans to sell the fleet, *Professor Koch* was valued at about £50,000. Two years later, when the vessel lay waiting for freight in Melbourne, Gustaf Erikson wrote to Clarksons that he would settle for £9,000 if they could find a buyer, even though sending the crew home, the bill for fitting-out in Frederikstad and other expenses would have reduced this sum by more than half. This may be taken as an indication of the fundamental collapse of the freight market.

The fully-rigged ship *Grace Harwar* was built in Glasgow in 1889 by Hamilton & Co for W Montgomery in London. She measured 1,564 tons net, 1,816 tons gross at her last measurement, and 2,950 tons deadweight. Her dimensions were 266ft 7in by 39ft 1in by 23ft 5in.

Alan Villiers, who, in his book *By Way of Cape Horn*, described a passage in *Grace Harwar* from Wallaroo to Queenstown for orders, says he was unable to find out much about her history before 1910. She was one of a thousand long-distance traders, no clipper, but not a typical slow-sailing merchantman either. In *Sea Breezes*, he tells —or rather he lets Captain T C Fearon tell — of an eventful stay in Iquique and a passage from there to Falmouth in 1911, during the course of which she suffered four collisions, sailed 12,000 nautical miles without a bowsprit, and on separate occasions lost both port and starboard anchors.

Grace Harwar sailed for her original owners until 1913, when she was sold to a shipowner in Helsinki. In the summer of 1916, she lay in Mobile. On 5 July (5 August according to another account), she was driven ashore in a violent hurricane, together with *Frieda,* a four-masted iron barque which had joined the Åland fleet four years earlier when she was bought by Mathias Lundqvist Junior. Her injuries were severe. Gustaf Erikson, who was considering buying *Grace Harwar,* wrote to Clarksons on 27 August that he was reluctant to buy in view of the damage. However, on 14 September the transaction was concluded, in spite of everything. The seller, the Delfin Company in Helsinki, undertook to meet the cost of repairing the damage she suffered in the accident in accordance with Lloyds' requirements. The purchase price was 940,000 Marks. Gustaf Erikson took over 69/100ths and increased this share to 75/100ths within a short time.

After such repairs as were possible had been completed (dry-docking had to be postponed), the vessel sailed on 6 November, bound for Delgoa Bay with pitchpine at 600/-, under the command of J Erikson, and arrived on 10 March 1917. She could not go into dry-dock here either. However, the Lloyds' surveyor allowed a postponement of certain classification work. Captain Anders Donner, who had been torpedoed in February in *Garnet Hill* after previously skippering *Hermes*, took over command, and on 16 July she sailed for Australia in ballast. *Grace Harwar* was chartered with wheat from Geelong to Europe, and arrived in Melbourne for dry-docking on 4 August. During this time, Gustaf Erikson succeeded, 'after a couple of months' hard work' he says in a letter, in getting the charter to the European danger zone cancelled. The port of destination was to be Durban instead. The freight rate was reduced, but a considerable sum was saved in war-risk premiums.

Grace Harwar sailed from Geelong on 4 October, arriving in Durban on 3 December, where she unloaded, took on a general cargo (wool, according to one account) for a lump sum of $14,500, completed her cargo in Algoa Bay and sailed for

Boston on 7 February 1918. The company had been able to pay out 500,000 Marks of the pitchpine freight from Mobile. In addition to this, Captain Donner had remitted £10,134 to Clarksons from Durban and, after certain advances had been deducted, the company had remaining a balance of some £8,000 — frozen, admittedly, on account of the political situation in Finland.

In Boston *Grace Harwar* encountered the same difficulties as *Professor Koch* and other Finnish vessels. She was unloaded by 26 April and chartered to Australia from New York with barrels of oil. But she was detained in New York for several months. After being released in July, and loading, she was stopped by a new embargo, which appears to have concerned her cargo of oil. In October Gustaf Erikson thought the vessel had finally left New York, but it was not in fact until 26 November that everything was ready for her departure. The long delay in the middle of the lucrative economic situation was naturally unwelcome. The legal action over compensation for the enforced lay-days, which Gustaf Erikson and other Finnish shipowners took against the American Government was as unproductive as it was lengthy.

Grace Harwar arrived in Melbourne on 15 March 1919 after a passage of 108 days, and sailed on 20 May for Norrköping with wheat at 150 Swedish Kroner per ton. Immediately after her departure, the cargo consignee in Sweden paid half the freight, with the exception of £5,000 which had been drawn in advance in Australia — about 113,000 Kroner, or 385,000 Finnish Marks at the current rate of exchange. 350,000 Marks were immediately paid out in dividends.

But now Cape Horn joined the game. The westerlies' *Johanne* (the midsummer festival of St John's Eve in Scandinavia) is the southern midwinter, and it is a season which scarcely lends itself to pleasure-cruising and dancing around the maypole. From 22 to 24 June, *Grace Harwar* battled through a violent storm in which she suffered a good deal of damage. On 29 June, at a position 57° 57′ S and 74° 54′ W, the storm suddenly struck again and increased to hurricane strength. The foresail and the lower mizzentopsail were blown to ribbons and the lee rail was driven underwater, rendering the lee braces inaccessible. The seas rolled ceaselessly across her decks, the starboard poop-door was stove in and the South Atlantic burst into the saloon, which became a ruin in an instant. Charts, ships's papers, instruments and clothes were swept away or destroyed. One chronometer was salvaged. The forecastle too was laid waste; the crew took refuge on the poop. Storm-covers were torn loose and casings broken; the running gear broke free from its belaying pins and became entangled in indescribable confusion.

Left, plate 81 *Grace Harwar* and Mathias Lundqvist's four-masted barque *Frieda* ashore at Mobile after the hurricane of July, 1916. (National Maritime Museum)

When the storm abated, the vessel was in bad shape. An attempt to reach Port Stanley in the Falkland Islands was unsuccessful. The signal flags had been blown away — but there remained a megaphone. This proved useful on 23 July when contact was made with an Italian steamer. Captain Donner succeeded in obtaining an elderly sextant and a chart of the mouth of the river Plate. The salvaged chronometer seems to have been of doubtful value, seeing that he asked the Italians for another. But they needed their chronometers as badly themselves. On 26 July, *Grace Harwar* anchored in Montevideo harbour.

Had this happened a couple of years later, *Grace Harwar's* story would also have been at an end. But the freight market was still flourishing and the vessel was repaired at a cost exceeding £13,000, of which the insurance covered less than half. She did not sail again until the beginning of December. Gustaf Erikson managed to get the port of destination for her cargo changed to Hälsingborg and Malmö — two places admittedly, but both ice-free.

On 3 March 1920, *Grace Harwar* put into Hälsingborg. In Malmö, she received a visit from her owner and her relief skipper, Captain K V Lindqvist, who succeeded Captain Donner.

Grace Harwar's decks had not completely passed the inspection in Melbourne, although they had been approved by survey Number 3 in 1918. Lloyds' surveyor in Malmö allowed a postponement to Buenos Aires, where she was bound when she sailed on 8 April, chartered to the UK and Continent with grain at 145/-. This was the last of the good years' charters. The gross freight exceeded £20,000 and Clarksons' advance for repairs could be settled. From Buenos Aires, the vessel was ordered to Falmouth, and from there she was towed to Antwerp to discharge her cargo of grain (linseed according to another source). 'All's well that ends well. 14 or 15 lay-days in Falmouth is good these days, you know. Now it is a matter of arranging it so we get at least as many in Antwerp,' Gustaf Erikson wrote to Captain Lindqvist on 25 November. Freights were plummeting, pre-war estimates were revived and lay-day compensation again became an agreeable factor to reckon with. In fact this rose to a total of £1,900 from Falmouth and Antwerp. After unloading, Gustaf Erikson decided, somewhat hesitantly, to let the vessel undergo the No 1 survey, and was pleasantly surprised when the cost amounted to no more than £1,500 despite the partial renewal of the deck which had been a matter of primary concern for so long.

A pleasant surprise of any sort was welcome. The world's sailing vessel tonnage was now definitely ripe for laying-up, and the major disposal at scrap-prices had begun. But *Grace Harwar* did not give up. She was towed to Frederikstad in February 1921 at a cost of £600, which had suddenly become a sizeable sum in a ship's budget. On 2 April, she was ready for sea with 800 standards planed boards at 85/- below decks. She arrived in Melbourne 92 days later. The return passage to Falmouth, with wheat at 45/-, took 111 days. 'You have sailed manfully in what was previously judged a lazy-sailer,' Gustaf Erikson wrote to Captain Lindqvist. After unloading in Bremen and sustaining some damage — which was a fairly serious matter seeing that *Grace Harwar* had sailed uninsured since February 1921 — she arrived in Frederickshald on 10 March 1922, where she took on a new cargo of timber for Australia at 75/- per standard. Here Captain Lindqvist was succeeded by Captain August Gustafsson, formerly skipper of *Mermerus* and *Lucipara* among other vessels.

When she arrived in Melbourne on 16 July 1922, *Grace Harwar* was still unchartered. There was no cargo of wheat to be had. For coal from Newcastle NSW to Chile, only 17/9d was offered and this was unacceptable. It was more worthwhile to sail in ballast to Tocopilla, where a cargo of saltpetre was available at 30/- per ton.

In a letter of 1 November 1923, Gustaf Erikson remarks that *Grace Harwar* had been followed by bad luck, but nevertheless had paid out 1.55 million Finnish Marks as well as paying for several instances of damage, the greatest being in Montevideo. Space allows only a summary account of her remaining freight passages. Sailings in ballast have not been included. Rates were low and returns hardly remarkable. What was remarkable was that the old full-rigger lasted as long as she did.

1923 Tocopilla/Falmouth. 105 days. Discharged in Bristol.
Restigouche/Buenos Aires. Timber. 65 days, arrived 6 Sept.
1924 Ingramport/Buenos Aires. Timber. 59 days, arrived 16 April.
Campbellton/Melbourne. Timber. Arrived 19 Dec.
1925 Melbourne/Falmouth for orders. Wheat @ 40/-. 125 days. Discharged Belfast.
Swansea/Luderitz Bay. Coal. 65 days, arrived 3 Dec.
1926 Campbellton/Buenos Aires. Timber. 81 days, arrived 27 Sept.
1927 Port Augusta/Queenstown for orders. Wheat. 136 days. Discharged Cardiff.
Swansea/Luderitz Bay. Coal. 73 days, arrived 5 Nov.
1928 Guanape Peru/Wilmington NC. Guano @ 52/6. 43 days. Passed Panama Canal 7 Aug, 14 days from Guanape.
1929 Wallaroo/Queenstown for orders. Wheat. 108 days, arrived Glasgow to discharge on 16 Sept.
1930 Swansea/LaGuayra. Coal @ 17/-. 57 days, arrived 21 Jan. Arrived Mariehamn and laid-up 10 June.
1931 Middlesborough/Port Louis, Mauritius. Fertilizer @ 21/-. 93 days, arrived 14 Sept.
1932 Juan de Novo/Auckland NZ. Guano. 73 days, arrived 2 Feb.
Port Victoria/Queenstown for orders. 132 days, arrived Falmouth 11 Sept.
Wheat @ 27/6. Discharged in London.
1933 Port Pirie/Falmouth for orders. Wheat @ 27/9. 130 days, arrived Glasgow to discharge 20 July. Mariehamn 28 Aug - 3 Oct.
1934 Wallaroo/Falmouth for orders. Wheat @ 25/6. 128 days, arrived Cork to discharge 22 July. Mariehamn 1 Sept - 9 Oct.
1935 Port Broughton/Falmouth for orders. Wheat @ 25/- 98 days, arrived London to discharge 5 July. Towed on 16 July from London to Charlestown Firth of Forth, to be broken up.

Grace Harwar was never rerigged as a barque, as were so many other full-riggers. She has been called the last full-rigger afloat, and she deserves this honoured title, if one takes into consideration her world-spanning sailings. In 1935, there were, admittedly, a score of fully-rigged training ships and floating museums left in the world, besides the American *Tusitala* ex *Inveruglas,* which was laid up, and *Calbuco* ex *Circe,* registered in Chile, and *Maipo*, owned by a guano company in Peru, which are reported to have sailed with cargo at least occasionally. But *Grace Harwar* was the only one to carry on the traditions of world-wide commercial deep-water sailing to the very last.

On 24 October 1917, Gustaf Erikson signed his boldest contract: he bought *Lawhill* from August Troberg for 2.5 million Finnish Marks.

This vessel was built by W B Thompson & Co in Dundee in 1892 for Captain Barrie. She later belonged to the Anglo-American Oil Co, was sold in 1911 to G Windram & Co for £5,500, and was bought by Troberg in 1914 for £8,500 — over 200,000 Marks. She visited Australia, the west coast of America, the Gulf and South Africa between 1914 and 1917, and was lying in Brest in the summer of 1917.

Lawhill was one of the giants in Gustaf Erikson's fleet. (See the table for a comparison in this respect.[1])

'The *Lawhill*' Lubbock writes, 'is rather an exceptional vessel'. He was thinking of her rig. She lacked royals and was a typical 'baldheader' but despite the weight and inelegance of her rig, she showed herself to be a good sailer. However, it was another peculiarity which Lubbock had in mind: her topgallant masts were rigged aft of the topmast heads — something which certainly gave rise to heated debate in the last sailing vessel ports around the world. Lubbock quotes a couple of British sea captains' pronouncements as to the advantages of *Lawhill's* rig. One thought the arrangement gave the rig increased strength; another, as her mate, had never found taking in her topgallants any more troublesome than on other vessels.

The acquisition of *Lawhill* was preceded by lengthy negotiations which have already been glimpsed in the text. In a letter of 7 June 1917 to Troberg, who was spending the summer in Helsinki, Gustaf Erikson offers 1.3 million Marks. The U-boat campaign had dragged down the price considerably, it seems, since the beginning of the year.

Troberg was invited to consider carefully what he had gained by selling *Margareta,* and lost by not selling *Garnet Hill* and *August*, before they were sunk. A new letter of 21 June increases the offer to 1.5 million, and refers to the possibility of a separate peace treaty between Russia and Germany and the consequences for Finland's merchant fleet beyond the North Sea. From the same letter, Troberg learns that Åland is having tropical weather with temperatures of 30°C in the shade, that his apple trees are snow white, and that no rain has fallen since they have been in blossom. This lyrical excursion does not seem to have cheered him up noticeably. He did not answer until 21 July: two million.

'Never intend to buy a *Lawhill* merely because she is the country's largest ship. No, vanity is the least of my weaknesses to date,' Gustaf Erikson announces immediately. He stands his ground with his offer of 1.5 million, but is willing to settle for 2 million 'if free from outgoing', ie if the seller pays the premiums for war and sea-risks from Brest to a port outside the Blockade zone.

The negotiations continued after Troberg's return to Mariehamn. It was not far to walk between the cousins' respective farmsteads. At the same time, *Lawhill* was undergoing classification for her No 3 survey in Brest. Her skipper was Captain

1 The vessels compared were all steel four-masted barques. Four of them were still afloat in 1977, *Moshulu* at Philadelphia, *Passat* at Travemünde, *Viking* at Goteborg and *Pommern* at Mariehamn. Only the latter is today virtually unaltered from her years as an active merchant vessel and only she conveys a true impression of what these ships were like in their prime.

	TONNAGE			DIMENSIONS (ft in)		
	Dwt	Gross	Net	Length	Breadth	Draught
Moshulu	4900	2120	2696	335 3	46 9	26
Passat	4700	3130	2585	322 0	47 2	26 5
Lawhill	4600	2816	2540	317 4	45 0	25 1
Pamir	4500	2798	2365	316 0	46 0	26 2
Olivebank	4400	2795	2427	326 0	43 1	24 5
Herzogin Cecilie	4350	3111	2584	314 8	46 3	24 2
Melbourne	4250	2691	2525	305 1	44 0	24 7
Pommern	4050	2376	2114	294 8	43 4	24 5
Viking	4000	2670	2154	293 8	42 5	23 2
Hougomont	4000	2378	2074	292 4	43 2	24 1
Archibald Russell	3950	2354	2048	291 3	42 9	24 0

Above, plate 82 *Lawhill*. Note that the jigger mast is a pole and the lower masts and topmasts are in one piece. The topgallant masts are fidded abaft the topmasts and there are no royals. She is setting sail off Falmouth in 1929. (National Maritime Museum)

August Jansson, a tried and proven deep-water sailor, and her first mate was Ruben de Cloux. Her price was finally agreed, as has been said, at 2.5 million. However, Troberg was to be responsible for all classification expenses up to 24 October.

Gustaf Erikson was well aware that it was a risky speculation. The day the contract was signed, he wrote to Clarksons, asking them for an advance to cover all expenses until further notice, premiums for an £80,000 harbour risk insurance among other things. The same letter says that it was virtually out of the question to order the vessel to sail from Brest before the end of the war. Another went to Captain Jansson, who was asked to remain at his post. Otherwise de Cloux was to take command for the time being, and possibly permanently, unless Gustaf Erikson's brother-in-law, Ekblom, who had priority, put in a claim. *Lawhill,* he wrote, was threatened by two dangers: a separate truce and requisition. While they waited for events to take their course, it was a matter of scraping and chipping rust, leading and painting, thereby keeping the crew on board, and not letting the mates go but rather signing them on for a couple of years, raising their salaries if necessary. The risks were great, but Gustaf Erikson thought less about them than about the vessel's three sets of sails and her donkey engine and two winches, with which it was possible to load or discharge through two hatches simultaneously.

His optimism suffered a blow when, on 18 June 1918, *Lawhill* was requisitioned by the French Government and valued at 1.8 million Francs. 'Present Scandinavian sale prices 40 Pounds dw', Gustaf Erikson telegraphed immediately to

Clarksons, who were instructed to protest and to protect his interests. £40 per ton deadweight meant £180,000, or about 5.5 million Marks. 'Since France has recognised Finland's independence, I am surprised at the way they requisition the vessel without the owner's permission and set a value on it at only half the Scandinavian market price. Be so good as to protest...', reads a letter to Clarksons of 26 September. Protests, of course, are easily drowned out by the thunder of guns.

Captain de Cloux remained in Brest to keep an eye on the vessel and its fittings. Immediately after the armistice on the Western Front, Gustaf Erikson asked Clarksons to take every possible step to secure the vessel's release from French seizure, and to offer de Cloux the command with a salary of 12,000 Marks, as he says in a letter of 19 November. The problem was to get the vessel back intact with all her fittings and fixtures. For a while nothing was heard about compensation. Not even the slightest hint of anything of the sort reached Mariehamn.

On the contrary, bad news came. *Lawhill* had been rigged down by the French authorities; only the lower masts were left standing. On 2 December, Gustaf Erikson wrote to Clarksons that he had learnt this 'from reliable quarters ... It is an unforgivable, unspeakable outrage against a private citizen's property. Consider that 4,600 tons d w are lying idle while people are starving. Why, one almost despairs, owning six vessels and having only one trading — even though the war ended on the 11th ultimo'. Confirmation of the rumoured rigging down was not long in coming. Every available means was now brought into operation both to get the vessel released and ready for sea, and to obtain compensation. Clarksons, for their part, were ordered to try to influence the French Government, not only in the matter of compensation, but also in getting permission to rerig the vessel on his own behalf. After all, de Cloux was in Brest. If the French authorities were left to see to the matter themselves, it could be expected to take 'not months but years in getting the claim through'. At the same time, councillor Sjöblom in Helsinki was instructed to make an official attack. 'It would be best for the French Government to receive reminders from several quarters'.

On 8 January 1919, the long-awaited telegram finally arrived with news of *Lawhill's* release. The news that the French authorities would themselves recondition the vessel was received with less pleasure; but they showed themselves quicker to act than Gustaf Erikson had expected. At this time, the question of a charter was very much to the fore. There was no lack of alternatives: wheat from the River Plate, pitchpine from Pensacola, petroleum from America to Australia. The first of these alternatives was chosen. *Lawhill* sailed in ballast on 17 April under the command of de Cloux, bound for Buenos Aires, insured at one third of her cost price and chartered with wheat at 200/-. She arrived on 6 June, sailed again on 20 July and arrived in Aarhus on 28 September. The total gross freight, about £45,000, could be drawn in advance in Buenos Aires. '*Lawhill* looks as if she is going to do splendid business after her long inactivity,' Gustaf Erikson wrote to Clarksons.

From 11 to 13 October the vessel was towed to Frederikshald for 10,000 Norwegian Kroner. Here she received a visit from her owner, who was more than well-satisfied with his ship. She sailed on 28 December with 1,383 standards planed boards and arrived in Melbourne on 5 April 1920 after 99 days at sea. It seems that wheat, at 150/-, was taken on in Geelong, where *Lawhill* sailed from on 15 June, uninsured. After a passage of 96 days, she arrived at La Palice, near La Rochelle, on 18 September. Here, as in Melbourne, certain minor repair work remaining from the classification for survey No 3 in Brest was carried out — among other things, nine new plates were put in. Captain de Cloux was urged to try to get Lloyds' final certificate dated 1920 instead of 1917, thus allowing her next classification for No 1 to be put forward by three years, a manoeuvre *Professor Koch* had succeeded with in Boston.

Lawhill managed to get yet one more freight before the boom ended: Wallaroo to Bordeaux at 120/-. She sailed from La Rochelle on 27 November, arriving at Port Lincoln for orders on 14 February 1921 after 78 days, sailed from Wallaroo on 13 March and arrived in Bordeaux on 3 July. From Australia she sailed uninsured, as did *Woodburn* some months later. 'My whole existence depends on both vessels' 120/- Australia freights,' Gustaf Erikson wrote to de Cloux on 13 January 1921. From the £27,210 gross freight, £21,450 remained to be drawn on arrival. A few hours after the arrival telegram from Bordeaux, a second cable arrived — *Grace Harwar*'s from Melbourne. 'The business is saved', Gustaf Erikson wrote. After the sudden fall of the Finnish Mark, he was able to sell £17,000 of *Lawhill's* net yield at rates of exchange between 212 and 220 Marks to the Pound, and settle his bank liabilities at home.

Lawhill's four freights had yielded excellent results. The vessel declared an income of 2.5 million Marks for 1920. But even as the large cargo of wheat was being loaded, freight rates were falling fast. While Clarksons tried to arrange a general cargo from Australia, wheat freights plunged to 60/-, 50/- and 40/-, or exactly one third of what they had been. Captain de Cloux was met by a letter in Bordeaux. There were two possibilities — Port Lincoln for orders, unchartered, or home to Mariehamn to lay-up. If he opted for the latter alternative, he was to come home with the vessel polished up and her brass gleaming, bringing with him a few bottles of something, as guests could be expected on board, eager to see Scandinavia's biggest sailing vessel.

It was to be Port Lincoln however, and a wheat freight at 40/-.[1] It was not until the following year (29 June) that *Lawhill* paid her first visit to Mariehamn, on her way to Skellefteå for timber.

In 1921, the dispute with the French government was finally settled with the payment of 25,000 Francs per month for the period between 18 June and 11 November, and 35,000 Francs per month from Armistice Day to 4 April 1919, a total of 286,000 Francs — exactly half of what Gustaf Erikson had claimed. The major portion of this amount had already been received in advances.

In Bordeaux, de Cloux left the command to his first mate, Captain J E Gustafsson, and became skipper of the newly acquired *Herzogin Cecilie*. After a passage in ballast to Adelaide, and with wheat at 40/- to England, Gustafsson was succeeded, in May 1922, by Captain A Öfverström.

Lawhill's continuing freight passages can be recorded in a brief summary:

1922 Skellefteå & Hargshamn/Melbourne. 118 days, arrived 30 Dec. 1,275 standards planed boards @ 75/-.
1923 Newcastle NSW/Iquique. 55 days. 4,600 tons coal @ 15/6d.
Iquique/Bordeaux. 105 days, arrived 3 Nov. Saltpetre @ 24/-.
Captain Julius Gustafsson skipper.
1924 Newcastle NSW/Tocopilla. 52 days, arrived 22 Aug. On 30 July, Captain Gustafsson died. 1st Mate Captain C Holmqvist took over command.
1925 Iquique/Ghent. Saltpetre @ 30/-. Arrived 5 March. Captain F Grönlund skipper.
Grangemouth/San Antonio. 104 days, 3,138 tons coke @ 15/9d and 850 tons ballast.
1926 Iquique/Queenstown for orders. 103 days. Saltpetre @ 27/6d. Discharged Bruges.
Campbellton/Melbourne. 124 days, arrived 12 December. Timber.
1927 Melbourne/Queenstown. 120 days, discharging London. Wheat.
1928 Taltal/Delfzijl, arrived 24 March. Saltpetre @ 30/-.
Port Lincoln/Falmouth. 130 days. Wheat @ 39/-. Discharged Le Havre.
1929 Hudiksvall/Melbourne. 117 days, arrived 31 Déc. Timber @ 86/3d.
1930 Wallaroo/Queenstown. 120 days. Wheat @ 22/-. Discharged in Rotterdam.
1931 Port Adelaide/Queenstown. 106 days, Wheat @ 32/6d. Discharged in Birkenhead. Lay in Mariehamn 14 July - 12 Sept.
1932 Port Victoria/Falmouth. 121 days, Wheat @ 30/-. Discharged in Birkenhead. Lay in Mariehamn 14 Aug - 21 Sept.
1933 Wallaroo/Falmouth. 126 days. Wheat@ 28/6d. Discharged in Cork. Lay in Mariehamn 20 Aug - 8 Sept.
Trångsund/London. 10 days, arrived 26 Oct. Lathwood @ 47/6d.
1934 Adelaide/Falmouth. 122 days. Wheat @ 24/9d. Discharged London.
1935 Wallaroo/Falmouth. 124 days. Wheat @ 25/-. Discharged at Barry Dock. Lay in Nystad 11 Aug - 2 Oct.
1936 Port Lincoln/Falmouth 118 days. Discharged in Belfast.
1937 Port Lincoln/Falmouth 107 days, arrived 16 June. Discharged London.
Trångsund/East London. 91 days. 73 days from Copenhagen.
1938 Port Victoria/Falmouth. 131 days. Discharging in Birkenhead.
1939 Port Lincoln/Falmouth. 140 days, arrived 16 Aug. Sailed in ballast Troon/Montevideo for orders 3 May 1940.
1940 Assumption, Seychelles/Auckland. Guano @ 46/-.
1941 Port Lincoln/East London. Wheat @ 55/-. Arrived 23 July after 68 days. Seized on 21 Aug. Condemned by prize court on 22 Sept 1942.

Lawhill was remarkably fast on some of her outward passages in ballast: 78 days from Bordeaux to Port Lincoln for orders in 1924, 88 days from London to Port Victoria in 1934, 87 days from Belfast

1 This passage is described in Alan Villiers' *The Set of the Sails*, London, 1949, and a number of subsequent editions.

to the same port in 1936 and 85 days from Birkenhead to Port Lincoln in 1938. The passage with timber from Trångsund in 1937 was also fast.

After being condemned by the prize court in 1942, *Lawhill* continued to sail between Australia and South Africa under the command of her former skipper, Captain Arthur Söderlund. She ended her days derelict at Lourenço Marques.

After the last year of the First World War, with its hazards and its misty horizons, 1919 the year of peace followed with brightening prospects. Vessels were sailing again, and war-risk premiums were gone, but the high wartime freight rates remained. Gustaf Erikson was on the lookout for new vessels. He considered *Perim* and *Katanga* among others and in March he offered £8 per ton deadweight for *Inversnaid*, which, however, was bought by Sir William Garthwaite, and rechristened *Garthsnaid*. After *Lawhill*'s departure from La Plata, at which point he had a £30,000 freight at his disposal, Gustaf Erikson went immediately to Clarksons. The French four-masted barque *Caroline* interested him, but was bought by a Norwegian company — she was destroyed by fire the following year in Antofagasta. *Jordan Hill* caught his fancy even more, but Clarksons evidently did not share his optimism. A month later, he asked impatiently why they had not arranged the purchase of the vessel, and wondered if his friend Ingman was on holiday. He personally had recourse to £50,000 and it should have been easy enough to arrange further credit.

Abroad, competition with Norwegians and others for vessels seems to have been too tough for his resources. In November, he bought the three-masted steel barque *Woodburn* through the Finnish Shipping Bureau in Åbo, with whom he was actively in communication. Blom, the director of a bank in Nystad, was the seller. The price was 2.9 million

Below, plate 83 *Garthsnaid* ex *Inversnaid* (Captain James Simpson). The photograph was taken by the second mate Mr Turner from the jibboom end after four hands had been sent aloft to secure a section of the foresail which had come free from the gaskets in very heavy weather, probably on a passage from Iquique to Delagoa Bay, in 1919. This is perhaps the finest and most revealing heavy weather photograph ever taken in a big merchant sailing vessel. (National Maritime Museum)

Above, plate 84 The steel barque *Woodburn.* (National Maritime Museum)

Marks. This sum cannot be compared numerically with *Lawhill*'s price two years earlier. In the autumn of 1919, inflation was in full swing. At the turn of the year 1919-20, the Pound already stood at 126 - 128 Marks. Three weeks later it had fallen to 86 Marks, but this was only temporary; the fall of the Finnish Mark continued inexorably with short intervals of improvement.

Woodburn was built by Russell & Co in Port Glasgow in 1896, and measured 1,552 tons gross, 1,445 tons net and 2,600 tons deadweight. Her dimensions were 242ft 0in by 37ft 5in by 21ft 8in. She was bought in Malmö, fully fitted out for a passage in ballast to Norfolk, Virginia. 'Sail as though the vessel were uninsured,' says a letter of 4 November to her skipper, Captain E W Hellsten. The vessel's hull was in fact insured for only 600,000 Marks, added to which there was 'missing' and mine-risk coverage for £30,000.

It seems that Captain Hellsten was not happy with the change of ownership. Captain A Öfverström took over the command and on 13 November, *Woodburn* was towed to Copenhagen to complete her fitting-out and provisioning at Schierbecks. The Norfolk charter was cancelled amicably and on 17 November she sailed for orders at Fayal, one of the islands of the Azores, often used as an order port.

But the autumn south-westerlies were severe and after a couple of days, *Woodburn* put into Frederikshald to shelter from a storm after her ballast had shifted, where she was met with somewhat mixed feelings by Gustaf Erikson himself, who had come to Norway to see *Lawhill.* In any case, he got the opportunity to look over his new vessel, which he found to be rather well-maintained, even if the outer plating above the ballast-line was 'seriously rusted and probably had not been chipped or painted for many years'. The rigging too was partially 'rusted-up'. As soon as he arrived home in Mariehamn, he saw to it that there was no need for bank director Blom in Nystad to be left in ignorance as to the extent of the rust.

At the beginning of December, *Woodburn* was once again driven back to Frederikshald by storms. On 19 January 1920, she reached Fayal after a passage of 43 days and the loss of a good number of sails. She was ordered to Buenos Aires, where she arrived on 26 February and was chartered with grain to Denmark at 13,550 Danish Kroner, with the possibility of the UK as an alternative destination at an increase of 10 Kroner. She sailed on 15 April from Buenos Aires, arrived in Queenstown on 27

June with a leak in the forepeak, and was ordered to Bremen. After discharging her cargo, she was towed to Norrköping from where she sailed on 12 August, bound for South Africa with timber at 240/-.

Woodburn arrived at Port Elizabeth on Christmas Day 1920. Part of her cargo was discharged at Port Natal. Her voyage continued in ballast by way of Cape Borda to Port Victoria, where she arrived on 12 April after struggling through a cyclone on 13 - 14 March at latitude 41°, longitude 63°, and losing sails. In Captain Öfverström's opinion, only the sacrifice of the sails saved the vessel from total loss. As it was, the loss was estimated at £560. *Woodburn* was partially insured with Allmänna Finska Försäkrings A/B in Helsinki. According to current practice, no compensation was payable for sails lost on the high seas. On the grounds that the canvas had been sacrificed to save the vessel, Gustaf Erikson claimed compensation nevertheless, but the insurers had no inclination to interpret the matter in the same way as Captain Öfverström.

The freight from Australia, 2,453 tons of wheat at 120/- (ie a total of £14,700,) was *Woodburn*'s last during the boom and it yielded a fine profit. £3,800 was drawn in advance in Port Victoria; among her expenses is an entry for £200 for two Germans who jumped ship. Falmouth was the order port and the wheat was discharged in Cardiff. Here there was a change of command, Captain M Nordberg taking over as skipper.

The golden years had now been and gone. 75/- was offered per standard from Viborg to Delgoa Bay, compared with 240/- from Noorköping to Port Elizabeth a year earlier! Would the vessel be reduced to hauling lathwood Gustaf Erikson wondered in a letter to Captain Nordberg. He thought the vessel was too small for long-distance routes. Nordberg didn't take kindly to talk of lathwood, and things didn't turn out so badly for *Woodburn*. She continued to sail on deep-water right to the end.

Her passages in freight after she discharged in Cardiff in the autumn of 1921, may be listed briefly. Sailings in ballast are not included.

1921-22 Cardiff/Port Mauritius. 105 days. Coal @ 20/-.
1922. Melbourne/London. 129 days. Wool, hides & talc. £5,100 lump sum freight.
1923. Frederikstad/Melbourne 118 days. 729 standards planed boards @ 70/-.
1923-24. Mejillones/Dunkirk 161 days. 2,600 tons saltpetre @ 39/-. After 140 days, arrived Azores for provisioning. In Dunkirk, Captain I Hägerstrand took command.
1924. Pictou, Nova Scotia/Preston 20 days, 18 days to Milford Haven, timber @ 65/-.
1924-25 Restigouche/Buenos Aires 56 days. Ordered to Rosario to discharge. Timber @ $15 per 1000 superficial ft. Captain F Ejder took command in Rosario.
1925. Guanape/Norfolk, Va via Panama Canal. Guano @ 52/6d.
1926. New York/Sydney. 109 days. Ordered to Newcastle NSW with oil at 21 Cents a barrel.

After discharging in Newcastle, *Woodburn* sailed for Suva, Fiji islands on 30 August, and arrived on 18 September. The barque was too small for deep-water sail's few remaining trades and had to be sold. Her buyers used her as a coal hulk.

'At the moment, the position is excellent both at home and abroad,' Gustaf Erikson wrote to Clarksons on Christmas Eve 1919. His debt of 3 million Marks to the Lantmannabank was a trifle, considering the value of his fleet. Reckoning £14 per ton deadweight, this had risen to more than 26 million Marks. He had staked a great deal and won more.

But staking did not always mean winning. A year later, the position was anything but excellent. Bank debts, primarily to the Unionbank, into which the Lantmannabank had been incorporated, had doubled. At the same time, the collapse of the freight market during the latter half of 1920 had reduced the market value of the fleet to a mere fraction of what it had been in the calculations of Christmas 1919.

The years 1920-21 can without doubt be described as the most crisis-ridden in the development of Gustaf Erikson's shipping concern. A couple of unfortunate new purchases in the eleventh hour of the boom, the steamships *Rigel* and *Edgar*, and the tightening up of the money market with rising interest rates and restricted credit opportunities imperilled his solvency. *Lawhill's* and *Woodburn*'s last good freights at 120/- from Australia and their successful passages back up to Europe definitely saved the situation. Inflation reduced the bank debts and counteracted the fall in the value of the vessels; and the freights converted into Finnish Marks, helped, of course, to consolidate the position when the crisis had passed its peak. Bank debts could be cut down to 2.5 million Marks after *Lawhill's* 17,000 Pounds Sterling were sold at 212 — 220 Marks to the Pound in July 1921. On 3 July came *Lawhill's* arrival telegram from Bordeaux, at the same time as the news of *Grace Harwar*'s unexpectedly fast passage to Australia with timber, as has already been said. Two days later, Gustaf Erikson wrote to the Mariehamn City Council donating 10,000 Marks 'towards covering any costs the city may be obliged to bear in respect of work done to aid Åland's reunion with Sweden.'

When *Woodburn* arrived in Cardiff in September, the Pound stood at 275 — 280 Finnish Marks, 'which put a better face on things', as he says in a letter to Captain Öfverström. Bank credit could then be reduced accordingly, and the acquisition of new vessels could again be considered. *Herzogin Cecilie* was purchased.

This chapter can be concluded with a few words about *Rigel* and *Edgar*, typical phenomena of the troubled times. In 1919, when Gustaf Erikson was unable to invest *Lawhill's* profits in a first-rate foreign sailing vessel, he bought *Woodburn*, as has already been mentioned. Trusting in good charters for both vessels in 1920, he bought the two tramp steamers in the late winter of that year, both newly built. *Rigel*, built at Sandviken's shipyard, loaded only 500 tons and cost 2.1 million Marks. After a few unprofitable freight-passages to England, she was sold for 1.85 million Marks to Finska Transoceana A/B as early as 15 September. *Edgar*, originally named *Stettin* and built at the Nya Varvet in Helsinki, loaded 1,250 tons and cost about 7 million. After sailing satisfactorily enough with relatively good charters for the summer of 1920, the sale of the steamer was considered. In February 1921, she was laid-up in Mariehamn, Prospective buyers proved extremely cool '*Edgar* is my cancer,' Gustaf Erikson wrote to Captain Törnqvist of *Mariechen* in September 1921. Clarksons did what they could in London, as did Olson & Wright in Stockholm — Gustaf Erikson's general factotum in the Swedish capital in respect of crews in transit and broker commissions of various sorts. Everything seemed to be in vain. The price gradually sank below £15,000. Only after endless correspondence with shipowners and brokers in Helsinki, Stockholm, Copenhagen, London, Leith, Hull and Christiansand — to name a few — was *Edgar* sold, on 15 May, to Schiffgesellschaft Dollast in Hamburg for £12,900. The loss was of the order of 5 million Marks; but the cancer had been removed and the patient was content. He decided immediately to use the money to buy one or two new sailing vessels, seeing that bank matters at home had been restored to balance by *Lawhill* and *Woodburn* — with the kindly assistance of the inflation of the Finnish Mark. On 18 May, he wrote two letters; one to Captain Öfverström asking him to look at *Peking* in London, and one to a broker in Paris with enquiries about *Pola*.

Like other Åland ships built at the end of the First World War, *Rigel* and *Edgar* seem to have been typical products of the crisis-period — thirsty for fuel and uneconomical to run, above all too expensive to yield any profit and pay insurance premiums on their purchase prices even with good freights. Added to this was the fact that in 1920, tramp operations in Finland still had special difficulties to contend with, a shortage of bunker coal among other things. *Rigel* sailed on her first passage from Lovisa on 30 April and arrived in London on 18 May. She burned wood instead of coal as far as Malmö. There the steamer lay from 3 to 13 May, initially waiting for a permit to fill her bunkers, and subsequently delayed by the authorities on the ground of her crankiness. Ten standards of her deck cargo had to be unloaded. By the time she was ready to sail, the stokers had all deserted.

The failure of these two tramp steamers led Gustaf Erikson to concentrate on developing his sail-powered fleet for a decade and a half. It was not until 1937 that he bought SS *Kirsta*. 'All's well that ends well' was his watchword. If *Rigel* and *Edgar* had come up to expectations, it is a valid question whether his achievement as the world's last major sailing vessel shipowner would have been so great.

CHAPTER 5

The Worldwide Abandonment Of Sail

In the 1870s, ports such as Calcutta, Sydney, Melbourne and San Francisco were overflowing with cargoes of jute, wool and grain for the holds of sailing vessels. In 1882, 550 windjammers loaded 1,250,000 tons of wheat for Europe in Oregon and California. In 1891, nearly 80 tall ships are reported to have taken on wool in Sydney for London's wool exchange. During the coal strike of 1896, considerably more than a hundred deep-water sailing vessels lay waiting for cargo off Newcastle, New South Wales. The examples could be expanded by examining the harbour records from Rangoon, Cape Town, Valparaiso and other overseas ports, not to mention the major seaports of the United Kingdom and the European continent.

But by the turn of the century, the beginnings of a worldwide trend towards selling off sail-tonnage were clearly visible. Chile's saltpetre deserts, America's oilfields, the coalmines of Britain and New South Wales, the wheat plains of Southern Australia and the sawmills of Scandinavia were still offering many good opportunities to sailing vessels, as was the timber of Canada and the West Coast of the United States, the Gulf's pitchpine and the West Indies' logwood. There were still guano islands, India's rice and jute had not been lost completely and the odd general cargo was still to be found. But the great maritime nations were more and more resolutely winding up their sailing-fleets, and their vessels were being offered on the world markets at prices which gradually approached scrap value.

The final disposal began in 1921. In the hectic economic climate of the Great War there had been no question of scrap prices. Many an old barque changed hands at a higher price than she had cost to build. In various parts of the world, smaller sailing vessels were even being built — mostly fore-and-aft schooners, but also some square-rigged vessels. Between 1917 and 1923, Åland shipyards saw the launching of two barques[1], two four-masted and six three-masted schooners or barquentines, five three-masted fore-and-aft schooners and a few motor-sailers — a total of 22 vessels and 5,500 tons net. At the same time, the Italians built a great number of small schooners. Those built in Åland at least were poor investments; production costs soared sky-high, materials were makeshift, and several of them were not even completed by the beginning of 1921 when the boom ended.[2]

It was then that the final abandonment began, as has been said. Hundreds of old ships which had been scantily maintained during the war were laid-

1 These were the *Fred* (Peace) launched into Bamböle Vik in Finström Parish in 1920 by the veteran Åland master shipbuilder Johan August Henriksson, then 78 years of age, and the *Carmen* launched at Granboda in Lemland in 1921. Both these vessels were rigged as barques instead of schooners, because the spars and rigging of old barques were available cheaply. The *Fred* was equipped with masts and gear from the *Per Brahe* built in Åland in 1877, the *Carmen* with gear from the *Southern Belle*, built in Nova Scotia in 1871.

2 They were mostly built to be fitted with motors as soon as they had earned the cost of doing so, but most of them never earned the money. The *Carmen* was lengthened to take a motor and her sternpost drilled out while she was building, but no motor was ever fitted. Despite these changes she sailed well, but she was very poorly and weakly built. *Fred* was also built to take a motor and was regarded as worn out by the time she was lost in 1933.

FRED

up ready for breaking up. Many good and relatively young vessels became redundant as well; their names appeared in brokers' lists under ships for sale, and their owners lived in hopes of finding an optimist. According to W L A Derby, in *The Tall Ships Pass*, 68 deep-water sailing vessels took on wheat for Europe in Australia in 1921; the following year the number was only seven. The maximum in the years 1922-39 was 22 in 1934. It should be noted however that in that year wheat was practically the only trade remaining, whereas during the 1920s sailing vessels had still had the possibility of other employment.

Left, plate 85 The barque *Fred* ('Peace') built at Bambole Vik in Finström parish in Åland in 1920, discharging timber at Great Yarmouth in 1930. Note that her home port is shown simply as Åland. (National Maritime Museum)
Right, plate 86 The *Fred* under sail off Southend. She was lost in the entrance to Mariehamn as the result of the parting of an anchor cable in the same gale of wind and snow as the iron barque *Plus* on 15 December 1933, but her whole crew got ashore on Svinö and were saved. The wreck was bought by Gustaf Erikson for her rigging and gear. (National Maritime Museum)
Below, plate 87 The building gang of a Lemland yard during the shipbuilding boom of the First World War (Ålands Sjöfartsmuseum)

The majority of the sailing vessels which were struck off shipping registers during that decade were broken up, perhaps after being condemned as the result of damage, dismasting, or something of the sort. But at least 70 square-riggers were lost between 1920 and 1929; a score of Norwegians, eight Britons, seven Germans and so on. Thirteen of the 70 were 'missing ships' which had disappeared with all hands.

The last British full-rigger, *William Mitchell*, arrived in Ostend in November 1927 carrying saltpetre from Tocopilla on her last freight passage before being broken up. One after another, the maritime nations began to talk of their last full-rigger, their last three- or four-masted barque, while the fore-and-aft rigs survived, living a modest life in the age of steam and diesel-powered ships. The *William Mitchell* belonged to John Stewart & Co in London, who started about 1880 with three barques and two full-riggers, and who, in the period up to 1927, owned a total of 38 sailing vessels, for the most part cheaply purchased second-hand tonnage. It was not one of the biggest and best known of British shipping concerns, and its attempt to continue the use of sail after the First World War was not successful. Their barque *Falkirk* was dismasted in the Bay of Biscay in 1924 and condemned; the full-rigger *Monkbarns* was sold to Norway in 1926 and became a coal hulk; and the barque *Kilmallie* was laid-up in Bordeaux and broken up in 1927 after an unprofitable voyage to Australia and Chile with three freights: rock salt to Sydney, coal to Chile from Newcastle, NSW, and saltpetre home.

A couple of years after *William Mitchell*'s last trip, the Canadians lost the last big barque flying the Red Ensign, disregarding the stationary training ship *Arethusa* (ex *Peking*), when, on 11 November 1929 *Garthpool* (ex *Juteopolis*) ran aground off the Cape Verde Islands.[1] Sir William Garthwaite's Garth Line was founded during the First World War and acquired a total of 11 square-riggers: *Inverneill* became *Garthneill*, *Inversnaid* became *Garthsnaid*, and so on. By 1917, five vessels had already been lost. In the years 1927-28, when only *Garthpool* remained, Sir William himself bought cargoes of wheat for this barque, an enterprise which is reported to have succeeded well.

1 Although often referred to as the last big British steel square-rigged merchant sailing vessel in fact the *Garthpool* was registered at Montreal as the property of the Marine Navigation Company of Canada Ltd and technically was the last big Canadian barque. The last British big steel deep sea square-rigged vessel registered at a port in the United Kingdom was the *William Mitchell* of London.

Above, plate 88 The four-masted barquentine *Dione* under construction in Jomala Parish in June, 1920. (Ålands Sjöfarts-museum.)

Below, plate 89 The *Dione* in Mariehamn western harbour in 1933. She sailed for Gustaf Erikson for many years. (National Maritime Museum)

Top left, plate 90 *William Mitchell* looking aft, starboard side during heavy weather in the fifties south. (National Maritime Museum)
Bottom left, plate 91 *William Mitchell*, lifelines rigged, in heavy weather in the Southern Ocean. (National Maritime Museum)
Centre, plate 92 *William Mitchell* in the Roaring Forties, April 1927. (National Maritime Museum)
Above, plate 93 *William Mitchell* — part of a watch at work on the mizzen upper topsail yard. (National Maritime Museum)
Below, plate 94 *Monkbarns* in heavy weather. (Malcolm Bruce Glasier)

Above, plate 95 The *Arethusa*, ex-*Peking*, built in Germany in 1911, lying in the Medway in 1948. She was a stationary training ship. (Basil Greenhill)

Below, plate 96 *Padua*, built at Geestemünde in 1926, the last steel four-masted barque ever to be built as a merchant vessel. In 1977 she was still afloat as a Russian training ship. (National Maritime Museum)

Below, plate 97 Hugo Lundqvist's steel four-masted barque *Ponape*. (National Maritime Museum)

Above, plate 98 The main deck of *Ponape*. (National Maritime Museum)

Laeisz in Hamburg, whose entire fleet of 14 large and renowned sailing vessels was lost as a result of the War and the Treaty of Versailles, bought back six of their former vessels after the War and had *Padua* and *Priwall* built in addition. The latter was completed in 1920, the former in 1926. But they kept only the new vessels, and went over to steamships which they employed in the fruit trade.

There were shipowners in other countries too who made more or less determined efforts to keep their sailing vessels carrying freight on the high seas; and there were buyers who tried to exploit the low prices for sail tonnage. Captain Hugo Lundqvist of Vårdö in the Åland Islands, later of Mariehamn, for example, was ship's husband for the barques *Prompt, Ponape, Plus and Zaritza,* as well as for the four-masted barquentine *Mozart.* But Gustaf Erikson was the major customer for vessels being sold around the world. Gradually he became the only customer, apart from the to a greater or lesser extent state-subsidised acquisition of training ships in various parts of the world.

A comparison between the numbers of vessels belonging to Åland in 1928 and 1939 respectively illustrates the speed with which developments took place:

	1928	1939
Iron or steel sailing vessels	21	11
Wooden barques	4	1
Wooden schooners and barquentines and fore-and-aft schooners over 100 tons	33	2
Auxiliary powered vessels	11	10
Steamships	1	38

Left, plate 99 The steel four-masted barque *Herzogin Cecilie* photographed off Gravesend on 18 July 1904 (National Maritime Museum)

Of the 21 iron and steel vessels in 1928, 13 belonged to Gustaf Erikson's fleet. In 1939, all 11 were his. In that year, he owned four of the 38 steamships, but he was a shareholder in the majority of steamship companies. The large number of steamships in 1939 includes some 'transferred' Swedish tramp steamers sailing under the Finnish flag.

Since *Lawhill's* and *Woodburn*'s last good freights from Australia had released the pressure on bank credit at home, and with the thought that in spite of everything SS *Edgar* could be expected to sell for £15,000, Gustaf Erikson was on the lookout for new sailing vessels — and there were plenty to be found in the autumn of 1921. He wrote to Clarksons in September: should he buy five vessels from the French Government for £17,500 - *Weser, Winterhude, Mimi, Mozart* and *Herzogin Cecilie* - or a 15-20 year old tramp steamer? The combined price for the five vessels was not much more than the repair bill *Grace Harwar* had run up in Montevideo a couple of years earlier. A few days later he wrote again; he was worried by the classification of two of the vessels, the tramp steamer was scarcely under serious consideration, but *Passat* for £13,000 and *Herzogin Cecilie* for £3,100 were worth thinking about - provided that Clarksons could advance the money until *Edgar* had been sold. *Passat* was virtually newly built, which was the reason for the high price. She was in fact bought back by Laeisz; but Gustaf Erikson became her owner in 1932. *Herzogin Cecilie* had lain interned in Chile from 1914 to 1920 and that year had made her last passage under the German flag with saltpetre from Antofagasta to Ostend. Her voyages as a training ship for Norddeutscher Lloyd in the years 1907-14 had covered all trades and earned her a reputation as a fine sailer, equal to the fastest P-vessels. A glimpse at a list of her ports of destination before 1914 reveals a great variety of names: Astoria, San Francisco, Philadelphia, Kobe, Singapore, Rangoon, Honolulu, Iquique and other saltpetre ports, Melbourne and Adelaide, to name a few.

In London the future of sail was generally viewed sceptically, and the suggestion of advance financing was greeted with particular scepticism. In his letter to Clarksons, Gustaf Erikson doesn't conceal his discontent over the firm's stubborn indifference, and there are hints of his anxiety that he might be outmanoeuvred by Captain Hugo Lundqvist, then his rival in the sailing vessel business but soon to become Åland's first successful steamship owner. At the end of September, Captain Lundqvist travelled abroad. Gustaf Erikson wrote to London that he smelled a rat. He urged discretion and loyalty. Clarksons, of course, were also brokers for Captain Lundqvist, who had in fact gone to look over some vessels. He inspected *Herzogin Cecilie*, but bought *Mozart*.[1]

Herzogin Cecilie also seemed unfavourable from a number of points of view to Captain de Cloux, who left Mariehamn in the middle of October with instructions from Gustaf Erikson to inspect this vessel, as well as others in Ostend, and to continue his journey to see *Passat* in Marseilles if the result was negative. '*Herzogin Cecilie* unserviceable for timber cargoes,' he telegraphed, 'suitable only for bulk cargoes and as a training ship.' Her accommodation for cadets encroached on her net tonnage, there were no brace and halyard winches, and so on. Otherwise it was a good vessel, de Cloux thought; certain drawbacks could be rectified relatively cheaply.

1 Captain Karl Kåhre who sailed in *Mozart* told me that Hugo Lundqvist bought her because she had water ballast tanks and required less alteration than *Herzogin Cecilie* to carry timber cargoes. Captain Lundqvist had a traumatic first passage in the *Mozart*. The water ballast tanks leaked and as a result the vessel would not sail. She took nearly two months to reach Bergen, having made her way there from Ostend largely on her beam ends. *Mozart*, one of the best remembered of the big steel vessels in Åland today, was the only Åland skonertskepp to sail continuously on deep-water. She was commercially very successful, but she was really too big for the four-masted rig. The weight of the huge sails and gear aloft working in a sea way caused frequent minor damage. The four-masted schooner or barquentine was highly efficient as a medium-sized vessel, like the American-built, Åland-owned *Atlas*, but in larger vessels it was really necessary to keep the sails and gear small by using more masts. The American barquentine *E R Sterling* was one of the most successful latter day sailing vessels. She was a little larger than *Mozart* but she had six masts. If the *Mozart* had had five masts she would have been even more profitable and made a great deal less work for her crews.

Her little known almost identical sister the *Beethoven*, built for the same German owners by the same British builders, was sold first to Norwegian owners and then in 1914 to owners in Trieste for use as a cargo carrying training ship. She went missing on her first voyage when on passage with coal from Australia towards Valparaiso, one of the first, but by no means the last, large sail training ship to be tragically lost.

When *Mozart* was broken up in Britain in 1935 her figurehead of the composer, perhaps the last big merchant sailing ship figurehead to be carved in Britain, was saved by Mrs Wingfield Digby. It is now on public display in the National Maritime Museum in the entrance to New Neptune Hall.

Clarksons were unenthusiastic. It was suspicious, admittedly, that the French wanted to sell the vessel while intending at the same time to equip another of the captured Laeisz vessels as a training ship — namely *Pola,* sistership to *Priwall,* later rechristened *Richelieu* and destroyed by fire in Baltimore in 1926. The final outcome was that in November Gustaf Erikson bought *Herzogin Cecilie* anyway for £4,250, added to which there were costs of £250 for repairs after a harbour accident in Ostend. An autumn storm had set her adrift and she

Left, plate 100 The steel four-masted barquentine *Mozart* built at Port Glasgow in 1904. (National Maritime Museum)

Below, plate 101 A rare photograph of *Mozart*'s sister ship *Beethoven*. She is being refitted and her topsail yards have been sent down. (National Maritime Museum)

Right, plate 102 The American steel six-masted barquentine *E R Sterling.* (National Maritime Museum)

Below, plate 103 Accommodation in iron and steel vessels (1) The saloon of an unknown steel four-masted barque of the 1890s. (National Maritime Museum)

Left, plate 104 Accommodation in iron and steel vessels (2) Captain Karl Kåhre, formerly Director of the Ålands Sjöfartsmuseum and formerly of the *Mozart*, at the table in the saloon of the *Herzogin Cecilie* as it is today re-erected in the Ålands Sjöfartsmuseum. (Basil Greenhill)

Right, plate 105 Accommodation in iron and steel vessels (3). Young Alanders of the crew of the steel four-masted barque *Olivebank* in the forecastle in the 1930s. (Handels-og Sjöfartsmuseum Helsingör)

Middle right, plate 106 Accommodation in iron and steel vessels (4). The small, simple saloon of the *Pommern* as she lies preserved in Mariehamn today. Note the photographs of Hilda and Gustaf Erikson, part of the furnishings of every Erikson sailing vessel. (Basil Greenhill)

Bottom right, plate 107 Accommodation in iron and steel vessels (5). The Mate's berth in *Pommern*. (Basil Greenhill)

had collided with a Norwegian steamer, sustaining a certain amount of damage.

After drydocking, repairs, modifications (described in a lengthy correspondence with de Cloux, who was to take command), and classification, 'The Duchess' inaugurated her new epoque by taking on timber for Australia in Frederikshald. Here, she also received a visit from her new owner, who fell completely under the spell of her charm. '*Herzogin Cecilie* was a good buy, a buy such as one makes only once in a lifetime,' he wrote to Captain Öfverström of *Lawhill* on 25 March 1923. She not only sailed excellently, but thanks to her several cargo hatches, she was able to load and discharge quickly. In Mejillones in 1922, she discharged ballast and loaded saltpetre in 19 days.

His enthusiasm for speculation was considerably dampened in the autumn of 1921 by *Lawhill's* 40/- wheat freight — exactly one third of the former rate. On top of that, the big barque ran aground on entering Port Lincoln — a matter of £1,000. At the same time, *Grace Harwar* suffered a lesser accident off Bremerhaven. The costly *Passat* was abandonned as a potential purchase, but her sistership *Peking,* which had fallen to the Italians in compensation (the French had got *Passat*) appears frequently in correspondence over a long period. Gustaf Erikson's first offer was for only £4,000. That was in the autumn of 1921. *Pinnas,* another former P-vessel, was also mentioned at this time.

The sale of *Edgar* in 1922, after so many tribulations, provided some Sterling and stimulated Gustaf Erikson's desire to purchase again. In his letters of the summer and autumn of 1922, a good number of the world's remaining deep-water sailing-vessels are reviewed with appropriate comments — especially former Germans, but also others: *Olivebank, Herö, Blankeness, Leni, Magdelene Vinnen, Perim, Olympia, Killoran, Archibald Russell, Weser, Edmund, Kensington, Windsor Park, Henriette,* the Belgian training ship *L'Avenir,* the Danish *Viking* and others. Again and again, Clarksons received curt reminders to show greater energy. At the same time, one gets the impression from the letters that Gustaf Erikson himself went ahead with care and vigilance, however resolute he was in his offensive and however liberal with his offers.

Peking, which lay in Antwerp (according to another account, in London), and which he had inspected himself, became the great dream of the year, but a vain dream. On 13 June he increased his offer to £7,500 through Clarksons. He wrote that he doubted the Germans, with their sickly currency, would be able to bid so high. But he was mistaken. His last offer, made as late as December, was for £9,000. Laeisz clearly could bid more, since he bought back his former vessel in 1923. Before this, Gustaf Erikson had succeeded in buying a considerable part of *Peking*'s sails, some thirty canvases which were eventually to unfurl from the yards and stays of Gustaf Erikson's growing fleet.

In July, Captain K V Lindqvist looked over *Herö* and *Olivebank* in Norway and then travelled to Dunkirk, to see *Edmund* and *Weser,* and finally to Antwerp, primarily to look at *Olympia.* In Dunkirk it looked as if it might turn into a very long trip for Captain Lindqvist. Gustaf Erikson wrote to him that a firm of ship brokers in London were offering the big four-master *Daylight* of 5,800 tons deadweight for $30,000 (about £6,700), and that he was awaiting particulars so that he could make an offer pending inspection. *Daylight* lay in San Francisco. It came to nothing however, and Captain Lindqvist did not have to make the long journey.

Below, plate 108 The iron *Loch Linnhe,* built in Glasgow in 1876 as a full-rigged ship, lying in Mariehamn with the yards stripped from the mizzen to make her into a barque. The Vårdö galeas *Rauha,* built in 1890, is half loaded and lying, in the local terminology, 'on the nose'. (Ålands Sjöfartsmuseum)

On the basis of Captain Lindqvist's reports on *Olivebank* and *Herö,* Gustaf Erikson bid 12 Shillings per ton deadweight for each vessel — 15 Shillings if they were delivered rust-free, painted, docked and classed. Only for exceptionally good vessels would he stretch his offer to a Pound or more. Negotiations for *Olivebank* continued long into the autumn. They came to an unexpectedly sorry end. In October, as Gustaf Erikson was preparing to go to Norway to attend personally the auction that had been arranged for the vessel, she was sold unexpectedly to a Norwegian rival without his having had the opportunity to renew his offer, an occurrence which angered him in the extreme and resulted in an animated exchange of letters with Norwegian brokers and lawyers. Legal proceedings against the vessel's seller, a Norwegian bank, were considered but shelved. Gustaf Erikson in fact bought *Olivebank* a couple of years later.

Other skippers in the fleet were also employed to inspect vessels. On 23 September, Captain August Gustafsson of *Grace Harwar,* en route to Tocopilla, was asked to hunt down ex-German windjammers in Chile, to inspect them and possibly to purchase them, taking command himself and leaving *Grace Harwar* to the mates. The same

day, a letter went to de Cloux, on his way to Taltal with *Herzogin Cecilie:* if *Potosi,* which the Italians had sold to a company in Chile, was for sale, he should 'inspect and telegraph per Scott's code'. The five-master *Potosi,* of 4,000 tons gross and built in 1895, was the best known of the P-Line's vessels after the loss of *Preussen,* widely renowned for her fast and very regular passages in the Chile trades before 1914. Captain de Cloux had nothing but praise for *Potosi* after getting reports from her German former skipper, who was still in Chile, but her new owners did not seem to have any desire to sell. Rechristened *Flora,* the famous five-master met her fate in September 1925, bound with coal, coke and oil from Cardiff to Mejillones. Fire broke out on board in the South Atlantic. The vessel was abandoned and scuttled by an Argentinian cruiser.

Pola too appears in correspondence from late autumn 1922. She had not yet been reconstructed as a French training ship. Gustaf Erikson wrote to the ship broker D Leroy in Dunkirk, offering to exchange *Herzogin Cecilie,* with her finished accommodation for 90 cadets, for *Pola* and a fee of £5,000. This sum was probably intended to allow a considerable margin for bargaining. After Captain Edvard Johnsson had inspected *Pola* on his way home from *Professor Koch* in Montevideo, and reported a negative verdict, Gustaf Erikson's interest in the exchange dwindled a little.

The year's intensive hunt for vessels among those being sold around the world ended modestly. For 400,000 Finnish Marks, Gustaf Erikson bought the Nystad barque *Loch Linnhe,* built of iron in 1876 and measuring 1460 tons gross; a small and elderly vessel compared with most of those that had previously been under consideration.

Gustaf Erikson's speculation continued and made more progress in the years that followed. The financial position had been consolidated at home. By the end of 1922, bank liabilities had been cut down 1.7 million Marks without having had to resort to the 2½ million Marks or so the sale of *Edgar* fetched.

In a letter to Captain Öfverström of *Lawhill* in January 1923, the British-built ex-German American *Moshulu* is mentioned for the first time as a desirable vessel. Gustaf Erikson bought her 12 years later. On 20 January, he cabled a broker in Antwerp with an offer of £5,000 for *L'Avenir,* and two days later he was asked to make an offer for *Mimosa* by a firm in Stockholm. On 27 January, *Herzogin Sophie Charlotte,* lying in Tönsberg, is mentioned in a letter to a broker in Frederikstad. Gustaf Erikson tentatively suggests £3,250, and wants to send Captain Nordberg, who is expected in Frederikstad with *Woodburn,* to look at the vessel. At the same time he could see the Danish *Valkyrian.*

In a very lengthy letter of 21 February 1923 to Captain de Cloux, who was in Ostend with *Herzogin Cecilie,* he outlined a complete programme for purchasing vessels. The prospective buys of former years had gained new interest.

Pola, lying in Dunkirk, had, admittedly, been inspected by Captain Johnsson, who remarked on her slack rigging, the water in her hold and so on; but the vessel was brand new and had not even made her maiden voyage. With *Peking's* and *Passat's* prices in mind, he bid £9,500 through Clarksons. If the offer was rejected, de Cloux was to make a new inspection.

Olympia, lying in Antwerp and loading 3,800 tons, unfortunately had bulkheads athwartships which divided the hull into four cargo holds, like *Herzogin Cecilie* had had at her purchase. Could these bulkheads be removed? Captain Lindqvist had thought well of the vessel. He had himself bid £3,500. The Italians wanted 175 Lire per ton deadweight: about £4,400.

Perim, also owned by the Italian State, had not yet been inspected. There would be grounds to inspect her if negotiations for *Pola* came to nothing. The vessel lay in Dordrecht.

Edmund and *Weser* could be seen in Dunkirk at the same time as *Pola.* Likewise *L'Hermite* which was offered for 290,000 Francs.

Besides these, *Magdelene Vinnen, Leni, Hackfield* and *Henriette* are also mentioned, but considered too old and rusted-up.

Gustaf Erikson bought none of these vessels. *Pola* occupied his thoughts particularly. Captain de Cloux inspected her twice, recommended purchase and declared that the set of sails bought from *Peking* the previous year should suit her well. On 26 March a Clarksons representative went to Paris to bring the matter to a conclusion. He had the authority to bid up to £10,500 if necessary.

When this attempt finally went on the rocks, Gustaf Erikson immediately turned his attention to a new prospect. *Pommern* was lying in Delfzijl, having gone to the Greeks at the dividing up of the German fleet. On 5 May Captain Lindqvist left to look at her. He had scarcely arrived in Delfzijl

when a telegram from his employer in Mariehamn informed him that *Pamir*, laid-up in Genoa, was also a vessel to think about. However, he completed his assignment, which turned out to be particularly pressing. Some days after his departure from Mariehamn, Gustaf Erikson received a cable from Clarksons: Accept or refuse by Monday 14 May. At the last moment, Lindqvist cabled '*Pommern* definitely worth buying'. On 16 May, Clarksons reported that the contract had been signed. The price was £3,750 plus £150 for provisions. Captain Lindqvist stayed aboard the vessel for classification and fitting-out, but would not take command. Captain Walfrid Gustafsson was skipper for her first passage to Chile, on which she sailed in ballast on 7 July, after dry-docking in Emden.

Left, plate 109 *Pommern* discharging in a London dock. (National Maritime Museum)
Bottom left, plate 110 *Pommern.* (Basil Greenhill)
Below, plate 111 *Carradale* (left) lying in Sharpness during the First World War. (National Maritime Museum)

Nitrate freights improved in the spring of 1923. *Lawhill* was chartered at 27/- on 3 March, and *Woodburn* at 34/- on 24 May. This reawakened Gustaf Erikson's interest in *Potosi,* the veteran of the saltpetre trade. However, after a vain sidelong glance in this direction, in June he suggested £3,000 for *Archibald Russell,* which was being offered by the well-known Glasgow shipowners John Hardie & Co, through Clarksons. If the vessel was delivered classed, he was willing to raise his bid to £4,250.

The negotiations became bogged down. Meanwhile, a couple of vessels were bought at home in Finland: *Carradale* in September for 417,000 Marks from Rederi A/B Aura in Åbo, and, in October, *Penang* from John Nurminen O/Y in Raumo for 540,000 Marks. *Penang* (ex-*Albert Rickmers*] was bought, without inspection, lying in Wilmington, USA chartered to Sydney with oil. At her departure, her cost was estimated at over £6,000, fully fitted-out — nearly two Pounds per deadweight ton.

On 24 November, Gustaf Erikson left for London, ready to do business and in high spirits. *Grace Harwar's* and *Loch Linnhe's* timber freights from Canada had yielded fine returns. *Herzogin Cecilie* had returned from Caleta Buena with her entire saltpetre freight money uncommitted; her outward coal freight had not only been enough to cover her expenses in Chile, but had allowed a remittance of £400 to Clarksons besides. Immediately upon arriving in London, he bought *Archibald Russell* for £7,500, and on 8 December, he sold *Carradale* for £2,950 to a German buyer for breaking up.

Archibald Russell was expensive, he considered; over £9,000 fitted-out and ready to sail from Milford Haven the following spring — more than two Pounds per ton deadweight. She was fitted-out in April by McSymons of Liverpool for £433 and by Appleby in London for £1,181.[1]

Carradale made only one freight passage. Captain Lindqvist took her to Uleåborg. From there, she sailed under Captain Isidor Eriksson's command with 677 cords of lathwood at 60/- per cord and 105 standards of planks at 50/- per standard, a fine gross freight of £2,800. She arrived in London on 8 December and was sold the same day — at a good profit, it should be added. *Carradale* was a distinguished deep-water sailer in her prime under the British ensign. Lubbock devotes several pages to her in the second volume of *The Last of the Windjammers.*

Gustaf Erikson had many irons in the fire while he was in London, both with brokers and ship chandlers. Sail canvas and manilla hemp were significant items in sailing vessel budgeting. After scrutinising quotations and examining samples, he decided on the two firms, Appleby in London and McSymons in Liverpool, for future supplies. He was not an easily satisfied customer. When Appleby complained, he wrote an answer straight from the heart after getting home to Mariehamn: 'If I were not to keep an eye on my affairs, and if I did not know

1 Captain Karl V Karlsson of Vårdö in 1977 described to me the fitting out of the *Archibald Russell* in which he took part at Milford Haven. She had been laid up for four years and there was not a rope yarn on board her. A lighter came alongside with 52 coils of manilla, coils of wire and barrels of oil and cans of paint and the newly arrived Åland crew rigged her with all running rigging.

Left, plate 112 *Penang* lying in Mariehamn. (Ålands Sjöfartsmuseum)

Below, plate 113 *Archibald Russell* photographed from the airship *Graf Zeppelin.* (Ålands Sjöfartsmuseum)

ARCHIBALD RUSSELL

what I pay and what quality and quantity I get for it, and otherwise look at everything from a business viewpoint, I would go bankrupt — to the detriment of myself, ship chandlers, ship brokers and circa 300 persons whom I feed and pay.'

Thus, in 1923, his fleet grew by three vessels with a combined tonnage of 11,250 tons deadweight: *Pommern, Penang* and *Archibald Russell.*

Content with his visit to London, Gustaf Erikson returned to Mariehamn on 9 January 1924. He did not rest long on his laurels. Ten days after arriving home, he lists nine desirable vessels in a letter to Clarksons: *Hougomont, Killoran, Bellhouse, Bellpool, Bellco, Pamir, Garthpool, Winterhude* and, still, *Pola*, 'the most attractive afloat'. That Clarksons had allowed *Peking, Passat* and *Pamir* to 'fall into the hands of the Germans' (they were bought back by Laeisz, as has been mentioned), was no recommendation for the firm, he stressed, intimating gloomily that *Pola's* fate would probably be the same, if his dear business friends in London did not pull themselves together.

A couple of days later, he made enquiries about *Winterhude* and *Mayotte* through a broker in Hamburg, and on 24 January, he asked his 'good friend', shipbroker Olsen in Kristianstad, if the price of *Herzogin Sophie Charlotte* had by any chance been reduced.

On 2 February, he offered £9,000 through Clarksons for *Hougomont, Killoran* and *Vimeira*, all belonging to J Hardie & Co, in Glasgow. At the same time, he reported that Captain Nordberg of *Woodburn*, in La Palice, would be travelling to Nantes to see the Frenchmen *Montmorency* and *Valparaiso* upon their arrival from Chile. The same day, he also sent a letter to Captain de Cloux: after

Left, plate 114 *Archibald Russell* in Mariehamn in 1930. (Ålands Sjöfartsmuseum)

Below, plate 115 *Killoran* discharging in London. (National Maritime Museum)

Left, plate 116 The figurehead of *Killoran.* (National Maritime Museum)
Above left, plate 117 *Olivebank.* (National Maritime Museum)
Above, plate 118 The wooden barque *Carmen* lying at Rochester with a high deck cargo of timber. Note the huge old fashioned wooden-stocked anchor of a type used in wooden vessels in the 1860s and 70s, still used in this vessel though she was built in 1921. (National Maritime Museum)

he had inspected the laid-up Frenchmen *Rhône, Atlantique* and *Dunkerque,* he should make the most of the opportunity and have a look at *Vimeira* in Calais.

The first transaction of the year was concluded on 7 February; *Killoran* was bought, without a bottom inspection, for £2650.

A couple of weeks later, Gustaf Erikson launched an offensive against his friends and rivals at home in Åland, the Lundqvists, sons of the great shipowner Mathias Lundqvist Jnr of Vårdö. Their *Parchim* had 'pinched a freight' on the Canada/ Buenos Aires trade. He had four of his own medium-sized vessels on this route, which he had had reason to be very glad of the previous year. He did not want any competitors on it, he wrote to Clarksons, and bid £2,600 for the vessel which was approximately her value on the scrap market. The offer did not lead to any result.

On the other hand, the acquisition of *Olivebank,* in the autumn, was relatively painless. This vessel, which was owned by Skibs A/S Ostra in Kristiansand and lay in Cardiff, was bought after an inspection by Captain Walfrid Gustafsson. She sailed on 12 November, bound for Port Lincoln for orders, favourably chartered with wheat at 42/6d and under the command of Captain K Troberg.

In 1924, lathwood began to yield good profits; *Tjerimai* was sailing in fine dividends and *Carradale*'s good rate has just been mentioned. Both Gustaf Erikson and Hugo Lundqvist were on the lookout for lathwood carriers. During the course of the autumn, Gustaf Erikson became the majority shareholder in Åland's last home-built barque *Carmen,* built in Lemland at Granboda after the War, and the fore-and-after schooner *Polstjernan,* built in Dragsfjärd in 1920, and the four-masted barquentine *Baltic,* built in Åland and launched after the War. *Polstjernan,* which is said to have cost ten million to build and now changed hands at 150,000 Finnish Marks, was bought purely for speculative purposes and was sold again as early as 7 March to Captain Seppinen from Björkö. *Carmen* and *Baltic* were put into the lathwood trade. The former was wrecked and abandoned by her crew near Bornholm on 2 September 1934, salvaged, towed into Karlshamn, and given over to her salvors. The latter was sold to Raumo in 1939, after having lived through many fluctuations in the lathwood market. After 1936 she sailed only in the Baltic.

Below, plate 119 The four-masted fore-and-aft schooner *Polstjernan* in front of the Royal Palace at Stockholm. (Ålands Sjöfartsmuseum)

Above, plate 120 The four-masted barquentine *Baltic.* In 1916 the Lemland Parish Council decided to sell a small forest for felling. A number of ship masters of Mariehamn, trapped in the war, bought it and set up a shipyard at Vesteränga in Lemland and there slowly built the *Baltic,* launched in 1919. (Ålands Sjöfartsmuseum)

Right, plate 121 *Hougomont,* a photograph which shows well the burdensome hull and the flat floors of the later steel sailing vessels. (National Maritime Museum)

The year's real contributions to the fleet were: *Killoran* and *Olivebank,* 7,450 tons deadweight, and *Carmen* and *Baltic,* 1,600 tons.

The fleet continued to grow in 1925. Increased wheat freights were an encouragement; vessels were sailing down to Australia in ballast, favourably chartered. The trends were good on all freight markets.

John Hardie's *Hougomont,* which in June 1921 had arrived in St Nazaire with wheat from Australia, belonged to the fleet the famous Glasgow shipowners were winding up. Gustaf Erikson had had his eye on the vessel for a long time. She was of the same size and type as *Archibald Russell* but eight years older. On 29 January 1925 he bought her for £3,500. Captain Walfrid Gustafsson inspected the vessel and began fitting out work until Captain Hägerstrand arrived from Rosario to take over

Above, plate 122 *Lingard* with a big deck cargo of timber about to be taken in tow by a steam tug off Southend. (National Maritime Museum)

Below, plate 123 *Winterhude.* (National Maritime Museum)

Above, plate 124 The fore and aft schooner *Ostrobotnia* with a deck cargo of timber. (Ålands Sjöfartsmuseum)

command. The latter left *Woodburn* to his first mate, Captain F Ejder, who received a bulky letter from his employer filled with instructions, good advice, and warnings on the subject of rocks, brokers, ship chandlers and deserters. On 14 March, *Hougomont* sailed for Callao for orders and to load guano in the Lobos Islands.

In February, *Penang*'s newly appointed skipper, Captain Mauritz Mattson, received instructions in Hull to look at *Wathara* (ex-*Lingard*) built in Norway and belonging to James Bell & Co in Hull. On 12 March, the vessel was purchased, unclassed, for £2,200.

James Bell & Co was one of the last sailing vessel lines in Britain. Apart from *Wathara,* in 1925 the firm owned several old deep-water sailing vessels which they were trying to sell: *Bellpool, Bellhouse, Bellco* and *Bellands,* all originally built for other companies and launched with other names. Some time before the War, *Bellco* and *Bellhouse* had belonged to Laeisz;the former had then been called *Pelikan,* and the latter *Ponape.* While Captain Gustafsson was in St Nazaire, measuring and fitting-out *Hougomont,* Gustaf Erikson wrote to him, outlining a plan to buy up Bell's entire fleet. In August 1924, Captain Hägerstrand had inspected *Bellpool* and found the vessel suitable for purchase; then the price had been too high: £6,000. By now the price should have sunk, after half a year's laying-up in Belfast. *Bellco* was expected in La Palice; Captain Gustafsson should inspect her. If the result was positive, Gustaf Erikson would bid one Pound per ton deadweight for the entire fleet.

This deal never came to anything. *Bellands, Bellco* and *Bellpool* were broken up sometime later. Captain Hugo Lundqvist bought *Bellhouse* and let her sail under her former Laeisz name *Ponape.* Built in Genoa, she had originally been called *Regina Elena.* When Gustaf Erikson bought her from Lundqvist in 1929, he preferred to let her keep her German P-name rather than giving her back her original Italian name. An analagous case was *Penang,* which was built for Rickmers Reismuhlen Reederei and originally named *Albert Rickmers,* only joining the P-Line a couple of years before the First World War. Similarly, *Winterhude* was originally the full-rigger *Mabel Rickmers.* She was trimmed down to a barque and given the name

Winterhude by her new owners in Hamburg, before getting the name *Selma Hemsoth* in 1923 from her third Hamburg owners, Hemsoth & Co.

Gustaf Erikson bought *Winterhude* in the autumn of 1925 for £1,950. Captain Gustafsson inspected, measured and fitted-out the vessel. Captain Nils Andersson took command.

There was yet one more purchase that year. In July, the three masted fore-and-aft schooner *Ostrobotnia* (named after a district in mainland Finland) was bought for 150,000 Marks from Jakobstads Varvs och Rederibolag, and was put into Baltic and North Sea trades, as were the barque *Lalla Rookh* and the three-masted barquentine *Estonia,* bought in 1926 and 1927.

The rapid growth of the fleet, worries over charters and the classification and maintainance of the deep-water sailing vessels, several of which were in poor condition at their purchase, and finally the sudden reduction in the stock of vessels being sold all put a stop to further purchases until 1929. In the summer of that year, *Melbourne* was bought for £4,000 from Herman Engel, a Hamburg shipowner, and then the Danish training ship *Viking,* for £6,500, and Hugo Lundqvist's *Ponape,* for £5,500.

There was a sad story behind the acquisition of *Viking*. The Danish United Steamship Company had two training ships, *Viking,* which had been acquired in 1915, having been a training ship from the beginning (she was launched by Burmeister & Wain in 1906 and cost over 250,000 dollars, fully fitted-out), and the considerably younger ill-fated five-master *Kjøbenhavn,* which sailed from Buenos Aires for Melbourne on 14 December 1928, and was never heard of again. This tragedy, which took the lives of so many young Danish Cadets, is said to have been responsible for the company changing their training ship practice and going over from cargo-

Below, plate 125 *Lalla Rookh* discharging timber in Regent's Canal Dock, London. Her sails have been cast off the jackstays and are hanging on the buntlines and clew lines to enable the crew to paint the yards. Her figurehead has been removed. (Ålands Sjöfartsmuseum)

Right, plate 126 The three-masted barquentine *Estonia.* (Ålands Sjöfartsmuseum)

Far right, plate 127 *Melbourne.* (National Maritime Museum)

Below right, plate 128 *Viking*, setting sail off Dover in 1936. (National Maritime Museum)

carrying sailing vessels to smaller vessels intended exclusively for nautical training. *Viking,* which had made her last freight passage under the Danish flag with guano from Peru to London at the end of 1927, was an expensive purchase for Gustaf Erikson. After discharging the guano, her hold was 'a sea of rust', she was unclassed and a new set of sails had to be made for her. The vessel is estimated to have cost £9,500 by the time she had been put in condition to sail.

The purchase of these three vessels put a considerable strain on Gustaf Erikson's credit. Clarksons did not conceal their disapproval. In April and May, there had been some talk of buying a British cargo steamer of 7,000 tons deadweight for £35,000. In connection with this, the firm had promised credit of £16,000, but they refused to participate in the financing of any sailing vessel purchases. Gustaf Erikson was annoyed at such a 'vote of no confidence'. His correspondence with his friend Ingman during the changeable years of the 1920s is rich in spicy remarks; whether the tone is humorous or serious, it is unreservedly outspoken. The two men knew each other well and had no fear of expressing their opinions directly. 'You tell me not to be nervous. It is all well and good for you to take things so lightly, but your debt at home is like a millstone around my neck. It doesn't seem to worry you in the least, but consider what it means to pay 10½% on such a debt,' Ingman writes (in English), in July 1926. 'The only way to reduce the debt is to sell at least two of your vessels', he adds, saying that he thinks Laeisz, with his secure saltpetre trade, would perhaps be willing to give £5,000, if not £6,000 for *Herzogin Cecilie* — a suggestion the addressee would certainly not have had the slightest inclination to consider. 'Do you think we're asleep in London?' Ingman asks in the same letter, discussing the chartering of vessels.

On other occasions, Gustaf Erikson gives frank expression to his supposition that the respected London firm *was* taking a nap.

From the end of the 1920s, Clarksons and other business friends were increasingly determined in their attempts to convince Gustaf Erikson of the necessity of winding up his fleet of sailing vessels and buying tramp steamers. He willingly conceded that the advice was probably sound, 'but as I have been brought up with these sailors since the age of ten, I cannot help loving them. Malicious tongues will even allege that these vessels are closer to me than my wife and child...' he writes in a letter to

Below, plate 129 The Swedish iron four-masted barque *Beatrice* (National Maritime Museum)
Right, plate 130 *Beatrice* from the jigger shrouds shortened down in a strong breeze. (National Maritime Museum)

Left, plate 131 *Pamir* discharging grain in Southampton in 1939. (Basil Greenhill)
Above, plate 132 *Passat*. (Anne Stanley)

London in July 1929 when he had just bought *Melbourne* and *Viking* and the purchase of *Ponape* was imminent.

By the early 1930s, there were, to the great delight of Clarksons one imagines, not many deep-sea sailing vessels left in the world to bid for. Laeisz owned the most distinguished of them: *Padua, Priwall, Peking, Parma, Passat* and *Pamir*. From 1929, at least three big four-masted barques belonging to the Alaska Packers Association were laid-up in Alameda, California: *Star of Lapland, Star of Shetland* and *Star of Zealand,* all bought in the mid 1930s by a Japanese company. A fourth 'Star', *Star of Greenland* was bought in 1929 by the Rydberg Foundation in Stockholm, inheriting the name of the foundation's earlier training ship *Abraham Rydberg,* which in her turn was renamed *Seven Seas* by her new owners in America. After 1928, *Moshulu* was laid-up in Seattle. Otherwise one might mention the Finnish training ship *Favell,* Hugo Lundqvist's *Mozart,* the Swedes' *Beatrice* and *CB Pedersen, L'Avenir* belonging to the Association Maritime Belge, and *Magdalene Vinnen,* which had, however, an auxiliary engine.

Gustaf Erikson bought four of the vessels mentioned above: *Pamir* in 1931, *Passat* and *L'Avenir* in 1932, and *Moshulu* in 1935, besides becoming a joint-owner of *Parma,* which was bought by de Cloux, and among whose owners was also Alan Villiers. After the loss of *Melbourne in* 1933, Gustaf Erikson wrote to Clarksons that he was thinking of replacing the lost vessel with *Priwall* but, like the purchase of *Padua* this idea was never more than a pipe dream.

But during the 1930s Gustaf Erikson purchased a number of smaller, mostly wooden, sailing vessels for use in the Baltic trade and on deep water which in total amounted to considerable investment in this class of tonnage. These wooden vessels in the Baltic and North Sea trades were an essential complement to the bigger steel sailing ships whose work took them all over the world, an essential part of the same economic and social complex. The management and sailing of these vessels was just as skilled a matter - in some ways more so - than that of the bigger ships. It will be noted from the list of masters which appears later in this book how many of them served in both classes of tonnage — and not always in the smaller vessels first.

The wooden barque 'Varma' [True] was built in Nystad in mainland Finland in 1922 and was the last wooden barque ever to be built in the western world. Her voyage to Genoa with china clay from Fowey in Cornwall and back to Gothenburg from Sicily with salt in 1930 was the last deep-water voyage ever made by a European wooden three-masted barque-rigged merchant sailing ship. The four-masted auxiliary fore-and-aft schooner 'Madare' was built in Sweden in 1919. The wooden barque 'Eläköön' [Long Life!] built at Nystad in 1920, justified her name by surviving to be Europe's last wooden three-masted barque. She made her last voyage with cargo in 1939, taking 412 standards of timber from Veitsluoto to Esbjerg in 27 days from 1 July and returning to Mariehamn in ballast, arriving on 29 August. She was laid up in Nystad during the War and taken to Åbo in 1944. In the spring of 1945 she was converted into a full powered motorship without sail, and thus ended almost five hundred years of shipping history. In 1977 her hull

was still in existence as part of a bridge between two islands in the Finnish Archipelago. The three-masted auxiliary schooner 'Vellamo' was also built at Nystad, but the four masted fore-and-aft schooner 'Valborg' had been built in British Columbia in 1919 and gave Gustaf Erikson good service for ten years. The steel barque 'Pestalozzi' was built in Hamburg in 1884 and the 'Kylemore' at Port Glasgow by J Reid and Co in 1880. The four-masted 'Odine' was another handsome big American built fore-and-aft schooner.[1] *The American style four-masted 'Regina' was built at Hammars in Borgå, east of Helsinki, in the Gulf of Finland. The four-masted barquentine 'Dione', acquired in 1934, had been built in Åland at Klinten in Jomala over the years 1919-1923 and was owned by Gustaf Erikson until 1939.*

The last sailing vessel ever to be acquired by Gustaf Erikson, who had, after the purchase of 'Moshulu' in 1935, acquired eight steamers and motorships, was the three-masted auxiliary fore-and-aft schooner 'Sirius', built in Sweden, bought in 1942, and disposed of to Norwegian owners four years later.[2]

1 The *Odine* was fitted with twin auxiliary oil engines and appears to have been purchased for these and her gear which were transferred to *Valborg*. She was then sold. She had been a well-known vessel in the lathwood trade to Regents Canal Dock, London, for many years. Despite her twin screws she could make only five knots under power and was therefore very difficult to manage in the London River. Captain Karl V Karlsson of Vårdö who commanded her for a short period told me in 1977 that when she was sighted off the Thames the pilots used to signal to one another, 'The enemy is in sight!'

2 The sentences in *italics* were added by the Editor.

Below, plate 133 *L'Avenir* in Milwall Dock, London, 13 June 1936. (National Maritime Museum)
Above, plate 134 *Moshulu* sailing under the United States flag. (National Maritime Museum)
Left, plate 135 *Arrow*, later *Parma*, photographed shortly after her launch in 1902. (National Maritime Museum)

No 7.
VARMA
VARMA
MARIEHAMN

CHAPTER 6

The Last Sailing-Fleet

In 1935, Gustaf Erikson's fleet reached its peak in the number of vessels and in total tonnage, though its market value increased considerably as a result of the steamship tonnage acquired in the years before the Second World War. The table below setting out the fleet as it was in 1935 was drawn up by my brother, managing clerk Hilding Kåhre. It shows the approximate value of each vessel, allowing a certain leeway, at the time in millions of Finnish Marks. There is no question of an actual market value, as a market for sailing vessels no longer existed. The vessels are listed in order of size.[1]

DEEP-SEA VESSELS	
Moshulu	1.3
Passat	1.8
Lawhill	1.35
Olivebank	1.35
Herzogin Cecilie	1.8
Pamir	1.5
Pommern	1.35
Viking	1.7
Archibald Russell	1.35
L'Avenir	1.4
Ponape	1.3
Penang	1.25
Winterhude	1.2
Killoran	1.0
Grace Harwar	0.85

NORTH SEA AND BALTIC SAILING VESSELS	
Kylemore	0.5
Lingard	0.5
Pestalozzi	0.5
Eläköön	0.25
Varma	0.25
Dione	0.2
Estonia	0.25
Baltic	0.2

AUXILIARY SAILING VESSELS	
Valborg	1.1
Regina	0.65
Madare	0.95
Vellamo	0.35

TOTAL VALUE 25.15 million Marks
(approximately £111,300)

Including the steam-tug *Johanna*, valued at 200,000 Marks, and two motorships without sails, the *Vera* and the *Sweden*, the fleet comprised 30 vessels. The combined deadweight was 75,200 tons, and the combined registered tonnage was 47,612 tons gross and 39,542 tons net. Deep-water sailers represented nearly 75% of the fleet's value and a somewhat higher percentage of its tonnage. The eight smaller sailing vessels corresponded to

1 The Finnish Mark then stood at 226 to the Pound.

Left, plate 136 *Varma* the last wooden three-masted barque ever to be built in Europe, discharging timber into barges in Regent's Canal Dock. Her steel main and fore yards, formerly upper topsail yards in *Arethusa*, ex *Peking*, were fitted in the winter of 1934-5. (Ålands Sjöfartsmuseum)

Above, plate 137 *Madare* with much reduced canvas as a motor schooner. (Ålands Sjöfartsmuseum)

Below, plate 138 *Eläköön*, deep laden, towing up the Thames behind the tug *Java* off Greenwich. (National Maritime Museum)

Right, plate 139 *Vellamo*, lying off Nystad. (Ålands Sjöfartsmuseum)

about 10% of the total value. If the fleet had been insured at its estimated value, the premiums would have approached 3 million Marks.

The table also includes other information of interest from the previous year, 1934. That year 22 million Marks were sailed in gross freights — only a little less than the total estimated value of the fleet. 540 people were employed in the fleet.

Skippers	29
First Mates	29
Second Mates	29
Third Mates	11
Galley personnel	50
Engine crew including donkeymen	34
Deckhands including apprentices	358

The previous year, Gustaf Erikson had bought the slipway at Nystad, in mainland Finland, picking up *Varma, Eläköön* and *Vellamo* in the deal, which was run on a modest scale in the period before the war, being used primarily for the repair of his own vessels. However, it was later considerably expanded, in order to handle war damage. In 1934, two master shipbuilders and an average of 74 workers were employed. Counting, in addition to these, a further three men working in the office in Mariehamn, and one in Nystad, the final total employed by the company was 620. A total of about 5 million Marks was paid out in wages. Provisioning bills for the vessels amounted to 2.5 million Marks, and the bill for sail-canvas was 0.9 million Marks. Roughly 0.6 million Marks were spent on Manilla hemp and wire, and 0.5 million on paint. A further 0.5 million Marks went on various other requirements. It might be of interest to compare these figures with the saving on insurance premiums.

Wages on shipboard varied within narrow limits (Marks per month).

Skipper	3,500 — 4,500
First Mate	1,900 — 2,100
Second Mate	1,500 — 1,600
Third Mate	1,000 — 1,100
Steward	1,700 — 2,000
Cook	800 — 1,200
Galley Boy	300 — 450
Sailmaker	900 — 1,300
Carpenter	900 — 1,200
Sailmaker's Mate	650 — 800
Donkeyman	900 — 1,300
Able Seaman	550 — 650
Ordinary Seaman	400 — 500
Junior Seaman	250 — 350

Above, plate 140 *Valborg*. (Ålands Sjöfartsmuseum)

Below, plate 141 *Valborg* with reduced canvas after being fitted with twin diesels from *Odine*. (Ålands Sjofartsmuseum)

Above, plate 142 *Pestalozzi*, with *Varma* in the distance, in 1935. (National Maritime Museum)

Below, plate 143 *Kylemore*, when under the British flag. (National Maritime Museum)

Apprentices paid a fee: Finns 6,000 Marks for two years with the right to draw 100 Marks per month in the first year, and 400 — 450 Marks per month in the second year, depending on the ability shown; Germans 850 Reichsmarks with the same conditions; Swedes 900 Kronor per year; British and others £50.

It is striking that stewards' and cooks' salaries were on a level with junior officers'. There was no shortage of mates who needed experience in sailing vessels for their masters examination. The fact that experience under sail was still required for nautical examination in many countries contributed to the last sailing-fleet's ability to squeeze past hidden economic reefs for so long.

Five of the 15 deep-sea vessels were gone from the oceans by the end of the decade: *Herzogin Cecilie, Ponape, Grace Harwar, L'Avenir,* and *Olivebank*. Among the eight Baltic and North Sea vessels the casualties were even greater; by 1937, five of them were no longer sailing: *Kylemore, Lingard, Pestalozzi, Varma* and *Estonia.*

Gustaf Erikson's ocean-going sailing-fleet had to face a continuing and irreversible decline in the number of available trades in the 1920s and '30s. This is evident from the following table:

TRADES	NUMBER OF FREIGHT PASSAGES	
	1920s	1930s
Australia/Europe. *Wheat*	30	115
Norway or the Baltic/Australia. *Timber*	22	—
Chile/Europe. *Saltpetre*	14	—
Newcastle NSW/Chile or Peru. *Coal*	8	—
West Indies/Europe. *Logwood*	8	4
Canada or USA/Buenos Aires or Rosario. *Timber*	6	—
Peruvian Islands/Europe. *Guano*	6	1
Peruvian Islands/East Coast USA. *Guano*	5	—
UK/South Africa. *Coal or coke*	5	1
UK/Chile. *Coke*	3	—
Canada/Australia. *Timber*	3	—
Norway or the Baltic/South Africa. *Timber*	2	16
Seychelles, Juan de Novo, Assumption/ New Zealand. *Guano*	2	8
Liverpool/Sydney. *Salt*	2	—
La Plata/Europe. *Grain*	2	—
New York/Australia. *Oil*	2	—
UK/South America. *Coal*	2	2
West Coast North America/South Africa. *Timber*	1	1
Chile/South Africa. *Saltpetre*	1	—
Australia/Peru. *Wheat*	1	4
Gulf of Mexico/Europe. *Timber*	1	—
Canada/Europe. *Timber*	1	—
Cardiff/Mauritius. *Coal*	1	—
Middlesborough/Mauritius. *Fertilizer*	—	4
Noumea NC/Bremen. *Ore*	—	1

Freight passages in the 1920s were made by *Archibald Russell, Grace Harwar, Herzogin Cecilie, Hougomont, Killoran, Lalla Rookh, Lawhill, Lingard, Loch Linnhe, Melbourne, Olivebank, Penang, Pommern, Professor Koch, Viking, Winterhude* and *Woodburn;* and in the 1930s by *Archibald Russell, Grace Harwar, Herzogin Cecilie, Hougomont, Killoran, L'Avenir, Lawhill, Lingard, Loch Linnhe, Melbourne, Moshulu, Olivebank, Pamir, Passat, Penang, Pommern, Ponape, Viking* and *Winterhude.* Of course the table only covers the sailings these vessels made under Gustaf Erikson's flag. The logwood carriers *Loch Linnhe, Lingard* and *Lalla Rookh* generally carried lathwood to Britain in their old age; their few sailings to the West Indies were rare excursions on deep-water. A rarer exception was *Lawhill*'s lathwood freight from Trångsund to London in 1933.

A quick glance at the table indicates that vessels made passages in ballast increasingly frequently over increasingly longer distances, in the 1930s. The opportunities for combining several charters in a long round trip became more and more scarce. In 1922-23 *Lawhill* sailed from Sweden to Melbourne with timber, from Newcastle NSW to Chile with coal, and from there to Bordeaux with saltpetre. This was followed by a long passage in ballast down to Australia. But *Lawhill* then sailed from Newcastle NSW to Tocopilla with coal, from Iquique to Ghent with saltpetre, from Grangemouth to Chile with coal, and back to Bruges with saltpetre, from Campbellton to Melbourne with timber and from there to London with wheat. From 1 July 1924, when *Lawhill* sailed for Tocopilla, until 22 June 1927, when she arrived in London, she sailed a bare 50 days in ballast: a day and a half between Tocopilla and Iquique, three days being towed from Ghent to Grangemouth, and 45 days to Campbellton.

By the 1930s, there were extremely few opportunities for such combinations, the working out and balancing of which had added some excitement to routine work in shipping offices during the heyday

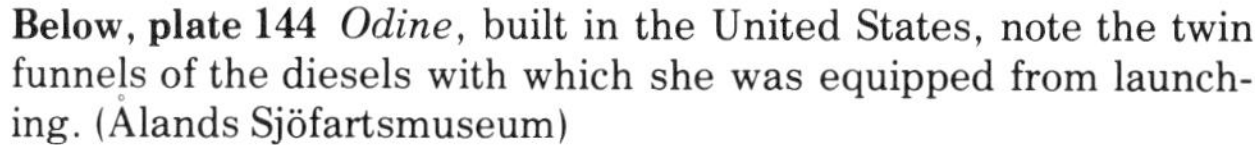

Below, plate 144 *Odine*, built in the United States, note the twin funnels of the diesels with which she was equipped from launching. (Ålands Sjöfartsmuseum)

Right, plate 145 *Regina* lying in the Erikson dockyard at Nystad. (Ålands Sjöfartsmuseum)

Above, plate 146 The motor schooner *Sirius*, the last sail-using vessel ever to be purchased by Gustaf Erikson. (Ålands Sjöfartsmuseum)

of sail. Australia-bound vessels sometimes had an outward freight of timber as far as South Africa. In four cases an outward freight of fertilizer to Mauritius was found. *Grace Harwar*, for example, had one such freight in 1931. After a short passage in ballast to Juan de Novo, she loaded guano for Auckland, and after 28 days in ballast from there to Port Victoria, she took on a cargo of wheat for Europe. Passages in ballast could turn out to be lengthy too. On 20 December 1928, *Killoran* sailed for Port Lincoln for orders, without a charter. She arrived on 3 March 1929, and immediately received orders for Ylo in Peru, a passage of a further 53 days. A cargo of guano was waiting in Santa Rosa. During the crisis of 1929-30, many vessels had similar experiences. After taking coal from Newport to Venezuela, *Killoran* was once again unchartered when she sailed from Tucacas for Falmouth for orders. She was ordered to Helsinki, and from there to Trångsund, where she arrived on 14 July, chartered with timber to South Africa at 66/3d — a lot of shouting for a little wool, as the Ålanders say. On 20 February the same year, *Penang* sailed in ballast from Sydney, bound for Falmouth for orders. *Grace Harwar* sailed on 12 January, also in ballast, from La Guayra in Venezuela to Elsinore for orders, and on to Mariehamn, where she was laid-up from 10 June 1930 to 13 May 1931 because of the shortage of freights.

An old-timer glancing at the table of routes might be struck by the flight of time and the transience of all things. It shows only one freight passage from the Gulf, where every year a score of wooden barques from Åland would take on their cargoes in the years around the turn of the century. Other trades too are pale spectres of their former greatness. The timber trade from the West Coast of North America, for example, is represented by only two freight passages; *Pommern's* from Tacoma to Port Natal in 1926, and *Hougomont*'s from Vancouver to the same port in 1930. A comparison of the two columns reveals the sudden departure of the Chile saltpetre trade from the scene. The last Åland vessels carrying saltpetre sailed in 1927: *Winterhude* on 27 September from Caleta Buena to Ostend, *Pommern* on 19 October from Tocopilla to Granville, and *Lawhill* from Taltal to Delfzijl on 3 December. *Winterhude* made her passage in 110 days, *Pommern* in 111 days and *Lawhill* in 112 days.

Left, plate 147 The timber trade (1). Women stevedores stowing the deck cargo of timber in the barque *Varma*, lying in the roadstead at Räfsö, August 1935. (Lars Grönstrand)

Above, plate 148 The timber trade (2). *Varma* with a big deck cargo in a light breeze on the port tack. Note the bowline on the weather of the mainsail. (Lars Grönstrand)

Below, plate 149 The timber trade (3). Hauling the spanker boom to windward, going about in *Varma*, August 1935. The master, Captain Lindqvist, has taken the wheel. (Lars Grönstrand)

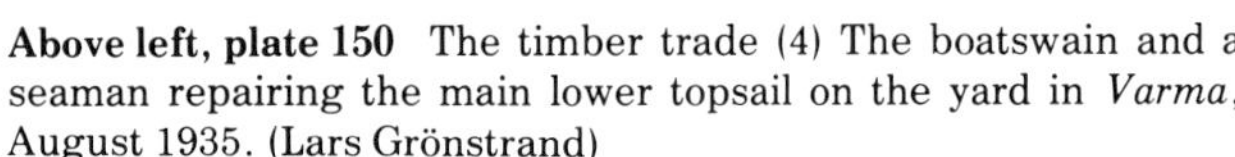

Above left, plate 150 The timber trade (4) The boatswain and a seaman repairing the main lower topsail on the yard in *Varma*, August 1935. (Lars Grönstrand)

Below, plate 151 The timber trade (5). A different type of deck cargo, staves, in the schooner *Lideborg* with her crew, 1928. *Lideborg* was built in Geta parish in Åland in 1921. (Ålands Sjöfartsmuseum)

Above right, plate 152 The timber trade (6). Discharging 'split wood', timber offcuts, from the small after hatch of *Lideborg* in Great Yarmouth. (National Maritime Museum)

The guano trades, one imagines, might awaken memories and feelings of a more unpleasant nature. There were two routes. In the 1920s, guano was taken mainly from the islands off Peru to the East Coast of the USA, or to Europe, through the Panama Canal, and in the 1930s, from the Seychelles to New Zealand. For skippers, a guano charter was seen almost as uncalled-for persecution by the owners and by providence, if not perhaps as amply distressing retribution for sins committed. As far as the crews were concerned, the guano islands were places where no seaman had deserted since the beginning of time. In February 1924, when *Archibald Russell* was chartered and ordered to the Peruvian guano paradise, Captain Isidor Eriksson was far from pleased, and he did nothing to conceal his opinion. Gustaf Erikson wrote long confiding letters, referring to Captain Blomfelt of *Penang,* 'Who had not had a bad word to say about guano cargoes', but on the contrary, had been able to remit 10,000 Dollars to his company. Expenses at the loading site had been kept down to about £600, the passage through the Panama Canal had cost £860, and Wilmington had been happy with £1500 in expenses. There were certain advantages to be taken into consideration; the men stayed on board and would collect a large sum in wages due, which was the surest measure against desertion, on reaching the guano's port of destination perhaps after as much as nine months. Besides, there would be plenty of time during the long passage in ballast for scraping and painting, which the vessel was certainly in need of.

Gustaf Erikson had no personal experience in the guano trade, which had been tried by very few Åland skippers before the First World War. August Gustafsson had taken one cargo from the Lobos Islands to London with *Mermerus*, and Emanual Eriksson too had sailed with one guano freight. After consulting him, Gustaf Erikson sent a new letter, loaded with good advice, to *Archibald Russell*'s worried and reluctant skipper. According to Emanual Eriksson, the deck had not suffered any direct damage, but the strong fumes had forced all tar and oil out of it, so that it turned as white as if it had been scrubbed with caustic soda. The sides of the hold, beams, and stanchions should be clothed in sacking, and 'dunnage' of planks and boards should be bedded under the cargo 'on the bottom as well as the 'tween decks.' If this was the case, it would be best to buy necessary materials while he was still in Milford Haven, where they would certainly be cheaper than in Peru. The greatest care should be taken of the water supply, and rationing introduced, but fish could be caught by the ton with dynamite and salted down. 'You must not be worried about this voyage. "All's well that ends well", the proverb says, and perhaps when the voyage is over, we will each be more satisfied with its result than we expect. And since you, Sir, are a practical and experienced skipper, you will no doubt soon familiarise yourself with this trade, even if it is one that is not well known to us Ålanders,' read the final comment. In one respect things did not go exactly according to plan; 11 men jumped ship in Savannah, where *Archibald Russell* arrived with her 3,950 tons of guano, and a gross freight of about £9,000, on 5 October, seven months after sailing from Britain. The passage from Callao was relatively fast — 35 days, 13 days from Callao to the Panama Canal.

In the summer of 1928, *Grace Harwar* took 14 days to sail from Guanape to the Panama Canal, and 29 days from there to Wilmington. The same year, about a month earlier, *Killoran* took 23 days to the Panama Canal from Don Martin Island, and 22 days the following year from Santa Rosa. All in all, the former passage took 91 days to London, and the latter only 77 days to Antwerp. In 1928, *Winterhude* took 14 days from Santa Rosa to the Canal and 81 days to Antwerp. The following year, she took 18 days from Guanape to the Canal, and 71 days from Guanape to London. *Ponape* took 73 days from Guanape to Dunkirk in 1930. *Hougomont* took 83 days from Lobos to London in 1925, and 36 days from Santa Rosa to Jacksonville in 1928. *Penang* took 87 days from Macabi Island to London in 1925, and 44 days to Jacksonville the following year from the same island.

The slow loading did not add to the pleasure. *Hougomont* arrived at Lobos on 20 July 1925 and left on 26 October. She spent more than two months loading at Santa Rosa in 1928. *Winterhude* lay there for almost two months at the same time. The two vessels sailed on the same day, 23 August. *Hougomont* reached the Panama Canal on 5 September, followed the next day by *Winterhude,* which loaded rapidly the next year at Guanape, in one month.

Guano from the Indian Ocean went to New Zealand, as has been said, mainly in the years 1931-33 and 1936-40:

Grace Harwar. Juan de Novo/Auckland 73 days. Arrived 2 Feb 1932.
Winterhude. Denis Is/Auckland 57 days. Arrived 27 Jan 1933.

Above, plate 153 The timber trade (7). *Lideborg* in Great Yarmouth. (National Maritime Museum)

Below, plate 154. The timber trade (8) The four-masted schooner *Atlas*, the steel barques *Oaklands* and *Lalla Rookh* discharging timber in Regent's Canal Dock, July 1927. (Ålands Sjöfartsmuseum)

Passat. Mahe, Seychelles/Auckland 75 days. Arrived 6 Feb 1933. Loaded at Assumption Island.

Winterhude. Mahe/Auckland 68 days. Arrived 10 Feb 1937. Loaded Astove Is.

Pamir. Astove Is/Auckland 73 days. Arrived 23 Jan 1938.

Penang. Juan de Novo/Auckland 71 days. Arrived 20 Feb 1938.

Penang. Juan de Novo/Auckland 69 days. Arrived 29 Feb 1940.

Pamir. Assumption/New Plymouth NZ. 63 days. Arrived 16 Dec 1940.

On 20 February 1941, *Pamir* sailed again to Mahe, arrived on 28 April, sailed on 18 June from Assumption, arrived in Wellington on 30 July after a passage of only 42 days, and was seized on 7 August.

This information has been taken from the company's position lists. One is tempted to doubt their accuracy regarding *Winterhude*'s and *Passat*'s sailings in 1932-33. The latter sailed from Mahe on 23 November, the former from nearby Denis Island eight days later, arriving in Auckland 10 days earlier. This story sounds almost too good to be true.

Under the command of K Troberg, *Olivebank* made two freight passages in this trade, in 1926 and 1928. The point of departure for the first was Port Lincoln, where the vessel had arrived too late to get a cargo of wheat for Europe. On 29 April, five days after sailing, *Olivebank* reached Queenscliff, where she spent a few days getting her breath back after a tussle with a storm in which she lost some canvas. The passage from Queenscliff to Mahe took 54 days, and from Mahe to Dunedin 89 days. The voyage of 1928 was more eventful. *Olivebank* arrived at Assumption five days too late and the charter-party was cancelled. After waiting at Mahe for three weeks, another freight was found from St Pierre Island. She sailed for St Pierre on 30 June, taking with her 84 negroes to do the loading. She arrived on 8 July and hung tightly on to the island with 80 fathoms of cable a ship's length from land. Two days later, her anchor dragged on the precipitous bottom and *Olivebank* drifted away. It took her two weeks to get back and anchor anew, 50 metres from land with 12 fathoms of water forward and 84 fathoms under her stern. *Olivebank* continued her voyage on 2 September, putting into Queenscliff on 13 November with sick crew, and not reaching Auckland until 20 December. Captain Troberg had had his due share of guano sailing. The fact that the vessel drifted away from the small island's non-existent anchorage was not so unusual however.

Freight rates from the islands off Peru remained at around 50/- per ton in the 1920s, but during the bad year 1930, *Ponape* had only 32/9d. From the Seychelles, 22/- to 23/- is recorded from 1931-33, but in 1937-38, *Pamir* and *Penang* had 37/6. *Pamir* had 46/- in 1940.

'From now on, we must save more on a penny than on a shilling earlier,' Gustaf Erikson wrote to Captain Nordberg of *Tjerimai* on 5 June 1921. An attitude of strict reserve should be taken towards ship chandlers, and the use of tugs should be avoided except in the case of extreme necessity. Other skippers received similar exhortations. 'The point is that freights will probably not rise. Expenses must be cut, even if we do not wish it,' to quote a prophetic sigh sent to Captain Lindqvist of *Grace Harwar* in February 1921.

The days of fabulous freights were finally at an end. A long sober working day began, ushered in by sudden failure or mere liquidation for many sailing ship companies which had been living extravagantly on expensively acquired tonnage. It was apparent without any calculations that thrift on shipboard had now to be a cardinal virtue in a fleet of sailing vessels which enjoyed no form of state subsidy; the massive sale of vessels around the world was evidence in itself. In fact, to shipowners and brokers abroad, it was a miracle that Gustaf Erikson's fleet continued to sail and, to judge by its steady expansion, to earn dividends and make profits. The secret of its success is no easier to pin down than the wanderings of the winds. The fact that, for historical reasons already explained, in the Åland Islands there were still officers who understood sailing ships from days of youth spent in wooden galeas and schooner and who were part of the small local community with all that this implies; stewards who were able to economise with provisions but still prepare them well; crews who tended to remain with the same ship for a long time — these all meant a lot, but not everything. One often hears good luck mentioned as the explanation, but anyone who has looked into the company's development has not the slightest desire to talk of luck and misfortune, he has discovered as much of one as of the other.

In order to counteract desertions, a guarantee was required in the form of a surety from the crew when they signed on. Another system was used, on *Hougomont* at least in 1925; some crewmen — able and ordinary seamen, donkeymen and boatswains — undertook not to draw cash until 5,000 Marks had been earned and left as wages due until they were paid off. The cheap labour provided by apprentices served to keep wages bills as low as possible.

I mentioned earlier that *Peking*'s sails were purchased. 'Go up to Bruges, where vessels are being broken up, and buy cheap blocks, sheaves, shackles, hawsers, wire etc,' reads a letter to *Lawhill*'s newly appointed skipper, Captain Grönlund, in Ghent in 1925. With a keen personal interest, Gustaf Erikson kept an eye open for various sorts of fittings, running gear, spars, sails and so on in those harbours where vessels were being scrapped. Vessels which he himself sold to be broken-up were meticulously stripped of anything which could be used by the fleet at sea. This too was a stroke of Gustaf Erikson's management in the later days of the sailing ship business.

In short, it paid to economise — but only up to a certain point. A skipper had to have enough of a seaman's eye to see where that point was. Desperate and ruthless exploitation was not tolerated, and vessels had to be maintained. A ship 'rusted-up' was an abomination before God. The principle of thrift was not applied to the same degree in oil and paint accounts that it was in others. That the fleet's skippers received fatherly instructions as to the necessity of stirring the paint well in the pail is a story in itself.

In the 1930s particularly, vessels often carried passengers — on long passages as well as on trips between England and Mariehamn, and sometimes from Mariehamn to Copenhagen when they sailed out in the autumn, bound for Australia. They were mostly sea-hungry Englishmen who contributed a modest sum to the credit side of the budget.

Thanks to the large number of vessels, the company was able to insure itself. One should not forget, however, that the insuring of cargoes, whether this was the obligation of shippers or consignees, constituted a heavy burden for sailing vessels. The company had nothing to do with the premiums, but these indirectly affected freight rates. Since the premium of a sailing vessel's cargo was several times higher than for a steamer's, the steamer's actual freight rate could be higher, of course. If 4,000 tons of wheat, with a value of £20,000 was carried on a sailing vessel, the premium

Left, plate 155 A nursery of seamen: sail is taken in as the schooner *Norden* comes up to an anchor. She was built in Geta parish in 1920 and her master was Eric Mattsson, formerly of the *Ingrid* (Plate 75). Among her seamen were Harald Lindfors, later to command *Archibald Russell* and Uno Mörn, later to command *Winterhude*, *Pamir*, *Olivebank* and *Viking*. (Ålands Sjöfartsmuseum)
Above, plate 156 The crew of *Valborg*. Captain Einar Palmqvist, later to command *Sigyn*, is seated right front. (Ålands Sjöfartsmuseum)
Right, plate 157 Captain K G Lindqvist in *Varma* August, 1935. He had formerly commanded *Grace Harwar*, *Carradale*, *Lingard*, *Pestalozzi* and *Kylemore*. (Lars Grönstrand)

for the cargo would be as high as 50/- per £100, ie 2½%, or a total of £500. A tramp steamer paid no more than £50 to £60. In other words, the difference of £450 meant that the steamer's freight rate could be set more than 2 Shillings higher per ton. When the number of sailing vessels in the fleet declined after 1935, the insurers naturally began to consider the insurance of the vessels' cargoes a risky gamble.[1]

Between the Wars, Gustaf Erikson's fleet lost two wheat cargoes: *Melbourne*'s and *Herzogin Cecilie*'s. The owners of MV *Seminole* were responsible for paying compensation for *Melbourne*'s. *Herzogin Cecilie*'s cargo constituted less than 1% of

1 This question of cargo insurance is dealt with at length and with great authority in W L A Derby's *The Tall Ships Pass*.

the total quantity of wheat transported by the fleet. Underwriters had reason to be satisfied, despite the fact that she was lost in 1936.

It would be interesting to know exactly to what extent the self-risk system paid off. Unfortunately, a calculation is impossible since damage that an insurance company would have covered was often repaired in conjunction with classification work and the like. There were of course vessels which it would have been a positive advantage to insure. In a cyclone on 12 October 1927, *Hougomont*, bound for Melbourne with timber, lost all her sails and a good part of her standing rigging besides. She was towed into Lisbon on 27 October. The cost of the damage reached £1,400, and her stay in Lisbon lasted a month. In 1932, this was followed by her final dismasting off Australia.

Hougomont collected an impressive run of misfortunes in her 35 year merit list. In 1903, while on a passage from San Francisco, she ran aground off Liverpool and lost her topgallant masts. In 1908, she struggled unsuccessfully against the current off the coast of Chile. Bound from Coquimbo to Tocopilla, about 500 miles further north along the Chilean coast, she drifted past her destination and, in the feather-light airs, was unable to get back. 400 nautical miles north of Tocopilla, her skipper took a quick decision; he sailed to Sydney, arriving after 80 days, by which time his vessel had been declared lost by Lloyds. In 1914, *Hougomont* ran aground off New York in a fog. She was salvaged and continued to sail for her original owners, James Hardie in Glasgow, during the First World War.

The dismasting in 1932 has been described by Derby, among others, in *The Tall Ships Pass*. It drew a lot of attention at the time, mostly perhaps because of the fine seamanship of Captain Ragnar Lindholm and his crew. On 21 April, shortly after midnight, *Hougomont* lost her rigging in a violent squall southwest of the Spencer Gulf, where she was bound, at latitude 39° 34′ and longitude 126° 53′. This time, the dismasting was complete. Her mainmast was broken six feet above the deck and bigger stumps were left of her remaining masts. *Hougomont* continued her passage under a jury rig. Captain Lindholm refused assistance from a steamer

Left, plate 158 Captain K F Lindgren takes his afternoon walk on the roof of the cabin in *Eläköön*, 26 June 1937, while awaiting the coming on board of the pilot off Räfsö. He had previously commanded *Olivebank*, *Ostrobotnia*, *Dione*, *Baltic*, and *Pestalozzi* and went on to the motorship *Vera*. Note his wooden shoes, the washing on the line, the windmill pump and the built up mainmast made of a number of timbers held together with iron bands. (Lars Grönstrand)

Above, plate 159 Captain Ivar Hägerstrand in *Viking*, July 1937. He had formerly commanded *Loch Linnhe*, *Woodburn*, *Hougomont* and *Winterhude* and went on to command the four-masted schooner *Yxpila* and *Passat* and was the last man but one ever to command a laden merchant sailing ship making a rounding of Cape Horn. (Basil Greenhill)

and a motor-vessel which sighted the damaged vessel, and reached Adelaide semaphore on 8 May unaided, thereby saving many hundreds of Pounds in salvage dues, to the benefit of her owner, as Derby remarks. *Herzogin Cecilie* took charge of everything that could be used by the fleet, including her figurehead, and seeing that no prospective buyers for her hull were forthcoming, *Hougomont* ended her days as a breakwater, a donation from Gustaf Erikson to the Spencer Gulf. Her charthouse went to *Penang*'s poop and *Killoran* took her wheelhouse.

Apart from the total losses, other vessels also suffered their accidents. But the self-insurance system seems to have paid off; in fact it seems to have been essential to the continuing economic viability of deep-water sailing. The cost of sails lost on the open sea would not have been the responsibility of any insurers anyway.

Partial damage seems to have been suffered to a greater extent by North Sea vessels. *Baltic,* for example, put into Gothenburg leaking in the autumns of 1931, 1934 and 1935. *Madare* took her cargoes to England.

After *Lingard*'s fateful collision with SS *Gerd* in 1935, and the resulting legal action over compensation for the steamer's crew who lost their lives, plans were realised for reshaping the company as a number of separate joint-stock companies, one for each vessel.

Those who are expecting me to portray an interesting cross-section of the fleet's skippers will be disappointed. The task would be beyond me; my knowledge of the finer points of nautical practice and of the skippers' individual qualities is inadequate. However, several of them have been characterised in English nautical literature. I have had the pleasure of knowing some of them personally, and I remember gratefully their wonderful hospitality in the saloons of their vessels in Mariehamn roads. Captain Seth Östling sent me a sparkling depiction of an admired skipper, Anders Donner of *Garnet Hill,* when he heard that I was dabbling in Åland's nautical history once again. But the fleet had had many captains in the days of the sailing ships. I retreat from any attempt to separate the chaff from the wheat, and limit myself to an alphabetical list — and I cannot even guarantee that it has the virtue of being complete.

For safety's sake, I point out that in many cases a single year denotes only part of the year in question. And years of command in the fleet's steamships have not been included. The steamer skipper still has his ship; the windjammer skipper has only a memory left of his vessel, though a number of these men went on to command the company's steam and motor vessels.

Karl Abrahamsson *Ostrobotnia* 1925. *Baltic* 1929-30
Nils Andersson *Winterhude* 1926
V Björkfelt *Killoran* 1933-37. *Pamir* 1937.
A Björklund *Borrowdale* 1917.
A G Blomfelt *Penang* 1923-Feb 1925
John Blomqvist *Vellamo* 1935
G Boman *Ostrobotnia* 1928-29. *Baltic* 1930. *Grace Harwar* 1930-34. *Moshulu* 1935-38
Karl Broman *Pommern* 1933-39. *Viking* 1946-47.
Ruben de Cloux *Lawhill* 1917-21. *Herzogin Cecilie* 1921-24 and 1925-29. *Viking* 1929 from Copenhagen to Mariehamn.
Hj Dahiblom *Loch Linnhe* 1924
L Dahlsten *Eläköön* 1936
Anders Donner *Grace Harwar* 1917-20. *Varma* 1933-34
F Ejder *Woodburn* 1925-26. *Winterhude* 1927.
E W Eriksson *Valborg* 1934-Feb 1937
Hj Erikson *Carmen* ?-?
Isidor Eriksson *Carradale* 1923. *Archibald Russell* 1924-26. *Lalla Rookh* 1926-28.
Julius Eriksson *Grace Harwar* 1916-17.
K J Eriksson *Loch Linnhe* 1922-23 and 1928? *Killoran* 1924-27. *Eläköön* 1933-35. *Kylemore* 1936. *Valborg* 1937.
Karl Eriksson *Madare* Nov 1931-Jan 1932.
Nils Erikson *Ostrobotnia* 1926. *L'Avenir* 1932-37. *Passat* 1937.
Sven Eriksson *Herzogin Cecilie* 1929-36.
A Fallström *Killoran* 1937-38.
W Geelnard *Ostrobotnia* autumn 1930 *Dione* 1935-36.
Carl Granith *Lingard* 1926-27. *Pommern* 1927-33. *Ponape* 1933-37, *Olivebank* 1937-39.
A Granlund *Baltic* 1936-37.
F Grönlund *Herzogin Cecilie* 1924. *Lawhill* 1925-30. *Penang* 1931-33 and 1934-36. *Pestalozzi* spring 1934. *Passat* 1936-37. *Madare* 1937-39. *Valborg* 1939-40
M A Gustafsson *Grace Harwar* 1922-28
Julius Gustafsson *Lawhill* 1924.

J W Gustafson *Pommern* 1923-24.
J E Gustafsson *Lawhill* 1921-22
I Hägerstrand *Loch Linnhe* 1923-24. *Woodburn* 1924-25. *Hougomont* 1925-27. *Winterhude* 1928-29. *Viking* 1929-37. *Passat* 1945-50.
G Holm *Grace Harwar* 1934. *Pestalozzi* 1935-36. *Winterhude* 1936-39. *Moshulu* 1941.
Carl Holmqvist *Lawhill* 1924-25.
E H Jansen *Hougomont* 1927-29.
J B Johansson *Lingard* 1927-28. *Melbourne* 1929-32.
Edv Johnsson *Margareta* 1917. *Professor Koch* 1919-22. *Pommern* 1924-27. *Madare* 1929-30.
Anton Karlsson *Winterhude* 1929-32.
Hugo D Karlsson *Ponape* 1932-33.
K E Karlsson *Tjerimai* 1917-19
K J Karlsson *Dione* 1937 *Baltic* 1937-38
K W Karlsson *Professor Koch* 1916-19. *Lalla Rookh* autumn 1928.
K V Karlsson *Penang* 1936-41.
Oskar Karlsson *Estonia* 1933-36.
U Karlsson *Ponape* 1929-32.
O Knahpe *Ostrobotnia* 1931. *Madare* 1932-37.
A Leman *Killoran* 1938-40.
K Lindblom *Ingrid* 1919.
H Lindeman *Baltic* 1933-34.
B Lindfors *Baltic* 1931-33.
H Lindfors *Carmen* 1930, *Archibald Russell* 1930-32.
KF Lindgren *Olivebank* 1929-31. *Ostrobotnia* 1932-33. *Dione* 1934-35 and 1938. *Baltic* 1935-36. *Pestalozzi* 1936. *Eläköön* 1937.
R Lindholm *Killoran* 1927-30. *Hougomont* 1931-32. *Loch Linnhe* 1933.
W Lindholm *Vellamo* 1937-39.
K V Lindqvist *Grace Harwar* 1920-22. *Carradale* 1923. *Lingard* 1931-33. *Pestalozzi* autumn 1934. *Kylemore* spring 1934. *Varma* 1935-36.
L Lindvall *Olivebank* 1933-37. *Pamir* 1937. *Passat* 1938-39.
G Lundberg *L'Avenir* 1932. *Baltic* 1925-29. *Estonia* May 1927. *Lingard* 1929-31. *Passat* 1932-33.
R. Mansnerus *Vellamo* 1933.
Bengt Mattsson *Valborg* 1938 - Jan 1939
Elis Mattsson *Tjerimai* 1924. *Lingard* 1925-26.
Emil Mattsson *Fredenborg* 1914.
Eric Mattsson *Ingrid* 1916
J M Mattsson *Penang* 1925-31. *Olivebank* 1931-33. *Pamir* 1933-36. *Passat* 1946
K W Mattsson *Lingard* 1935. *Varma* autumn 1936.
U. Mattsson *Penang* 1933-34.
U Mörn *Winterhude* 1932-36. *Pamir* 1936. *Olivebank* 1937. *Viking* 1937-39.
M Nordberg *Åland* 1913-14. *Tjerimai* 1915-17, and 1920-21. *Woodburn* 1921-24.
E Näsänen *Tjerimai* 1921-23.
Fritz Pettersson *Vellamo* 1934, April 1935 and 1936. *Regina* 1935.
B A Sandström *Hougomont* 1929-31.
K G Sjögren *Archibald Russell* 1928-30. *Madare* 1931. *Pamir* 1931-33. *Passat* 1933-36.
M Sjögren *Archibald Russell* 1933-38. *Moshulu* 1938-40.
S Sjölund *Tjerimai* 1925.
P Sommarlund *Archibald Russell* 1938-39
K G Svensson *Baltic* spring 1925. *Grace Harwar* 1928-30. *Ostrobotnia* autumn 1929.
A Söderlund *Killoran* 1932-33. *Lawhill* 1933 —.
L A Söderlund *Dione* 1939.
J A Söderlund *Ostrobotnia* 1930. *Lawhill* 1930-33.
J Tallqvist *Vellamo* autumn 1933.
N Törnqvist *Estonia* 1927.
K Troberg *Borrowdale* 1916. *Olivebank* 1924-29.
J A Westerberg *Tjerimai* 1913-14.
J Wilhelmsson *Ostrobotnia* 1927. *Estonia* 1928-32.
A Öfverström *Woodburn* 1919-1921. *Lawhill* 1922-23.
W Öjst *Archibald Russell* 1932-33

CHAPTER 7

The Wheat Trade

During the first months of 1936, Gustaf Erikson's wheat-loading tonnage in the Spencer Gulf reached its maximum. Compared with the previous year, the difference was not great, a matter of barely 2,000 tons. *Moshulu* had taken the place of *Grace Harwar,* which had ended her long career on the oceans with a fine trip of 88 days in ballast from Copenhagen to Port Lincoln, and an even better 98 days with freight from Port Broughton back to Falmouth for orders.

The following schedule covering the wheat fleet in 1936 was drawn up according to the company's position lists. The vessels are listed in the order they sailed from Australia.

Herzogin Cecilie. About 4,200 tons wheat. Sailed from Port Lincoln 28 Jan, arrived Falmouth 23 April. 86 days. Her cargo was lost with the vessel.
Pamir. 4,301 tons @ 25/6d. Pt Victoria 5 Feb — Queenstown 13 May. 98 days. Discharged at Birkenhead.
Pommern. About 4,000 tons. Pt Lincoln 7 Feb — Falmouth 11 May. 94 days. Discharged at Ipswich.
Viking. 4,001 tons @ 25/9d. Pt Lincoln 15 Feb — Falmouth 9 June. 115 days. Discharged at Hull.
Ponape. 3,374 @ 25/9d. Pt Germein 15 Feb — Falmouth 9 June. 115 days. Discharged at London.
Passat. 4,584 tons @ 25/3d. Pt Victoria 15 Feb — Queenstown 12 May. 87 days. Discharged at Barry Dock.
Moshulu. 4,835 tons @ 25/-. Pt Victoria 17 Feb — Queenstown 8 June. 112 days. Discharged at Cork.
L'Avenir. 3,518 tons @ 25/9d. Pt Lincoln 18 Feb — Falmouth 4 June. 107 days. Discharged at London.
Penang. 3,123 tons @ 26/-. Pt Lincoln 18 Feb — Falmouth 10 June. 113 days. Discharged on the Tyne.
Olivebank. 4,301 tons @ 25/3d. Pt Lincoln 21 Feb — Falmouth 8 June. 108 days. Discharged at Glasgow.
Archibald Russell. 3,814 tons @ 25/9d. Pt Lincoln 21 Feb — Falmouth 8 June. 108 days. Discharged at Glasgow.
Winterhude. About 3,100 tons. Pt Germein 7 March — Falmouth 3 July. 118 days. Discharged at London.
Lawhill. About 4,500 tons. Pt Lincoln 7 March — Falmouth 3 July. 118 days. Discharged at Belfast.
Killoran. 2,991 tons @ 26/-. Pt Victoria 14 April — Falmouth 7 Aug. 115 days (120 days according to Derby). Discharged at Ipswich.

The same year, *Abraham Rydberg, C B Pedersen* and *Parma,* owned by de Cloux and his partners,[1] also loaded in the Spencer Gulf. They had homeward passages of 130, 117 and 117 days respectively. *Padua* and *Priwall,* which for a couple of years had given fine performances in the wheat trade (the former in 1934-35, and the latter in 1933-35), had been put back into the saltpetre trade by Laeisz.

Thus Gustaf Erikson's 14 windjammers loaded a total of over 50,000 tons of wheat in 1936. Gross freights amounted to a total of £68,000. It was not a good year; rates were low and none of the vessels had outward freights from Europe. In 1921, when *Lawhill* and *Woodburn* sailed home with the last of the postwar boom's splendid freights, they had about £42,000 in combined gross freights for their 7,000 tons wheat, which I quote for the sake of comparison.

In 1938, the situation was completely different. Favourable winds were blowing on the deep-water sailing vessels' freight market. Their number in the Spencer Gulf had diminished. *Herzogin Cecilie, L'Avenir* and *Ponape* were gone

1 Who included Algot Johanson, who later became Finland's largest ship-owner, he began his career by purchasing one tenth of the four-masted barque *Parma*: later he purchased an old steamer and gave her the name *Parma.*

Above, plate 160 Masters in sail photographed in 1975. From left to right: Mauritz Mattson of *Penang, Oliverbank, Pamir* and *Passat*; Uno Mörn of *Winterhude, Pamir, Olivebank,* and *Viking*; Gerhard Sjögren of *Archibald Russell, Madare, Pamir* and *Passat;* (see also Plate 163), Arthur Söderlund, *Killoran* and *Lawhill;* Karl V Karlsson *Nils, Atlas, Odine,* and *Parma;* Mikael Sjögren *Archibald Russell* and *Moshulu* (Ålands Sjöfartsmuseum).

Below, plate 161 Sailmaking in *Archibald Russell,* 1930. The man on the right is Karl Kåhre, brother of the author, later a captain who became Director of the Ålands Sjöfartsmuseum (Kårl Kahre)

Above, plate 162 A watch of the crew of *Viking*, 1931. (Karl Kåhre)

Below, plate 163 Captain Arthur Söderlund and the crew of *Lawhill* in 1933. (Ålands Sjöfartsmuseum)

Below right, plate 164 Captain Uno Karlsson and the crew of *Ponape* about 1930. (Ålands Sjöfartsmuseum)

for ever, and *Pamir* was loading in New Caledonia. But all had outward freights. *Penang* and *Winterhude* took guano from the Seychelles to New Zealand and the others carried timber to South Africa. Passages to England were slower that year, admittedly.

Viking. 4,059 tons @ 41/9d. Pt Victoria 16 Feb — Lizard 12 June. 116 days. Discharged at London.
Passat. 4,611 tons @ 41/-. Pt Victoria 4 March — Falmouth 10 June. 98 days. Discharged at Hull.
Winterhude. About 3,100 tons. Pt Victoria 5 March — Falmouth 17 Aug. 165 days. Discharged at London.
Killoran. 2,976 tons @ 40/6d. Pt Germein 8 March — Falmouth 14 July. 128 days. Discharged on the Tyne.
Pommern. About 4,000 tons. Pt Germein 28 March — Falmouth 26 July. 120 days. Discharged at Belfast.
Lawhill. About 4,500 tons. Pt Victoria 8 April — Falmouth 17 Aug. 131 days. Discharged at Birkenhead.
Moshulu. 4,877 tons @ 41/3d. Pt Victoria 25 April — Falmouth 23 Aug. 120 days. Discharged at Belfast.
Olivebank. 4,301 tons @ 36/6d. Pt Victoria 10 May — Falmouth 22 Sept. 135 days. Discharged at Glasgow.
Archibald Russell. About 3,900 tons @ 35/-. Pt Germein 11 May — Queenstown 21 Sept. 133 days. Discharged in Cork.
Penang. 3,174 tons @ 37/6d. Sailed from Pt Victoria on 19 May, put into Otago Harbour N Z on 12 June with broken main topmast, towed to Dunedin, repaired and sailed on 14 Aug. Arrived off the Lizard on 15 Dec. 210 days from Pt Victoria, 123 from Dunedin. Discharged in London.

This time wheat cargoes amount to 39,000 — 40,000 tons in total, while combined gross freights were of the order of £75,000 to £80,000 — some £10,000 more than in 1936 despite the reduction in tonnage.

Outward freights served to increase net profits, even if they carried with them significant drawbacks. Late loading at the wheat ports often meant lower rates and unfavourable weather conditions on the passage home. In this context, it might be worth looking briefly at the timber freights to South Africa and in the autumn of 1937,

beginning with *Lawhill*, which on this occasion had the fastest passage from Copenhagen, where vessels carrying timber habitually stayed a few days for provisioning and fitting-out. Schierbecks got the opportunity to relive the traditions of the heyday of North Sea sailing, as a little headquarters abroad for Åland ships and skippers.

Lawhill. About 1,100 standards. Copenhagen/East London 73 days. 91 days from Trångsund, 4 of these in Copenhagen.
Moshulu. 1,172 standards @ 68/9d. Copenhagen/Lourenço Marques 77 days. 94 days from Trångsund, 4 in Copenhagen.
Viking. 1,019 standards @ 68/9d. Copenhagen/East London 80 days. 92 days from Kotka, 4 in Copenhagen.
Pommern. About 1,000 standards. Copenhagen/Durban 84 days. 103 days from Kemi, 4 in Copenhagen.
Passat. 1,100 standards @ 68/9d. Copenhagen/East London 86 days. 105 days from Trångsund, 7 in Copenhagen.
Archibald Russell. £3,471 gross freight @ 75/- per standard. Copenhagen/Lourenço Marques 87 days. 100 days from Kemi, 3 in Copenhagen.
Olivebank. 1,074 standards @ 68/9d. Copenhagen/Durban 91 days. 100 days from Kotka, 3 in Copenhagen, 5 in Elsinore.
Killoran. 701 standards @ 61/3d. Oslo/East London 92 days.

The gross timber freights amounted to a total of about £28,000, the guano *Penang* and *Winterhude* took to Auckland brought in about £12,000, and *Pamir* got £7,960 for her guano and about £11,000 from Noumea to Bremen, the highest freight of the year. Outward freights therefore amounted to about £48,000 and homeward freights approached £90,000. In other words, between autumn 1937 and autumn 1938, the fleet brought in, or rather sailed in between £135,000 and £140,000, compared with £68,000 two years earlier when the fleet was three ships and 11,500 tons bigger. Of course a large part of the increased gross went to cover increased expenses for loading, discharging and so on. By 1939, the recession had come with freights down to an average of 25/-.

Below, plate 165 The anchorage, Port Victoria. Five big sailing vessels lie offshore, *Mozart* on the extreme right. The small ketches and schooners by which they were loaded with bagged grain lie inshore. (Ålands Sjöfartsmuseum)
Right, plate 166 Vessels loading at Port Lincoln. (Ålands Sjöfartsmuseum)

Freight rates for Australian wheat gradually became the critical factor in the last sailing-fleet's economy. They varied greatly from year to year, and even during the same season, being sensitive to general trends on the world freight markets, the result of the harvest in Australia, prospects in the USA, Canada and the USSR, and trading policies in the wheat exporting and importing countries. It has already been said that late loading often meant a lower freight rate; a cargo should of course reach its destination before the harvest in the northern hemisphere. At times when the trend was generally rising freights, the opposite might be encountered, as for example, when the late-sailing *Olivebank* had 31/- in 1937, whereas the rest of the fleet sailed for 29/- or thereabouts.

The fluctuations are illustrated by the list below, beginning in 1922 after the post-war boom had run its course. The year indicates the time of shipping; the contract might have been made the previous year.

1922 *Lawhill & Woodburn*. 40/-
1923 None of Gustaf Erikson's vessels loaded wheat.
1924 None of Gustaf Erikson's vessels loaded wheat.
1925 *Grace Harwar* 40/-. *Olivebank* 42/6d. *Archibald Russell* 45/-.
1926 *Herzogin Cecilie*?
1927 From *Lawhill's* 33/9d, loading at Melbourne, to *Olivebank*'s 35/6d.
1928 *Archibald Russell* 26/3d. *Penang* 36/3d.
1929 *Grace Harwar, Penang* and *Lawhill* 39/-. *Pommern* 38/6d. *Archibald Russell* 32/6d. *Olivebank* 32/-.
1930 *Viking, Herzogin Cecilie, Lawhill, Archibald Russell, Pommern,* and *Melbourne* from 21/3d to 23/-. *Hougomont* and *Ponape* 20/- to Callao. The same year, *C B Pedersen* had 16/6d. *Penang* and H Lundqvist's *Mozart* sailed home in ballast. *Olivebank,* which arrived in Melbourne with timber from Hudiksvall on 19 May after a long passage of 157 days, was laid-up in Geelong in June, and loaded in Melbourne in December-January.
1931 Varying between 29/- for *Ponape* and 33/9d for *Archibald Russell. Herzogin Cecilie* 31/-, *Lawhill* 32/6d, etc.
1932 30/- to 31/6d, but *Grace Harwar* and *Pamir* 27/6d.
1933 From 29/- for *Penang* to 27/3d for *Pamir, Olivebank, Passat, Viking* and *Archibald Russell.*

1934 25/6d for most. 24/6d for *Pamir,* 24/9d for *Lawhill* and 25/9d for *Killoran.*
1935 25/-, but 19/6d for *Pamir.*
1936 Between 25/- for *Moshulu* and 26/- for *Penang* and *Killoran.*
1937 Between 28/9d for *Viking, Passat,* and *Pamir,* and 31/- for *Olivebank*
1938 *Viking* 41/9d. *Moshulu* 41/3d. *Passat* 41/-. But *Olivebank* 36/6d and *Archibald Russell* 35/-.
1939 Around 25/-.
1940 *Penang* 130/-. Vessel disappeared with cargo and all hands.

For the many sailing vessel enthusiasts ashore, these sailings in the wheat trade provided an interesting spectacle during the last year, not as freight traffic but as a sport. Games, competitions and gambles have always appealed to man's imagination, as on the whole has everything hazardous and uncertain, not least at sea, where the navigator in his sailing vessel weighs his skill and insight against the whims and habits of the ocean, his sea instinct, one might say, against brutal and unbridled natural forces. Racing at sea is an old sport. In long-distance traffic, it experienced its heyday during the age of the clipper ship, when a fast passage was not only a sporting achievement but also a matter of great importance to skippers and shipowners. During the second half of the nineteenth century, when the world's sailing-fleet was at its zenith, the right conditions existed for true deep-sea regattas: simultaneous departure, clean hulls, with adequate crews. In the China tea trade from Foochow to London, the emigrant trade to Australia, and the gold-digger trade from Boston or New York round Cape Horn to California, it was not only days that were taken into account; sometimes only a few hours separated competing vessels at the finish. The names of vessels were renowned around the world, skippers became legendary characters in fo'c'sles and after saloons, times from pilot to pilot were recorded, and the oceans became a battleground of competition and record-hunting.

For the sake of comparison, I give a few details of the fastest clippers' achievements.

Lightning, was built in the winter of 1853-54 and cost £30,000 in addition to being equipped for the emigrant traffic in Liverpool at a cost of £2,000. Her length was 244ft, her beam 44ft and her draught 23ft. Her mainmast measured 164ft, her foremast 151ft and her mizzenmast 115ft. The mainyard measured 95ft, attached to which were her mighty studdingsail booms. Apart from studdingsails, she carried thirty sails. Her mainmast carried a course, single topsail, single topgallant, royal, skysail and, at one time at least, a moonraker. The foremast too carried a skysail.

Lightning's first outward passage from Liverpool to Melbourne was a 77 day trip in light winds with topgallants set from start to finish, a rather mediocre achievement for a newly-built clipper. The passage home was better. *Lightning* sailed from Melbourne on 20 August 1854 and arrived in Liverpool after 64 days, a record that has stood through the years. Some of her positions might be of interest:

Port Phillip Heads/Cape Horn **19 days**
Cape Horn/Equator **22 days**
Equator/Azores **12 days**
Azores/Liverpool **11 days**

Between the World Wars, the fastest passage with wheat from Australia was made by *Parma,* commanded by de Cloux, in 1933: 83 days from Port Victoria to Falmouth:

Kangaroo Island/Cape Horn **27 days**
Cape Horn/Equator **28 days**
Equator/Falmouth **27 days**

Unlike *Parma*, *Lightning* was not carrying wheat. According to Lubbock, the record in the wheat trade was set by the four-masted steel barque *Svanhilda,* built in England in 1890 for a company in Nova Scotia: 66 days from Wallaroo to Queenstown in 1894.

But to return to the clippers, *Lightning* made four voyages from Liverpool to Melbourne and back between January 1855 and August 1859. Her outward passages took 73, 81, 68 and 69 days, and her homeward passages: 79, 86, 84 and 82 days. According to her logbook, *Lightning* once sailed 436 nautical miles in a day, and 430 nautical miles on another occasion, ie an average of 18 knots over 24 consecutive hours. These figures have been noted with a certain scepticism by nautical historians. There is of course no absolute guarantee for the trustworthiness of the logbook or of the observations recorded there.

Lightning belonged to the Black Ball Line of Liverpool. The founder of this firm, James Baines,

Left, plate 167 The watch making fast the main course in *Archibald Russell* (Karl Kåhre)
Inset, plate 168 The watch coming down the topmast shrouds having made fast the fore lower topgallant in *Passat* (Anne Stanley)

put his own name on the stern of another renowned clipper, and himself in a high hat as her figurehead. *James Baines* made her maiden voyage from Boston to Liverpool in 12 days and 6 hours in September 1854. She sailed from Liverpool on 9 December with 700 passengers, 1,400 tons of cargo and 350 bags of mail. She sailed 423 nautical miles on 6 February 1855 and found herself at longitude 123° south of Australia after 59 days, arriving in Melbourne after a passage of 63½ days. Her homeward passage took 69 days 12 hours and the round trip, including 27 days in Melbourne, took 5 months and 10 days. The same year, according to Lubbock, *Red Jacket* broke a record in her class, and, in June, sailed 5,033 nautical miles between longitude 34°, east of Good Hope, and Melbourne in 17 days: 296 miles per day, or an average of over 12 knots. *Red Jacket*'s voyage that year took 5 months and 11 days, including time in Melbourne.

The tea trade was a fast passage trade. Tea was believed to lose its aroma during a long passage. When some ten of the oceans' fastest sailers weighed anchor together in Foochow, and when a freight advance awaited the shipowner whose chests of tea samples were the first on the quayside in London, the conditions were right for a true regatta from China to England. After the opening of the Suez Canal in the autumn of 1869, the regattas soon came to an end: many of Britain's tea clippers were already sailing to Australia.

They never achieved the same records for nautical miles per day as their rivals from New York and Boston shipyards, but they out-distanced them in light winds. *Thermopylae* of Aberdeen, which, at 991 tons gross, was one of the larger tea clippers, is reported to have slipped along at 7 knots in a light air that was not even strong enough to extinguish a burning candle; but she also bore well the ardours of the westerlies. Her log could show up to 14 knots in tradewinds. Her maiden voyage from Gravesend to Melbourne took 63 days. Over ten passages from the Lizard to Melbourne, her average was 68 to 69 days, varying between 60 and 80 days. If *Thermopylae* achieved her best performance on her outward passages, *Cutty Sark,* one year her junior, made herself known for her excellent passages home with wool in the 1880s, with an average nearer 70 than 80 days. From Sydney to Ushant in 67 days in 1885 was an extraordinary achievement. After a long Portuguese interlude under another name, from 1895 to 1922 (barquentine-rigged after 1916), *Cutty Sark* returned to her homeland. She received back her original full-rig and was used as a stationary training ship in Falmouth, the last deep-water sailing vessels' most frequented order port. *Cutty Sark* is now preserved in the care of the Maritime Trust in a dry dock at Greenwich in London, next door to the National Maritime Museum.

One or two of the British iron full-rigged ships of the 1870s, which Lubbock calls wool-clippers, were bought by Åland shipowners before 1914. After belonging to a company in Åbo for a couple of years, *Mermerus* joined Robert Mattsson's fleet, to continue her illustrious tradition as a fast-sailer, under the command of Captain M A Gustafsson. Another, *Thomasina* (ex-*Thomasina McLellan*), McMillan's masterpiece, to quote Lubbock, made fine passages under Captain K A Frederiksson's command. In 1902 *Mermerus* sailed from Cardiff to Port Pirie in the Spencer Gulf in 71 days, carrying rails and bricks, and in 1903 she sailed from Frederikshald to Port Adelaide, carrying timber, in 72 days — 68 days from the Suez Canal. However, Lubbock is mistaken when he reports that *Mermerus* sailed back from Australia in 69 days in 1904.

But after this excursion into the days of the clippers, something should be said in passing about the achievements of the last sailing-fleet. It would be best to begin with a few cool facts which should be borne in mind when making comparisons. A long time had passed since fast sailing was the same as economically profitable sailing. In the last days of sail, Gustaf Erikson, and men like him, were more inclined, or perhaps compelled, like a number of moral philosophers, to consider gambling-fever to be one of the most evil weapons in the devil's arsenal, since a few sails blown away could well spoil the chances of a modest profit on a wheat freight. On the other hand, if a cargo reached its destination a few weeks earlier or later, it had very little effect on the expense bill. This should certainly not be taken to mean that Gustaf Erikson did not care for fast sailing. He was himself a seaman, and no one

Below, plate 169 The watch making fast the crossjack in *Viking*, July 1937. (Basil Greenhill).
Right, plate 170 Clearing a jammed slide on the luff of the gaff topsail on the jigger in *Viking*, July 1937. (Basil Greenhilll)

appreciated *Herzogin Cecilie's* achievements more than he. But he was, above all else, a shipowner.

Occasionally a slow-sailer arrived too late and had her freight cancelled; but once vessels had their wheat cargoes in their holds, their charterers did not expect them to be in any hurry. On the contrary they might serve usefully as a grain store during the passages home, while their cargoes were the subject of speculation on the grain exchange.

The table below, illustrating the wheat-ships' homeward passages in 1936, shows the form a grain race took. For the sake of clarity, I have listed the vessels in two columns: the first in the order they sailed from Port Lincoln, Port Victoria or Port Germein, and the other according to the dates of their arrival in Falmouth or Queenstown:

Herzogin Cecilie	*Herzogin Cecilie*, 86 days
Pamir	*Pommern,* 94 days
Pommern	*Passat,* 87 days
Viking	*Pamir,* 98 days
Ponape	*L'Avenir,* 107 days
Passat	*Moshulu,* 112 days
Moshulu	*Olivebank,* 108 days
L'Avenir	*Archibald Russell,* 108 days
Penang	*Viking,* 115 days
Olivebank	*Ponape,* 115 days
Archibald Russell	*Penang,* 113 days
Winterhude	*Winterhude,* 118 days
Lawhill	*Lawhill,* 118 days
Killoran	*Killoran,* 115 days

Passat passed two competitors, and *Pommern* passed one. Captain Hägerstrand of *Viking* and Captain Granith of *Ponape* weighed anchor the same day and had passages of the same length, as did Captain Lindvall of *Olivebank* and Captain M Sjögren of *Archibald Russell. Olivebank* was a surprise, sailing tenth and arriving seventh after passing *Penang, Viking* and *Ponape. Archibald Russell* did the same, less surprisingly however, since she was considered a better sailer. It was generally thought that the earlier in the year a vessel's departure, the better her chances were for a fast passage.

Left, plate 171 *Viking* shortened down in a summer gale off the mouth of the Bristol Channel, July 1937. (Basil Greenhill)
Top Inset, plate 172 Southern Ocean, a sea breaking on board *Archibald Russell.* (Karl Kåhre)
Middle Inset, plate 173 *Archibald Russell* (Karl Kåhre)
Bottom inset, plate 174 Southern Ocean, *Archibald Russell* rolling heavily in a very high sea. (Karl Kåhre)

The following list shows grain race prize-winners according to W L A Derby. Details for 1937-39 are taken from Gustaf Erikson's position lists:

1921 *Marlborough Hill* **91 days**
1922 *Milverton* **90 days**
1923 *Beatrice* **88 days**
1924 *Greif* **110 days**
1925 *Beatrice* **103 days**
1926 *L'Avenir* **110 days**
1927 *Herzogin Cecilie* **98 days**
1928 *Herzogin Cecilie* **96 days**
1929 *Archibald Russell* **93 days**
1930 *Pommern* **105 days**
1931 *Herzogin Cecilie* **93 days**
1932 *Parma & Pamir* **103 days**
1933 *Parma* **83 days**
1934 *Passat* **106 days**
1935 *Priwall* **91 days**
1936 *Herzogin Cecilie* **86 days**
1937 *Pommern & Passat* **94 days**
1938 *Passat* **98 days**
1939 *Moshulu* **91 days**

Left, plate 175 South Atlantic, *Mozart* off the Falkland Islands in 1930. Big barquentines with the wind abaft the beam in a big sea were frequently sailed under squaresails only. Here the upper topsail has blown out. (Karl Kåhre)
Right, plate 176 *Herzogin Cecilie* from *Archibald Russell.* (National Maritime Museum)
Below, plate 177 The figurehead of *Herzogin Cecilie,* now preserved at the Ålands Sjöfartsmuseum. (National Maritime Museum)

But statistics are known liars, and the deep-sea sailing ships' day-figures are not an entirely reliable indication of their sailing abilities. The evidence of logbooks as to the whims of the winds and the play of chance might breathe life into the dry figures but, even if the information existed, that story would be too long. Much depended on the skipper, not only on his skill, but also on his interest in the grand regatta and his inclination to risk sails and so on for the sake of a good position. Even if skippers participated in the betting, there was more than one who in his heart felt antipathy for the racing-mentality which expected an under-manned vessel to be pushed to breaking-point, after decades of faithful service, to no purpose except the satisfaction of gamblers ashore.

The following table shows the average number of days each vessel took from the Spencer Gulf to Falmouth or Queenstown, or in some cases The Lizard, arranged in order beginning with the fastest:

	Average No of days	over No of passages	Years
Passat	99	7	1933-39
Pamir	102	7	1932-39
Moshulu	106	4	1936-39
Herzogin Cecilie	107	11	1926-36
Pommern	108	11	1929-39
L'Avenir	113	5	1933-37
Ponape	114	7	1929-36
Archibald Russell	115	14	1925-39
Viking	116	9	1931-39
Penang	121	10	1928-37
Olivebank	121	13	1924-39
Lawhill	121	14	1921-39
Killoran	125	10	1927-39
Grace Harwar	127	8	1921-36
Winterhude	133	8	1932-39

Penang's long passage in 1938 with delays and repairs in Dunedin is not included in the reckoning. *Herzogin Cecilie's* 137 day passage of 1926 increases her average, which otherwise would have been 104.5 days. *Passat* has the honour of the inter-war period's best performance on the wheat route, with an average of 95 days over five passages between 1935 and 1939, the same number of days that the German four-masted barque *Magdelene Vinnen,* with her auxiliary engine, averaged over four passages between 1932 and 1935.

According to Derby, *Padua* took 109 and 100 days respectively for her passages of 1934 and 1935, *Priwall* took 106, 108 and 91 days for her passages between 1933 and 1935, *Beatrice* averaged 110 days over seven passages between 1921 and 1930, and *C B Pedersen* averaged 120 days over 10 passages between 1927 and 1936.

Passages of 100 days or less were fast passages and made by the following vessels:

Passat 100, 87, 94, 98, 98 days 1935-39.
Pamir 92 days, 1932, 98 days 1936,
98 days 1937, 96 days 1939.
Herzogin Cecilie 98,96 days 1927-28, 93 days 1931,
86 days 1936.
Pommern 98 days 1933, 95, 94, 94 days 1935-7
Archibald Russell 93 days 1929, 98 days 1931,
97 days 1937.
Moshulu 91 days 1939.
L'Avenir 95 days 1937.
Viking 97 days 1935.
Ponape 98 days 1929. According to Derby,
99 days 1931.
Grace Harwar 98 days 1936.

As has been said already, *Parma* had 83 days in 1933, but her average over five passages between 1932 and 1936 was no lower than 115 days.

Outward passages in ballast also provided opportunities for racing, especially in the 1930s, when the vessels sailed from Copenhagen in the autumn. A few figures might be noted, even if any readers with an inclination to scepticism find the great number of statistics disagreeable:

Pamir averaged 83-84 days over five trips, 3 from Copenhagen, one from Hamburg and one from Dublin. Best: 77 days Copenhagen/Port Victoria in 1932. Worst: 89 days, autumn 1934.
Passat averaged 93 days over 5 passages. Best: 86 days (83 from Elsinore) Copenhagen/Pt Victoria in autumn 1934. 3 passages of 92 days, 1 of 102 days. *Passat* made her best passage the same autumn *Pamir* made her longest. *Passat* sailed from Elsinore on 17 October, *Pamir* from Copenhagen the same day. But in 1936, both vessels sailed from Copenhagen the same day, and *Pamir* arrived at Pt Lincoln two weeks before her rival reached Pt Victoria.
Pommern averaged 85 days over 7 passages, 4 from Copenhagen, 1 from Falmouth, 1 from Gothenburg and 1 from Belfast. Best: 76 days from Copenhagen in 1932. Worst: 96 days. 1933.
Archibald Russell shows an even series from 86 days in 1936 to 97 days in autumn 1934. Mean 91-92 days over 7 passages.
Lawhill averaged 92 days over 6 passages, 2 from Copenhagen, 2 from London, 1 from Gothenburg and 1 from Belfast. Best: 83 days from Copenhagen Nov 1935 - Jan 1936. *Lawhill* put into Pt Lincoln on 30 Jan, 6 days after *Viking*, which had weighed anchor in Copenhagen exactly 4 weeks before her.
Viking averaged 97 days over 7 passages from Copenhagen. 84 days in 1932. 88 days in 1938.
Olivebank 97 days over 6 passages, among them one of 85 days from Glasgow in 1939. Best: 84 days from Copenhagen to Pt Lincoln Oct 1934 - Jan 1935.
Ponape: 89 and 88 days on 2 passages from Copenhagen.
Herzogin Cecilie had 3 passages between 80 and 85 days.

The Germans *Padua* and *Priwall* made the fastest passages in ballast during the inter-war period:67 days from Hamburg in 1933. They sailed on 31 October and dropped anchor on 6 January, the

Left, plate 178 *Mozart* sailing well on the port tack in a smooth sea. Note the preventer tackle on the main boom, the huge lower mast and the big mast hoops. (Karl Kåhre)
Right, plate 179 Wet decks in *Viking* running up Channel. (Basil Greenhill)

former at Port Broughton and the latter at Port Victoria. In 1936, *C B Pedersen,* which had not otherwise distinguished herself particularly as a fast-sailer, sailed from Gothenburg to Port Germein in 71 days, and, the same year, *Parma* sailed from Barry to Port Victoria in 73 days. Apart from these four, only *Pommern* and *Pamir* were faster than 80 days, the latter twice, in 1932 and 1936.

Outward passages with timber were generally slower. *Archibald Russell* had 126 days from Sundsvall to Melbourne in 1926, 124 days from Hudiksvall to Melbourne in 1927, 94 days from Larvik to Melbourne in 1928-29, and 110 days from Harnösand to Port Adelaide in autumn 1929. *Pommern* had 121 from Larvik to Melbourne in 1925, but only 87 days from Oslo to Melbourne in 1929.

Herzogin Cecilie laid the foundations for the popularity and publicity which Gustaf Erikson and his entire fleet enjoyed during the 1930s. The beautiful 'Duchess' became his flagship and his yacht, and she did justice to her honourable title, even if *Pommern* and the youngsters *Passat* and *Pamir* rivalled her in the speed of their passages. According to the company's position lists, her sailings under Gustaf Erikson's flag were as follows:

Skipper: Ruben de Cloux.

1922 Ostend/Kristiania in ballast.
Kristiania/Frederikstad.
Frederikstad/Melbourne, planed boards. 28 April-1 Aug, 95 days.
Melbourne/Taltal in ballast. 15 Sept - 20 Oct, 35 days, excellent!
Taltal/Mejillones, 5 days.
1922-23 Mejillones/Falmouth for orders Saltpetre. 15 Nov - 19 Feb, 96 days.
1923 Falmouth/Ostend under tow.
Ostend/Grangemouth. 26 - 29 March.
Grangemouth/San Antonio. Coke 12 May - 23 Aug, 103 days.
San Antonio/Caleta Buena. 27 days for discharging in San Antonio and the passage to Caleta Buena.
1923-24 Caleta Buena/Fayal for orders Saltpetre. 4 Oct - 3 Jan, 90 days.
1924 Fayal/Falmouth for new orders. 3 - 10 Jan, 7 days.
Falmouth/Ostend under tow.

Skipper: F Grönlund.
Ostend/Taltal for orders, in ballast. 19 March - 10 July, 113 days.
Taltal/Mejillones. 5 days.
Mejillones/Dunkirk. Saltpetre. 13 Aug - 29 Nov, 108 days, towed from Deal roads.

Skipper: de Cloux.
1925 Dunkirk/Albany for orders in ballast. 5 Jan - 16 April, 101 days.
Albany/Pt Lincoln. 11 days.
Pt Lincoln/Callao. Wheat. 2 June - 23 July, 51 days
Callao/Pt Lincoln for orders in ballast. 9 Sept - 12 Nov, 63 days.
1926 Pt Lincoln/Falmouth for orders. Wheat. 3 Feb 20 June, 137 days.
Falmouth/Hamburg. 7 days.
Hamburg/Pt Lincoln for orders, in ballast. 4 Sept - 11 Dec, 99 days.
1927 Pt Lincoln/Queenstown for orders, 24 Jan - 3 May, 99 days.
Queenstown/Hamburg.
Hamburg/Sundsvall in ballast, 16 - 30 June, 14 days. Towed to Friederichshafen after running aground off the West coast of Jutland on 18 June, inspected by divers and continued passage on 23 June.
Moved to Gävle 21 July.
Gävle/Melbourne. Timber. 12 Aug - 16 Nov, 96 days 86 days from the Skaw, 79 days from Beachy Head and 69 days from Cape Finisterre.
Melbourne/Pt Lincoln. 17 - 19 Dec.
1928 Pt Lincoln/Falmouth for orders. Wheat. 19 - 24 April, 97 days.
Falmouth/Cardiff. 2 days.
Cardiff/Mariehamn. 2 - 11 June.
Mariehamn/Pt Lincoln in ballast. 31 Aug - 4 Dec, 95 days. In a south-westerly gale north of Scotland on 15 Sept, her ballast shifted, she lost sails and developed a severe list. It was four days before the vessel was capable of being sailed, and then only as a result of the Captain and crew exerting their utmost efforts to save themselves and their ship.
1929 Pt Lincoln/Falmouth for orders. Wheat. 18 Jan - 3 May, 106 days.
Falmouth/Liverpool. 3 days
Liverpool/Frederikstad. 28 May - 6 June

Skipper: Sven Eriksson
Frederikstad/Melbourne. Timber. 30 July - 21 Nov. 114 days.
Melbourne/Wallaroo. 22 - 28 Dec.
1930 Wallaroo/Falmouth for orders. Wheat. 28 Jan - 15 May, 107 days
Falmouth/Birkenhead. 24 - 31 May.
Birkenhead/Mariehamn. 7 - 26 June, 19 days.
Mariehamn/Copenhagen. 9 - 12 Sept.
Copenhagen/Port Lincoln. 19 Sept - 12 Dec, 84 days.
Wallaroo to load. 18 Dec.
1931 Wallaroo/Falmouth for orders. Wheat. 23 Jan - 26 April, 93 days.
Falmouth/Barry Dock. 28 April - 4 May.
Barry Dock/Mariehamn. 21 May - 6 June. 16 days
Mariehamn/Trångsund. 28 June - 3 July.
Viborg/Kotka under tow on 11 July to complete cargo.
Kotka/Lourenço Marques. Timber. 30 July - 2 Nov, 95 days (Copenhagen 7 - 14 Aug).
Lourenço Marques/Beira to continue discharging. 19 - 24 Nov.
1931-32 Beira/Pt Lincoln in ballast. 12 Dec - 18 Jan 37 days.
1932 Pt Augusta/Queenstown for orders. Wheat. 9 Feb - 27 May, 108 days.
Queenstown/Birkenhead. 27 May - 2 June.
Birkenhead/Mariehamn. 14 - 28 June, 2 days from Copenhagen.
Mariehamn/Pt Adelaide. 6 Sept - 16 Dec. Sailed from Copenhagen 23 Sept, 84 days from there.
1933 Pt Adelaide/Falmouth for orders. Wheat. 25 Jan - 20 May, 115 days.
Falmouth/London. 25 - 30 May.
London/Mariehamn. 28 June - 8 July, 10 days.
Mariehamn/Kotka. 20 - 23 July.
Moved to Trångsund on 9 Aug to complete cargo.
Trångsund/Lourenço Marques. 17 Aug - 5 Dec. (Copenhagen 27 - 30 Aug, 97 days from there.)
Lourenço Marques/Beira. 30 Dec - 8 Jan 1934.
1934 Beira/Pt Lincoln in ballast. 16 Jan - 1 March, 34 days.
Wallaroo/Falmouth for orders. Wheat. 5 April - 3 Aug, 120 days.
Falmouth/Belfast. 3 - 9 Aug.
Belfast/Pt. Lincoln for orders in ballast. 7 Sept - 7 Dec, 91 days.
1935 Pt Lincoln/Falmouth for orders. Wheat. 22 Jan - 18 May, 116 days.
Falmouth/Belfast. 25 May - 1 June.
Belfast/Nystad. 12 - 29 July.
Nystad/Copenhagen. 30 Sept - 7 Oct.
Copenhagen/Pt Lincoln for orders in ballast. 17 Oct - 5 Jan 1936, 80 days.
1936 Pt Lincoln/Falmouth for orders. Wheat. 28 Jan - 23 April, 86 days.
Falmouth/Ipswich. Sailed 24 April and wrecked.

A comparison between the above data and those in Derby and in L Grönstrand's *Reports from the Åbo Acadamy Museum of Nautical History No 5*, reveals a number of discrepancies of the odd day here and there. Like Lubbock and Villiers, Grönstrand gives 88 days for the northward passage of 1927, 10 days too few; *Herzogin Cecilie* weighed anchor on 24 January, not 3 February.

At dusk on Friday 24 April, *Herzogin Cecilie* sailed from Falmouth. After sailing 49 nautical miles in 7½ hours in a light southwesterly breeze and thickening fog, she ran aground at dawn off Sewer Mill Cove, near Bolt Head, Devon, several miles from where she should have been according to her log book. To what extent the fog, the tide and possibly magnetic disturbances contributed to the shipwreck is a mystery, and will remain so. The salvage attempt, when the vessel was successfully refloated and towed to Starehole Cove, Salcombe, on 19 June, and the disappointment on 17 July when her keel was broken in an onshore gale and the salvage attempt had to be abandoned, has been described in detail in Derby's much-quoted work, *The Tall Ships Pass*. In fact Derby's book is a monograph on the beautiful duchess during her German and Åland periods. 'It is more sorrowful that I can say, especially for me, as I lived aboard her for eight years and learnt to love her more each year. You have a true conclusion to your history of *Herzogin Cecilie,*' Captain Sven Eriksson wrote after the disaster to Derby, who was then in the middle of his work.

As a training ship for Norddeutscher Lloyd, she distinguished herself in the saltpetre trade, and in 1909 sailed from Bremerhaven to Taltal in 68 days, and back to Rotterdam in the same number of days. A meeting with her is described by Captain Lundqvist of the full-rigger *Pera*, who in July 1911 was sailing close-hauled in a topsail breeze off Staten Island, bound for Valparaiso. 'In the cold and hazy air, visibility was extremely poor, so we were very surprised when suddenly the outline of a huge mass of sails appeared to windward. Somewhat amazed by the amount of sail the vessel was carrying in the strong headwind, we were also curious to know who it was, and when, at that moment, the vessel made preparations to wear ship just astern of us, we were able to establish that it was the German four-masted barque *Herzogin Cecilie*. Then we were no longer surprised at the sails she was carrying, as there were of course more than enough crew aboard to handle them.'

Herzogin Cecilie has been the subject of a number of descriptions. In *Falmouth for Orders*, Alan Villiers describes her race with *Beatrice* in

Below, plate 180 The midships wheel in *Viking* in good North Sea sailing weather. (Basil Greenhill)

1928, though it was not exactly a race, considering that *Herzogin Cecilie* sailed via Cape Horn, and her Swedish rival via Good Hope. The most sensational point was provided by a female stowaway. W L Leclercq's *Wind in de Zeilen* is a Dutch work. In *Out of this World*, Pamela Bourne describes the passage from Australia in 1934. As Captain Sven Eriksson's wife, she experienced personally the disaster and the salvage attempt. I don't think she or her husband (now on a farm in South Africa, if I am not mistaken) would have anything against my borrowing a feather from her cap and quoting a few lines from an article signed Pamela Eriksson and published in *Min Bästa Seglats II* (*My Best Passage II*), edited by E Lindström and published by Förlaget Bro in 1943.

'Under ideal conditions, she set a record of 20 knots in the Kattegat, but 16, 17 and 18 knots were not unusual, sailing with a strong and steady breeze, slightly abaft the beam. If her sails held in hard weather, she seemed to want to set her course for the moon itself, throwing off the sea and rising from the waves like a bird, without it costing her any effort. That was the secret of her sailing. She never buried her head in the water, thanks to the well judged placing of her foremast'.

On her last passage home, *Herzogin Cecilie* achieved one of her finest performances, sailing from Port Lincoln to Falmouth in 86 days.

Regrettably, skippers have left all too scanty a contribution to nautical literature. It has been said that those who can write cannot sail, and those who can sail cannot write. Captain Granith conclusively proves the fallacy of this maxim when, in the old pre-war *Sea Breezes,* he describes *Pommern's* voyage to Australia and back in 1932-33. His account concludes this meagre description of deep-water sail's last trade. As skipper of *Olivebank,* Captain Granith was one of the first of the Second World War's sacrifices to the sea.

With Port Victoria, South Australia, as our destination, the *Pommern* sailed from Mariehamn in ballast on October 2nd, 1932. She was the last of Captain Gustaf Erikson's fleet to sail from the home port, where most of his ships had been laid up during the summer.

After four days out, we anchored at Copenhagen to take on board some stores and water, and then sailed away again in the evening of October 8th. Being favoured by a fresh south-easterly wind, we made an average speed of 14 knots to the Skaw. In the smooth waters around these districts there is great pleasure in sailing these ships, especially with a leading wind, but, unfortunately, headwinds and bad visibility only too frequently occur.

During that first night at sea, we passed a score of steamers and smaller sailing craft, but owing to the darkness we were unable to show them what a sailing ship could do, under favourable conditions, so the mates were rather disappointed. When passing the Skaw Lightship the wind hauled more to the east, accompanied by heavy rain squalls, which made it necessary for some of our lighter canvas to be furled.

Under the prevailing weather conditions, I decided to take the route north of Scotland instead of by way of the English Channel. Once, between the rain squalls, we sighted the Norwegian coast, and a course was now shaped for Fair Island.

The easterly wind had by this time increased to gale force, sending us along at a very good rate, so that after only 39 hours from Copenhagen we passed that green storm-thrashed piece of land.

In order to keep well away from the Scottish coast, the course was changed to due west, but as the wind, which has so much to say in these ships, kept backing around to the north and west, we only just managed to steer clear of the coast. Abreast of St. Kilda the wind was S.W., blowing fairly hard.

After heading north-westward, close-hauled for a day, the wind suddenly veered into the N.W., the ship was taken full aback, which caused a certain amount of confusion amongst our untrained crew; but, fortunately, we had the lower courses and all the light sails furled at the time, so with all hands pulling at the braces, we soon had the ship on her course again, heading south. The wind continued to blow a moderate gale, accompanied by occasional hard squalls.

As all mariners know, north of Scotland is no picnic ground, so with all sails set we were anxious to get away from there as soon as possible. When the squalls struck the ship, she was luffed up in the wind in order to take the greatest part of the strain off the rigging, and when the hardest part of the squall had passed, the ship was put back on her course. This process caused a tremendous clattering and flapping of the sails, but it saved us from clewing them up.

On the parallel of Cape Finistere we sighted the four-masted barque *Pamir*, also belonging to Capt. Gustaf Erikson; she left Copenhagen 2½ days ahead of us, and was bound for the same port. We kept her in sight the following day, but we parted again during the night.

The next day offered us a fresh south-westerly gale: the hardest blow we had experienced during the whole voyage. Still it could not be termed as really bad weather; it did not last very long before it wore round to the north, and without further delay set us right into the north-east Trade and fine weather.

For five days we weredetainedin the Doldrums with light and unsteady winds — as usual. One day a school of dolphins made an appearance, and we caught a good many fine specimens, which gave us a welcome change in our menu.

During the afternoon of November 5th, we picked up the south-east Trades, and how glad we were to know that for the next week or ten days we'd have a steady wind. The only good thing about the Doldrums is that they offer an excellent opportunity for an inexperienced crew to learn how to pull the braces and gather rain water while waiting for the next shift of wind.

At daybreak, on November 7th, we sighted another sailing vessel astern, and at first we thought she was overtaking us, so we immediately set about trimming out kites aloft to a T — sheeting home a little more here and slacking a little there — until nothing further could be done to them. After a couple of hours it was quite evident that our earlier fears were quite unnecessary. We recognised her to be the three-masted barque *Penang*, another of the fleet of Capt. Erikson. Failing to catch us, we backed out mainyards until she came abreast, when we exchanged signals, and after wishing each other "a pleasant voyage" continued on our respective courses. The *Pommern* proved to be the faster ship, although the difference in speed was only slight. We kept her in sight for three days before she finally disappeared astern.

The same day we sighted the *Penang* we crossed the Line, and at 4 p.m. Neptune and his Staff paid us a visit. We continue to keep up this old sea-custom of initiating those members of the crew who experience their first Crossing of the Line.

The performance being over, and the boys having washed themselves clean, they felt rather elated at the thought of having been initiated into the realm of Neptune, but the certificate to this effect, signed by the Master, is much sought after and is taken great care of, as it is not many who wish to go through this performance a second time.

We lost the south-east Trade in latitude 9 south, and on coming to the Calm Belt of Capricorn we again sighted the *Pamir* ahead of us; the wind being free we slowly gained on her. Shortly afterwards we were both becalmed for two days, lying idly on a high swell without steerage way. When the wind came up again, from the south-west, we saw to our disgust the *Pamir* drawing ahead, and finally disappearing altogether. There was no mistake about it —close-hauled she was the faster ship.

I intended to sail in sight of the Island of Tristan da Cunha in order to ascertain the correctness of the chronometers, and probably heave the ship to for a couple of hours for the purpose of bartering with the islanders and leaving with them a parcel of books, newspapers and a few other things. They are always very grateful to any ship that comes to stop and exchange greetings, etc., with them. However, thick weather set in and we did not even sight the island.

We crossed the 0 meridian in 40 south, and from now on commenced the best piece of sailing I have ever had the pleasure to take part in. The westerlies blew strong and steady, so that for the first five days we had the following runs:— 300, 303, 304, 296 and 304 miles.

In a squall off the Cape of Good Hope, with all square sails set, the two helmsmen allowed the ship to run up into the wind. I thought for a few dreadful moments that some of our spars must carry away; the topgallant masts bent at a dangerous angle, but fortunately everything held. A third man was now sent to the wheel, and the officer of the watch stood continually by the compass.

On the parallel of 44, we ran the easting down across the Indian Ocean. The winds only slackened twice during the run down, and then they soon came up strong again from the westerly quadrants thus it happened that we had only two day's run below 200 miles.

In the eastern portion of the Indian Ocean the winds were very steady, and it was here that we made our record run of 330 miles from noon to noon: this distance is by log, and does not include the easterly set of the current.

The most she made per watch was 60 miles, and taking an average of our daily runs from 0 meridian till we arrived at Port Victoria, we had made 265 miles for 24 consecutive days.

Eventually we arrived at Port Victoria on December 23rd, thus completing the passage from Copenhagen in 75 days 3 hours.

The same day the *Pamir* arrived at Port Lincoln with a passage of 77 days.

At one time there were 10 deep-water sailing ships in Port Victoria — a rare sight nowadays. All of them had made good passages, but the *Pommern* had made the trip in the shortest time — she was lucky.

The first ship to leave Port Victoria was the German four-masted barque *Priwall,* on January 18th, then followed the *Mozart* and *Olivebank* on February 1st, and the *Viking* sailed away four days later.

We had rather a slow dispatch, and did not leave for Falmouth (f.o.) until the morning of February 11th, 1933.

A leading wind soon took us out of the Spencer Gulf, but shortly after reaching "open waters" the wind wore ahead.

I had intended to take the usual route homeward around the Horn, but as the S.S.E-ly wind was a dead muzzler for the Eastern route, I abandoned the idea and after a short attempt at beating, squared-off for Cape Leeuwin.

After sailing westward for three days, we again struck headwinds. I was by this time quite undecided what to do — to turn back meant loss of time and increased distance; on the other hand, I knew of ships beating against the westerlies for weeks in vain efforts to weather Cape Leeuwin, and then had to finally turn east. Thinking this would probably happen to us, I decided that as we had already lost enough time it was as well that we should revert to our original intentions to come around the Horn.

For several days we had a nasty south-east swell and light westerly winds, so that we were unable to get a proper go on the ship; however, we finally drifted by Tasmania, and on March 3rd we passed Campbell Island (S. of New Zealand). Thence to the Horn we made a smart run.

Two days before we rounded the Horn, we sighted a windjammer on our port bow. At once we set every stitch of canvas hoping that we should be able to catch her, but unfortunately rain and darkness separated us before we could identify her.

On March 24th, forty-one days out from Port Victoria, we rounded that dreaded Cape with the finest weather imaginable, a high and steady barometer and an exceptionally smooth sea. I have been around the Horn more than a dozen times, and I have never passed it under such favourable weather conditions.

At Easter we enjoyed some eggs, and killed one of our four pigs which we had aboard.

From Cape Horn to the Line, which we crossed on April 20th, it took us some 26 days. The winds were light, but we were favoured by an unusually strong current setting east.

Off the Falkland Islands we struck a northerly gale, the hardest blow we had had so far on the homeward run.

Along this section of the route, between the 50th and 40th parallels, is situated the district I dread more than any other on the Globe. Owing to the numerous icebergs we passed there during our passage in 1927, it is impossible for me to pass through this region without remembering this experience. For in that year we had ice constantly in sight for more than 700 miles, with several close calls for collisions.

I have since sailed six times through this same zone, but without seeing any icebergs at all.

The Doldrums treated us extremely well this time: the wind was easterly, light but steady. We were fortunate not to strike any dead calms, so close-hauled we slipped through into the north-east Trades without touching a brace.

Similar conditions were experienced in the Horse latitudes. As soon as we entered the Anti-Trade winds we picked up a fresh S.S.W. breeze, which became so strong that, on May 13th, we made a record run for the homeward passage — 276 miles.

Our light canvas was suffering badly, but there was nothing to do but let the sails stay there: if we had touched them they would have surely gone to tatters.

From the Azores we had only slight winds to the Channel. At daybreak on May 19th we sighted a large sailing vessel ahead of us; at first we thought her to be the *Viking,* but as we gained on her we recognised the four-masted barque *Herzogin Cecilie.* She had sailed from Adelaide 17 days ahead of us.

At noon, Bishop Rock was abeam, our chronometers being more than four minutes out. I rather expected this, as twice during the voyage we had tried to sail some islands in sight, but we were unable to see anything of them.

We arrived at Falmouth Bay at 2 a.m. on May 20th, having made the passage in 97½ days.

Thus ended the finest and the most pleasant round trip to Australia and back I have ever made — without a storm and any damages to the ship or loss of valuable canvas.

Pommern's outward passage to Australia was the fastest of the year. But other vessels made fine passages as well. *Penang* took only a day longer after the meeting in the southeast trades, and 75 days from Dungeness.

On the homeward passage *Pamir* got her revenge with her 92 days, but, as was mentioned earlier, *Parma* won the wheat regatta that year with 83 days, followed most closely by *Pamir* and *Pommern.*

CHAPTER 8

The Headquarters

At the same time as Gustaf Erikson was starting his shipping concern in Mariehamn the horizons of Åland seafaring were darkening. The shipping magnates Robert Mattsson and August Troberg, who owned the majority of Åland's deep-water sailing vessels, moved to Helsinki. Their fleets retained their Åland home registration, but there was no guarantee this would be the case for much longer. In 1917, Gustaf Erikson contemplated following their example and going to live in the Finnish capital. On 27 April, he wrote to Troberg that he set great store by what he thought about this matter — 'whether we Ålanders, with such lovely homes and gardens as yours and mine on Mariehamn's beautiful esplanade, will be able to take up residence in a completely strange city.' I do not know what advice he was given, but later in the year he bought a house on Armfeltvägen in Helsinki. The property was under lease however, there were tenancy regulations then as now; the tenants could not be given notice to quit. The separatist expectations of the following year probably cooled his eagerness to move, and Gustaf Erikson remained a Mariehamner. Admittedly, in the spring of 1919 he wrote to Victor Sandman informing him that a property on Armfeltvägen was expected to be vacated in the autumn, and that he would probably move in with his family. But some time later, he sold the house in Helsinki.

He owned the well-known garden on the esplanade in Mariehamn from 1915 and amongst the copies of his correspondence, teeming with business, one finds an idyll from 4 May: he asks the garden's former owner, postmaster Karhunen in St Michael, about the age of the three strawberry plots, and whether the roses should be covered for the winter. One might well suppose that the comforts of his beautifully situated home helped to diminish the attraction of the capital. Plans to move were finally shelved after Styrsö, formerly an island, now linked with adjoining land, had become his summer home and his darling.

He bought a lease on Styrsö in April 1919. It belonged to Kastelholm and was consequently state property. Many years later, a dream came true; he succeeded in getting permission to buy the property. It lies on a waterway used by the travellers of the medieval itinerary mentioned earlier when they crossed the sea from Roslagen and ran into Lemböte. To the west, towards Mariehamn's outer roadsteads, the Åland Sea opened out.

The family home in Hellestorp lay too far away from the office in Mariehamn and the anchorage. It was sold in 1930. However, a farm estate in miniature grew up on idyllic Styrsö, and competed with the sailing-vessels for its owner's heart. It was there, one midsummer evening, that his eventful life[1] came to a peaceful end.

'Come home and look after the headquarters. As for myself, I'm going to take a trip around the world as skipper of *Lawhill*', So he wrote in a letter of spring 1921 to Ingman in London. The office work was taxing, Gustaf Erikson's nerves needed a rest and he felt an increasing longing to get away 'after nine years of plodding ashore'. I don't know how seriously the suggestion to Ingman was meant, but Gustaf Erikson himself could scarcely have believed in his dream of a trip round the world as a skipper. Company matters had become too extensive and they demanded all his attention. The abrupt

Left, plate 181 The pattern of white sails, *Viking*. (Basil Greenhill)

1 Styrsö is still in the possession and use of the family and has retained its character as a maritime rural retreat. Deep-water comes near the shore below the garden and here one summer Gustaf Erikson had *Lawhill* spend her annual lay up, so that, 'I can see my lucky *Lawhill*!'

recession in the freight market allowed no pleasure trips away from the headquarters.

His correspondence bears witness to his untiring pen. Letter after letter was sent to ship brokers about charters and prospective vessel purchases, and to skippers with instructions, good advice and admonitions — and occasionally with words of praise. Skippers do not generally like writing, nor receiving detailed instructions from shipowners concerning the necessity of turning over casks of salted meat every two weeks, or of stirring the paint well in the pails. For Gustaf Erikson, it was a matter of course to send such reminders. He lived aboard his vessels wherever they sailed, loaded or discharged; he knew the order of the day on board down to the last detail. If he could not give his orders from the poop, he would give them from his office chair, in the hope that they would be effective. 'It is worth...being sure to protect the bottom at least two or three times every voyage with the best anti-fouling compound available, containing the greatest amount of arsenic and other poison and keeping paint well stirred at the time of application, as the thicker layer at the bottom is the most valuable poison against barnacles,' he wrote in a letter to Captain H Lindblom, who was urged at the same time to sail *Ingrid* carefully in heavy headseas, as the vessel was not so young as she had been.[1] When Captain Nordberg took command of *Åland*, he was exhorted to let ship chandlers understand from the start that everything would be checked by weighing. Supplies must not be delivered at the eleventh hour but at least a week before sailing so that everything could be checked. Manilla hemp should be thoroughly inspected — 'open the yarns and comb them out. The longer the threads, the better the quality.' It was worth taking great care with provisions; 'Meat is a very important factor on board; and Australian meat is probably better than American.' As for salted meat, the American was to be preferred. 'Extra Indian Mess Beef may keep longest in the heat, but half of it is just fat, which will not be eaten by the men.'

In most cases, the advice concerned the vessels' economic management, their fitting-out, maintenance and provisioning, but also nautical questions sometimes. During the critical years 1921-22 especially, when the change from boom to recession necessarily demanded a reduction of running costs, conflicts with skippers could not always be avoided. A moral tale about one of Zachariassen's skippers who had been forced to resign because he had 'wartime boom expenses, but freights in accordance with the recession' appears in letters to several skippers in December 1922. One of the addressees clearly thought the intention was all too obvious and promptly cabled: 'send more economical skipper if my resignation is desired.' Gustaf Erikson replied coldly, 'Those of my skippers who consider themselves unable or unwilling to receive a criticism...may make their choice, to continue or to end their service.' The conflict was resolved amicably.

In letters to especially trusted skippers, de Cloux for example, the tone is often friendly, not to say patriarchal. They received real reports on the development of the company, prospects on the freight market, the positions of vessels, planned

1 Gustaf Erikson's letters in connection with the *Ingrid* provide a good example in detail of his methods and his business correspondence. Two are quoted in the essay "My Girlfriend *Ingrid*" in National Maritime Museum Monograph No 36.

Below, plate 182 Styrsö in 1977 stood very little changed in the thirty years since Gustaf Erikson died there. (Basil Greenhill)

Right, plate 183 The kitchen in Styrsö. Note the traditional stove, the American wall clock, known in Åland as a 'skipper's clock; like many others brought back at the end of a season on the Atlantic, and the ' rogbrödkaker' in the ceiling. (Basil Greenhill)

Below right, plate 184 Gustaf Erikson sitting on the visitors' sofa in the old office. The globe is the trophy won by *Herzogin Cecilie* in her race with *Beatrice* in 1928. (Ålands Sjöfartsmuseum)

purchases, and inspections that had been carried out, as well as oddments of news from Mariehamn, and their opinions were sought regarding charters for one or another of the fleet's vessels.

Although Clarksons attended to the routine work surrounding the chartering of the deep-water sailing vessels, it was not possible in the long run, to deal with the increasingly complex business matters with an office having no other personnel than the chief himself. Captain Oscar Reader began working in the office in April 1922 and remained at his job until the autumn of 1926. There was more than enough work, he relates, mentioning as an example that nearly 8,000 coded telegrams were sent during his time. But although the work was heavy and the responsibility taxing (particularly as Gustaf Erikson periodically suffered ill-health and had to spend occasional sojourns at the spa in Nådendal), he cherished the memory of those four years. It was the right job for a seaman with a declared sense of the romance of sail, to be able to work for the development of the last sailing-fleet.

Letters, telegrams, circulars and documents from all points of the compass accumulated on the desk. The office had to become an office in function as well as name, and it needed personnel. In 1924, the typewriter began to clatter under the energetic management of Miss Gerda Applegren. She remained at her job until 1930, when, as might be expected in such circumstances, she married one of the company's skippers, Captain Harald Lindfors. In 1927 Captain Victor Sundman, an old friend of Gustaf Erikson's and a deep-water man besides, worked in the office for a while. The following year, Captain K A Frederiksson and my brother, economist Hilding Kåhre, began their long service with the company, the former in April, the latter in July. They complemented each other's abilities. K A Frederiksson had a long and varied nautical career behind him, having been skipper of the full-rigger *Thomasina,* the steel barque *August* and the four-masted barquentine *Mozart* among others. Nautical expertise was his responsibility, whereas economic matters were the responsibility of Hilding Kåhre, who had practised both in Hamburg and with Clarksons in London after graduating from the School of Economics and Business Administration in Helsinki.

Gustaf Erikson's son Edgar began to work in the office in 1935, after commercial studies in the

Left, plate 185 The old office as it is today, dismantled and recreated in every detail in the office block of the Rederiaktibolaget Gustaf Erikson. (Basil Greenhill)

Below, plate 186 Mrs Solveig Erikson, wife of Edgar Erikson, (right) with Ann Giffard outside the house that was the Erikson home for two generations. (Basil Greenhill)

home country and experience abroad. In the next twelve years, before his father's death, he thoroughly established himself in the company and gradually gathered the extensive threads of its business in his hand. In 1935, the fleet was a sailing-fleet. Before his death twelve years later Gustaf Erikson had bought sixteen steamers and eight motorships and his last acquisition was the brand new steamer *Kungsö*, built for him at Åbo. Edgar Erikson saw the changeover to steam and later motor-driven tonnage and collected experience to help him in his demanding task of commanding the ship on its continuing voyage.

In the late 1970s as a result of his initiative and business leadership, the Gustaf Erikson Company operates a large fleet of specialised motorships in different trades all over the world from a modern office block in Mariehamn with a staff of twenty-four. In the basement, besides the extremely comprehensive company archives, from which this book was compiled, is a fully equipped professional theatre run by Solveig, Mrs Edgar Erikson. Their son Björn, after extensive experience in command at sea, has now joined the Headquarters. [1]

As a rule, the officers on the last deep-water sailing vessels were young and the crews very youthful. The ports they visited were young in the history of shipping, undistinguished and away from the mainstream of the world's business; Mariehamn under the Pole Star and under the Southern Cross, the ports of the Spencer Gulf, each with its handful of shops, its post office, its dances to pianola music, and its wooden pier pointing out into the gulf. There was a pier for vessels to load at in Port Lincoln, Port Augusta, Wallaroo and Port Germein, whereas Port Victoria and Port Broughton had only roadsteads far out from land and wheat-ketches to call on. According to reliable authority, Port Germein with its pier, over an English mile in length, became famous for its sailings to shore. A single-track railway ran out to the end of the pier,

1 The sentences in *italics* were added by the Editor.

where one windjammer loaded at a time. After the day's work, the men sailed ashore before an onshore breeze in an empty railway truck that had deliberately been left behind, returning later with the night's offshore breeze. Even the ancient Romans said that it was more important to sail than to live.

In the 1930s, visiting vessels added lustre to the summers in Mariehamn. For a shipowner, it was not in itself particularly pleasing to see his vessels lying idle for weeks, perhaps even months but the home port also had its small advantages. It was the most suitable place for signing on and paying off, since not only the officers but a great proportion of the crews were Ålanders. And minor repair work, and perhaps the odd item of provisioning, could be provided more cheaply than abroad. Officers and crew were spurred on to do their best to present their vessel in as perfect, and above all rust-free, condition as possible before the awaited visit on board — not only from the owner, but also from family and friends who, without wasting time, appeared in the saloon, armed with a good thirst, a splendid appetite and nautical expertise — the latter often in inverted commas. For Gustaf Erikson himself, the personal inspection was a delight. A vessel's condition was never so faultless that the famous walking stick could not find some small detail to point out.

For many Mariehamners, and no doubt for many visiting tourists as well, the image of the idyllic western harbour, with the hulls, masts and spars of the Australia-sailers, became an unforgettable memory.

Mariehamn's western harbour is a busy enough shipping place today and something of the old atmosphere is ensured by the presence of Pommern lying in one of the old berths, her towering masts visible for miles as you approach Mariehamn by sea. [1]

Anchoring in home waters after a voyage around the world naturally had its pleasure for the men on board. But sailing in the Baltic and the Åland Sea in a big four-masted barque was by no means always a pleasant summer diversion. On many occasions, it was like sailing in a bathtub. The fact that the bathtub could match the storm squalls of Cape Horn in its bad temper, was demonstrated to *Pamir* one September night in 1934.

Under the command of Captain Maurice Mattson, *Pamir* sailed in ballast from Cork on 17 August, bound for Mariehamn. She passed the

Left, plate 187 Edgar Erikson with a portrait of his father as a young man. (Ålands Sjöfartsmuseum)

Below, plate 188 *Herzogin Cecilie, Olivebank, Viking, Mozart, Winterhude*, and *Archibald Russell*, lying at the southern end of the western harbour at Mariehamn. (Ålands Sjöfartsmuseum)

1 The sentence in *italics* was added by the Editor.

Above, plate 189 *Pommern* in 1977 (Basil Greenhill)
Below, plate 190 Mariehamn Harbour today from the bare red granite rocks of Klinten, above the town. The masts of *Pommern* tower above the trees. A Lundqvist tanker lies at the south end. Entering the harbour through the outer islands in a four-masted barque under sail called for consumate skill that was taken for granted until the Second World War. (Basil Greenhill)

Lizard on 19, Dungeness on 20, Elsinore on 25 August, and the passage looked as if it would be quick and pleasant with southwesterly winds in the North Sea. One thing was needed to make the atmosphere on board fully satisfying; they searched in vain for a sight of *Grace Harwar*, which had sailed from Cork 18 hours before them. They also had a fine passage across the Baltic with easterly winds. In the afternoon of Saturday 1 September, Svenska Björn (The Swedish Bear — a landmark) was sighted and at the same time *Grace Harwar* was seen ahead. The outlook was not good. The wind was increasing and, what was worse, veering from East to East Northeast. *Pamir* lay closehauled up to Kobba Klintar, but the change of wind spoiled her chances of sailing into Mariehamn roads under her own sails. Admittedly the company's tug *Johanna* could be relied on from Mariehamn, but *Grace Harwar* was there, and first in line.

The wind continued to freshen steadily. When *Pamir* lay to at nightfall to take the pilot aboard at Kobba, she was carrying topgallants, but one sail after another was taken in during the course of the night. The tug towed *Grace Harwar* into the home harbour. It grew dark. It became increasingly clear that a real storm was on the way. *Johanna* returned with bad news; she would no longer risk it, it was blowing too hard. Captain Mattson was given the order to stay at sea for the night and to wait for better weather.

Pamir now found that she was lacking stability. Ballast was expensive in Britain and the intention had been to make it up in Mariehamn for the passage down to Australia. Lying-to would mean drifting across towards the Swedish coast at a speed of several knots, and the distance to Roslagen's treacherous outer skerries was shorter than a long September night. There was another alternative: to sail closehauled on the Åland Sea, southwards towards Lågskär or northwards towards Gislan. It was not an attractive alternative, but there was no other choice. In a good breeze, carrying all sails and sufficient ballast, *Pamir* would tack without difficulty — which was by no means the case with all deep-water sailing vessels. But with scant canvas and poor steerage, tacking was out of the question. Wearing ship meant a half hour manoeuvre and sailing several miles down to leeward — precious miles in a bathtub.

So began the nocturnal round-dance. Helm hard-a-lee! Haul in the spanker! Stand by mizzen braces! It was a laborious night for the crew, taking in sails and wearing ship, hauling in tacks to windward and sheets to leeward, and tidying up the braces and other cordage on the deck. There was no longer any time for reflection.

The gale became a storm. At nightfall, the strength of the wind had been estimated at force 4 to 5 on the Beaufort scale; a couple of hours after midnight, force 11 was recorded in the log. Visibility deteriorated periodically in violent rain squalls. About 1 o'clock, a strange interlude occurred. The regular boat from Stockholm to Finland appeared on the scene, heading out to sea between Tjärven and Söderarm on a northeasterly course. From the North came *Pamir*, heading southwards, closehauled. And as surely as if the Devil had charted each vessel's course with his own hands, they approached each other. *Pamir* blazed with blue lights and paraffin flares, but to no effect. Three men struggled with the wheel to turn her head to leeward, and after a few endless minutes in the storm, the manoeuvre was successful. *Pamir* fell away and shot past, clearing the steamer's stern by half a ship's length, while the steamer continued on her course undisturbed, a ghostly apparition with her rows of lighted portholes and not a sign of life on board.

At the end of the dogwatch, Captain Mattsson held council with his first mate and the pilot. Every time they wore ship, the Swedish coast came a few miles nearer, and every sail that was taken in increased their leeway. The way back out into the Baltic was closed; beating to windward around Svenska Björn would be impossible. The way out to the Gulf of Bothnia was also obstructed; they might possibly clear Understen, but not Grundkallen. There remained only one alternative — to look for an anchorage among the Swedish islands. It was a hazardous proposition. Detailed charts were lacking and if a rain squall obscured the beacons, the game would be lost. The entrance between Söderarm and Tjärven was chosen, and, after the last sails had been taken in, *Pamir* ran in between the two lights at a speed of 10 knots under bare rigging. The Pilots on Söderarm saw her signals, but had no chance of catching up with the ghost ship drifting past. At first light, *Pamir* lay riding gently at double anchors between Båskärsbådan and Tviklåva, according to one who was there, but was not entirely certain that these names were right. He more certainly remembered the rocks which stuck up out of the water barely a ship's length astern of the vessel, and which were surveyed with mixed feelings by *Pamir's* officers and crew when the morning broke.

A couple of days later, she was towed home across the Åland sea in a glittering calm.

CHAPTER 9

Epilogue

Vessels sailed, loaded and discharged, departure and arrival telegrams flowed in; the days were filled with assignments. Good times alternated with bad but the magic wand of success never seemed to fail its master. His business affairs stretched over an ever wider area. When other Åland shipowners began to buy steam tramp tonnage in the 1930s, Gustaf Erikson invested in the majority of companies. He gave Ålands Aktiebank a helping hand in a difficult situation and acquired the majority of shares in the bank which developed into a sound and robust enterprise. He bought the shipyard in Nystad when it was on the verge of bankruptcy. He was one of the pioneers of fur farming in Åland. Everything was successful. His fleet became famous all over the world, and he received his share of that fame himself.

For nautical journalists in Britain, Australia and elsewhere, the last sailing-fleet was nothing short of a miracle; he was the man behind that miracle. Many people made his personal acquaintance, either abroad, or in the office in Mariehamn. It was not difficult to get to know him. Whether he was talking of shipping or, in festive company, playing *Hela Världens Vals* on his fiddle, he was original and always himself, vital and positive in attitude, unassuming, but straightforwardly conscious of the achievements of his fleet. 'The Maritime Counsellor is an interesting and dynamic personality. When we first made his acquaintance, one fine July Sunday, it was as if one was in the presence of a character straight out of Joseph Conrad's or Jack London's novels,' Helen af Enehjelm wrote in a newspaper in 1935.

Aboard his vessels, the lads who fought storms for a meagre wage were of course considerably cooler in their judgement. Seamen are not given to hero-worship. A skipper might be admired in the fo'c's'le, but to admire a shipowner would go against nature. He is parsimonious, which is a deadly sin at sea. Many deckhands liked to joke about the owner's 'lecture' on the company's fine future prospects, which he gave when signing on crew in the office. As for himself, he was not joking. Once anyone had sailed under his flag, they had no

Below, plate 191 Kobba Klintar, the old pilot station, now abandoned, stands on a skerry of the eastern Skärgård. Beyond is the Åland Sea. (Basil Greenhill)

Inset, plate 192 The end of the sailing-fleet (1). The wreck of the barquentine *Estonia*. (Ålands Sjöfartsmuseum)

Right, plate 193 The end of the sailing-fleet (2). The wreck of the *Herzogin Cecilie*. (National Maritime Museum)

reason to fear redundancy. That was his honest intention and he had no cause to conceal it.

He became a Maritime Counsellor. A title is nothing remarkable. It fulfills its function on the vanity market if it gives a little lustre to its bearer. But if, on the contrary, it is he who gives the title its lustre, it acquires meaning and life. It became a proper name. There was no doubt in any Åland home as to whom *'Sjöfartsrådet'* - or *'Sjöfartsrådinnan'* (the Maritime Counsellor's lady) - referred. There is no doubt that Gustaf Erikson enjoyed this fact, as he also enjoyed being able to receive President Svinhufvud and his wife on board *L'Avenir*, in the western harbour, or being able to dance a whirling

Above, plate 194 The end of the sailing-fleet (3). The four-masted schooner *Regina* on fire. (Ålands Sjöfartsmuseum)
Above right, plate 195 The end of the sailing-fleet (4). The deck of the schooner *Ingrid* in her old age, derelict at Fowey, Cornwall, in 1937. (Basil Greenhill)
Right, plate 196 The end of the sailing-fleet (5). *Mozart* in the hands of the shipbreakers in 1935. (National Maritime Museum)

waltz with the Crown Princess of Norway on board the same vessel in the summer of 1933, the festive summer of Baltic cruises. The honour was not only his, it was his fleet's.

But whatever the magic wand of success can do, it cannot stop the inexorable passage of time, it cannot cure sickness, it is powerless against death.

On 13th June 1942, SS *Argo* sailed from Lübeck, bound for Helsinki with a cargo of saltpetre. Three days later, she was torpedoed south of the Åland skerries at latitude 59° 21′, longitude 20° 14′. Nine men died. Among them was Gustaf Erikson's younger son, Gustaf-Adolf. The blow hit hard.

Four years later, in my capacity as a teacher of the mother tongue (Swedish) at the Åland Nautical High School, I happened to read an essay written by one of the officers and entitled *A Shipmate I Will Never Forget*.

'An ordinary seaman from Mariehamn by the name of Erikson, son of Maritime Counsellor Gustaf Erikson, taught me a great deal about seamanship', the essay began. It continued with a description of a stormy night off Cape Horn when the two shipmates helped each other furl the main upper top-gallant. 'We worked until we thought our finger nails would tear loose. When we finally got hold of the sail with both hands, we put our knees against the yard and heaved. The sail came up more quickly than we expected. I lost my balance, and the footrope swung forward. But just as I was about to fall, I felt a hand push me back up to the yard. It was what one might call a push at the right time. And if he had not been there on the yard, I would never have had the chance to write about a shipmate I will never forget.'

In the autumn of the year his son died, Gustaf Erikson reached the age of 70. He donated considerable sums to the Åbo Academy School of Business Administration, the Åland Cultural Foundation, the Åland Maritime Museum and the Lemland Parish Home, as well as starting two funds, one of a million Marks, bearing his own and his wife's names, whose purpose was to provide for seamen's widows and unsupported children, and the other, named after First Officer Gustaf-Adolf Erikson, to support the widows and children of Åland Merchant Naval officers. The chapel in Mariehamn cemetry is also a gift from him to the town.

Some years later, he followed his daughter Greta to her last resting place. Shadows lengthened across the road. When *Viking* and *Passat* were fitting-out in the western harbour for new sailings on the high seas after the second world war, he experienced once more a period of intense craving for activity,[1] but when reports came of the vessels' hard struggles against winter storms in the North Atlantic, he was himself struggling hard against the illness which, on 15th August 1947, ended his life.

I remember a few words from the copy of a letter written in his prime. The letter, addressed to one of his skippers in 1923, describes the successful purchase of *Herzogin Cecilie*. It bubbles over with optimism, but under the signature there is the postscript 'Don't forget that we have a God who sails above us all...'

Left, plate 197 The end of the sailing-fleet (6). The last days of *Mozart*. (National Maritime Museum)

Below, plate 198 The end of the sailing-fleet (7). When northerly gales have pushed the sea out of the Gulf of Bothnia and lowered the water level around Åland the frames of the schooner *Leo* show above the Lumparsund like the bones of a great animal where she has lain since 1897. Built in 1870 she was so successful that she was dubbed 'the money dragon' by the shareholders in Lemland in the great days of the farmer-shipowner-shipmasters a hundred years ago. (Basil Greenhill)

1 The eventual fates of the sailing vessels still owned by Gustaf Erikson at the outbreak of the second world war are summarised in Appendix 1 of this book.

Three big steel barques, *Viking, Pommern* and *Passat* and the wooden barque *Eläköön* were caught by the war in Mariehamn and the steel vessels lay there, apart from voyages under tow to Stockholm and Åbo, until 1945. *Eläköön* was moved to Nystad, sold, and converted to a motorship early in 1945. *Pommern* was never refitted. In 1952 she was presented by Edgar Erikson and his sister Mrs Eva Hohenthal to the town of Mariehamn as a museum ship. She has been magnificently maintained and is today the finest large merchant sailing ship in the world and the only one preserved in her working state without extensive alteration or reconstruction. She lies alongside the Åland Sjöfartsmuseum, opened in 1954, which is itself a model regional merchant shipping museum. The relationship between the *Pommern* and the Museum is similar to that between the National Maritime Museum in Britain and the *Cutty Sark*, in that they are administered by separate bodies with the management of the Museum represented in the management of the ship.

Viking was recommissioned and sailed under Edgar Erikson's management until 1949 when she was sold and, much altered, is preserved today in Gothenburg.

Passat was also recommissioned and returned to sea. After the war *Pamir*, which had been seized by the New Zealand Government when Finland became a combatant, was returned to the Erikson family. In 1949 *Pamir* under Captain Verner Björkfeldt and *Passat* under Captain Ivar Hägerstrand both sailed from Australia with grain cargoes for Europe. *Passat* left Port Victoria on 2 June and arrived at Queenstown for orders on 19 September, 109 days out. *Pamir* sailed from Port Victoria on 28 May and arrived at Falmouth for orders on 2 October, 127 days. *Passat* passed *Pamir* between Australia and the Horn. She had a clean bottom and simply sailed faster, so she rounded the Horn a few days ahead of *Pamir* which, on 11 July 1949, made the last rounding of the Horn ever made by a merchant sailing vessel carrying cargo on an ordinary commercial voyage. These passages of *Pamir* and *Passat* ended the real history of Cape Horn sailing. On their arrival in Europe there was no further possibility of operating commercial sailing vessels successfully, even had masters and crews been obtainable, so Edgar Erikson sold both vessels. Both were eventually converted to be auxiliary training ships under the German flag. In 1957 *Pamir* was disastrously lost with all but 6 of her crew of 86 including many cadets. *Passat* was withdrawn from sea and is today preserved at Travemünde, again greatly changed from her days as a merchant vessel.

Left, plate 199 The end of the sailing-fleet (8). Arthur Lundqvist's (Plate 53) composite barque *Sverre*, built at Nystad in 1872 as the steamer *Aalto*, the last composite sailing vessel and the last barque to earn her living at sea, lost near the lighthouse of Lagskär, south of Mariehamn on 7 December, 1941. (National Maritime Museum)

Above, plate 200 The end of the sailing-fleet (9), and the end of a vital tool of western man for five centuries. Gustaf Erikson's *Eläköön*, the last engineless wooden three-masted barque to earn her living as a merchant vessel at sea, lying at anchor off Åbo in December 1944. In the spring of 1945 she was stripped of her masts and rigging and fitted with engines. (Lars Grönstrand)

Right, plate 201 Gustaf Erikson in old age. (Ålands Sjöfartsmuseum)

Over page, plate 202 *Viking*, *Passat*, and *Pommern*, laid up in Mariehamn during the Second World War. (Ålands Sjöfartsmuseum)

Appendix I List of Sailing Vessels in Gustaf Erikson's Fleet

Date of Ownership	Type of Vessel	Name of Vessel	Deadweight Tonnage	Material	When Built	Builder	Where Built
1913-1925	3 bk	TJERIMAI	1,550	Composite	1883	J F Meusing	Amsterdam
1913-1914	4 bk	ÅLAND ex Renee Rickmers	3,300	Iron	1887	Russell & Co	Port Glasgow
1914-1916	3 bk	FREDENBORG	600	Wood	1881	Johan August Henriksson	Isaksö, Geta, Åland
1916-1917	3 bk	BORROWDALE	1,850	Iron	1868	W H Potter & Co	Liverpool
1916-1935	S	GRACE HARWAR	2,950	Steel	1889	W Hamilton & Co	Port Glasgow
1916-1923	3 bk	PROFESSOR KOCH	2,350	Steel	1891	Russell & Co	Port Glasgow
1917-1919	3 Sr	INGRID	650	Wood	1907	E Söderström	Knutnäs, Geta, Åland
1917-1919	3 bk	SOUTHERN BELLE	850	Wood	1871	J Mulcaha	Church Point, Digby, Nova Scotia
1917-1942	4 bk	LAWHILL	4,600	Steel	1892	W B Thompson & Co	Dundee
1917	4 bk	MARGARETA ex Craigerne	3,100	Steel	1889	R Duncan & Co	Port Glasgow
1919-1924	3 bk	WOODBURN	2,600	Steel	1896	Russell & Co	Port Glasgow
1921-1936	4 bk	HERZOGIN CECILIE	4,350	Steel	1902	Rickmers A/G	Bremerhaven
1922-1933	3 bk	LOCH LINNHE	2,200	Iron	1876	J & G Thomson	Glasgow
1922-1953	4 bk	POMMERN ex Mneme	4,050	Steel	1903	J Reid & Co	Glasgow
1923-1924	4 bk	CARRADALE	3,300	Steel	1889	A Stephen & Sons	Glasgow
1923-1941	3 bk	PENANG ex Albert Rickmers	3,250	Steel	1905	Rickmers A/G	Bremerhaven
1924-1939	4 bk	OLIVEBANK	4,400	Steel	1892	Mackie & Thompson	Glasgow
1924-1940	3 bk	KILLORAN	3,050	Steel	1900	Ailsa SB Co	Troon
1924-1934	3 bk	CARMEN	850	Wood	1921	Lemlands Varv	Granboda, Lemland, Åland
1924	4 Sr	POLSTJERNAN	1,600	Wood	1920	Skinnarviks Varf	Dragsfjärd
1924-1939	4 bkn	BALTIC	750	Wood	1919	A/B Baltic	Vasterangå, Lemland, Aland
1924-1949	4 bk	ARCHIBALD RUSSELL	3,950	Steel	1905	Scott & Co	Greenock
1925-1932	4 bk	HOUGOMONT	4,000	Steel	1897	Scott & Co	Greenock

NOTE The vessels in this list are those in which Gustaf Erikson was at one time or another the largest single shareholder. The list does not include a number of vessels in which he had shares. It does not include fully powered steam and motor vessels which were not dependent on sails in any way.

Gross Tonnage	Net Tonnage	Dimensions (ft in) L	B	D	From Whom Bought	Price	Notes
976	827	188 3	36 7	21 1	N Tarasoff m fl, Lovisa	F Mk42,500	Lost in collision with Dutch trawler in the North Sea, 22 August 1925
2,135	2,064	283 0	40 5	24 6	Rickmers Reismullhlen, Rederei & Schiffbau, AG	£6,500	Stranded on the coast of New Caledonia in August 1914.
435	431	131 8	31 2	15 4	Alandskt rederi	£300	Sold in 1916. Broken up shortly afterwards.
1,268	1,191	226 4	36 4	22 0	August Troberg, Mariehamn	F Mk300,000	Torpedoed in 1917 in North Atlantic.
1,816	1,564	266 7	39 1	23 5	Rederi A/B Delfin, Helsingfors	F Mk940,000	Sold for Breaking up, 1935.
1,453	1,357	236 2	36 2	21 7	August Troberg, Mariehamn	F Mk750,000	Condemned at Montevideo after collision with iceberg, 1923.
305	291	132 0	27 0	13 0	Ålandskt rederi		Sold to British owners in 1919 fitted with auxiliary engine and used in West Indies and home trades under the name *Rigdin.* Broken up 1939. Only Åland built vessel to become British.
	588	146 0	31 4	18 8	Ålandskt rederi		Sold for breaking up, 1919. Part of masts and rigging incorporated in new barque *Carmen* (qv)
2,816	2,540	317 4	45 0	25 1	August Troberg, Mariehamn	F Mk2,500,000	Condemned by Prize Court, 1942, in South Africa. Fell to pieces at Laurenco Marques.
1,873	1,748	270 2	40 0	23 6	August, Troberg, Mariehamn	F Mk1,100,000	Torpedoed March 1917 in the Irish Sea.
1,552	1,445	242 0	37 5	21 8	A Blom, Nystad	F Mk2,900,000	Sold and reduced to a coal hulk, 1924.
3,111	2,584	314 8	46 3	24 2	French Government	£4,250	Wrecked Salcombe, South Devon, England, 1936.
1,460	1,175	235 9	37 1	22 1	C Lundstrom m fl, Nystad	F Mk400,000	Wrecked in the Åland Islands, 1933.
2,376	2,114	294 8	43 4	24 5	Greek Government	£3,750	Preserved intact as a merchant vessel at Mariehamn.
1,967	1,881	285 7	41 0	23 7	Rederi A/B Aura, Åbo	F Mk417,000	Sold for breaking up, 1924.
2,019	1,743	265 7	40 2	24 3	John Nurminen O/Y, Raume	F Mk540,000	Missing on passage from Port Lincoln towards Cork for orders, 1940.
2,795	2,427	326 0	43 1	24 5	Skibs A/S Ostra, Kristiansand		Sunk by a mine in the North Sea, 1939.
1,817	1,523	261 5	39 1	22 7	J Hardie & Co Glasgow	£2,650	Sunk by enemy action, August 1940.
558	445	176 1	33 9	12 9	Ålandskt rederi		Abandoned near Bornholm, 1934.
1,028	733	202 9	40 3	16 0	Dragsfjärds Rederi A/B	F Mk150,000	Sold, March 1925.
451	354	171 4	33 7	11 3	A/B Baltic, Lemland	F Mk163,500	Sold, May 1939
2,354	2,048	291 3	42 9	24 0	J Hardie & Co Glasgow	£5,500	Sold for breaking up, 1948
2,074	2,084	292 4	43 2	24 1	J Hardie & Co Glasgow	£3,500	Dismasted and presented to Waratah Gypsum Co for use as a breakwater, at Stenhouse Bay, Spencer Gulf, Australia, 1932.

Date of Ownership	Type of Vessel	Name of Vessel	Deadweight Tonnage	Material	When Built	Builder	Where Built
1925-1935	3 bk	LINGARD ex Wathara	1,600	Steel	1893	Fevigs Jernskibsbygerri	Arendal
1925-1934	3 Sr	OSTROBOTNIA	800	Wood	1919	J Lundqvist	Jakobstad
1925-1944	3 bk	WINTERHUDE ex Mabel Rickmers	3,250	Steel	1898	Rickmers A/G	Bremerhaven
1926-1928	3 bk	LALLA ROOKH ex Karhu ex Effendi	1,450	Iron	1876	R & J Evans & Co	Liverpool
1927-1936	3 bkn	ESTONIA	800	Wood	1921	A Wammus	Gutmannsbach
1929-1932	4 bk	MELBOURNE ex Gustav ex Austrasia	4,250	Steel	1892	Russel & Co	Port Glasgow
1929-1939	Aux 4 Sr	MADARE ex Fox III	900	Wood	1919	Arveskjobings Skibsverft	Arveskjobing
1929-1951	4 bk	VIKING	4,000	Steel	1907	Burmeister & Wain	Copenhagen
1929-1936	4 bk	PONAPE ex Bellhouse ex Regina Elena	3,500	Steel	1903	Bacini	Genoa
1931-1951	4 bk	PAMIR	4,500	Steel	1905	Blohm & Voss	Hamburg
1932-1936	4 bk	L'AVENIR	3,650	Steel	1908	Rickmers A/G	Bremerhaven
1932-1951	4 bk	PASSAT	4,700	Steel	1911	Blohm & Voss	Hamburg
1933	Aux twin screw 4 Sr	ODINE ex Astrella, ex Odine ex Pauline	1,600	Wood	1917	McEachern Ship Co	Astoria, Oregon
1933-1937	3 bk	VARMA	1,400	Wood	1922	Nystads Slip	Nystad
1933-1943	3 bk	ELÄKÖÖN	1,400	Wood	1920	Nystads Slip	Nystad
1933-1939	Aux 3 Sr	VELLAMO	550	Wood	1919	Nystads Slip	Nystad
1933-1943	Aux 4 Sr	VALBORG	1,500	Wood	1919	Cholberg Shipyard	Victoria B C
1934-1937	3 bk	KYLEMORE ex Suzanne	1,900	Steel	1880	J Reid & Co	Port Glasgow
1934-1937	3 bk	PESTALOZZI ex Claudia	1,600	Iron	1884	Blohm &Voss	Hamburg
1934-1935	4 Sr	REGINA	1,000	Wood	1919	G Kyntzell	Borga
1934-1942	4 bkn	DIONE	1,000	Wood	1923	B Donner	Jomala
1935-1947	4 bk	MOSHULU ex Kurt	4,900	Steel	1904	W Hamilton & Co	Port Glasgow
1942-1946	Aux 3 Sr	SIRIUS ex Bjerkvik ex Marten	180	Wood	1901	E Norstom	Västervik Sweden

Gross Tonnage	Net Tonnage	Dimensions (ft in) L	B	D	From Whom Bought	Price	Notes
1,039	882	213 0	33 9	17 7	James Bell & Co, Hull	£2,200	Sold in Gothenburg in 1936 after collision damage. Preserved as museum ship at Oslo but broken up in the late 1940s.
500	434	163 9	32 8	15 2	Jakobstads Varv & Rederi A/B	F Mk150,000	Hulked at Nystad, 1934
1,972	1,709	267 2	40 5	24 1	French Government	£1,950	Sold to German Navy, 1944
824	741	196 5	31 8	19 6	Werner Hacklin, Räfso		Sold for breaking up, 1928
481	414	151 5	33 9	13 6	T & S Oates	N Kr12,000	Wrecked in Baltic, 1936
2,691	2,525	305 1	44 0	24 7	Hermann Engel, Hamburg	£4,000	Sunk in collision off Irish Coast, 1932.
544	366	155 9	34 6	16 1	R Boxberg, Helsingfors	F Mk750,000	Sequestrated in Bremen after collision and sold.
2,670	2,154	293 8	42 5	23 2	De Forenede Dampskibs Selskab,	£6,500	Preserved at Gothenburg, Sweden, in much altered state.
2,342	1,974	283 8	42 5	23 2	Hugo Lundqvist m fl, Mariehamn	£5,500	Sold for breaking up, 1936.
2,798	2,365	316 0	46 0	26 2	F Laeisz, Hamburg		Sold to German owners and lost at sea in 1957.
2,754	1,871	278 2	44 8	26 5	Belgian Government	£2,820	Sold to German owners and lost at sea in 1938.
3,130	2,585	322 0	47 2	26 5	F Laeisz, Hamburg	£6,500	Preserved at Travemünde, Germany, in much altered state.
1,723	1,349	248 2	44 5	19 7	Erik Nylund, Mariehamn		Rigged down and sold at the Nystad yard, motors transferred to *Valborg*. She appears to have been bought for her motors and gear.
718	649	201 7	35 0	17 2	Undenkaupungin Laiva O/Y, Nystad		Condemned and sold to German owner, 1937.
827	756	209 5	36 0	17 1	Undenkaupungin Laiva O/Y, Nystad		Sold 1943 to Finnish owners and converted in 1945 to a motor vessel. Hull still in existence 1977 as bridge between two islands in the Finnish Archipelago.
337	201	139 4	28 6	12 2	Uudenkaupungin Laiva O/Y, Nystad		Sold to Finnish Owners in 1939
964	472	197 5	40 0	16 5	Hugo Lundqvist m fl, Mariehamn	F Mk225,000	Fitted with engines from *Odine* on purchase. Sailed on Norwegian coast during Second World War. Condemned after fire and sold to Norwegian owners.
1,229	1,001	226 2	36 4	22 1	H Marechal, Havre	£800	Sold for breaking up, 1937
1,046	851	206 6	34 1	19 6	H Marechal, Havre	£800	Sold for breaking up, 1937
681	545	182 0	34 5	16 2	A Ekbom m fl, Mariehamn	F Mk35,000	Lost in the Baltic by fire, 1935
502	428	160 2	33 0	13 2	O Engman m fl, Mariehamn	F Mk95,500	Sold to Finnish owners, 1942
3,120	2,696	335 3	46 9	26 6	Charles Nelson Co, San Francisco	$12,000	Preserved at Philadelphia in much altered state.
116	72	93 5	23 0	8 5	Karl J Fremling, Lemland		Sailed on Norwegian coast during Second World War. Sold to Norwegian owners, 1946.

Appendix II
List of Books for Further Reading

ATTIWILL, Ken
Horizon. London: Newnes 1930.

BOURNE, Pamela
The Life and death of the Duchess. Boston: Houghton Mifflin, 1959.
Out of the world. London: G Bles, 1975.

BOWKER, F E
Blue water coaster. Camden, Maine: International Marine Publishing Co, 1972.
Hull down. New Bedford: Reynolds Printing, 1963.

BOWNESS, Edward
Modelling the 'Archibald Russell'. London: P. Marshall, 1947.

BUTLIN, C M
White sails crowding. London: Cape, 1935.

COLTON, J F
Last of the square rigged ships. New York: G P Putnam's Sons, 1937.
Windjammers significant: an account of the finest deepwater square-rigged sailing vessels ever constructed. Flagstaff, Arizona: the author, 1954.

COURSE, A G
The wheel's kick and the wind's song: the story of the John Stewart Line of sailing ships 1877-1928. London: Percival Marshall, 1951. Newton Abbott: David & Charles, 1968.

DERBY, W L A
The tall ships pass. The story of the last years of deepwater square-rigged sail, embodying therein the history and detailed description of the Finnish four-masted steel barque 'Herzogin Cecilie'. London: Cape, 1937. Newton Abbott: David & Charles, 1970.

DESMOND, Shaw
Windjammer: the book of the Horn. London: Hutchinson, 1932.

FREDRICKSON, Nils
Endless voyage. London: Harrap, 1939.

GREENHILL, Basil
The merchant schooners. London: Percival Marshall, 1951, 1957. Newton Abbott: David & Charles, 1968. London: National Maritime Museum, 1978.
My girlfriend 'Ingrid'. National Maritime Museum Monograph 36, 1978.
The Life and Death of the Merchant Sailing Ship. London: H.M. Stationery Office, 1980.
Karlsson: The Story of an Åland Seafarer. London: National Maritime Museum Monograph 55, 1982.
The Merchant Schooners. London: Conway Maritime Press, 1988.

GREENHILL, Basil & GIFFARD, Ann
Women under sail: letters and journals concerning eight women travelling or working in sailing vessels between 1829 and 1949. Newton Abbott: David & Charles, 1970.
The British Assault on Finland: A Forgotten Naval War. London: Conway Maritime Press, 1988.

GREENHILL, Basil & HACKMAN, John
The Grain Races: The Baltic Background. London: Conway Maritime Press, 1986.

HURST, A A
The call of high canvas. London: Cassell, 1959.
Ghosts on the sea-line. London: Cassell, 1957.
The music of five oceans. London: Harrap, 1960.
Square-riggers: the final epoch, 1921-1958. Brighton: Teredo Books, 1972.

HUTTON, W M
Cape Horn passage. London: Blackie, 1934.

KARLSSON, Elis
Mother sea. London: Oxford University Press, 1964.
Pulley-haul: the story of a voyage. London: Oxford University Press, 1966.

LEAVITT, J
Wake of the coasters. Middleton, Connecticut: Wesleyan University Press, 1970.

LUBBOCK, Basil
The down easters; American deepwater sailing ships 1869 - 1929. Glasgow: Brown, Son & Ferguson, 1929.
The last of the windjammers. 2 vols. Glasgow: Brown, Son & Ferguson, 1927, 1929.
The nitrate clippers. Glasgow: Brown, Son & Ferguson, 1932, 1966.

MEAD, W R & JAATINEN, S H
The Åland Islands. Newton Abbott: David & Charles, 1975.

MUNCASTER, Claude
Rolling round the Horn. London: Rich & Cowan, 1935.

NEWBY, Eric
Grain race: pictures of life before the mast in a windjammer. London: Allen & Unwin, 1968.
The last grain race. London, Secker & Warburg, 1956.

PARKER, W J Lewis
The great coal schooners of New England 1870-1909. Mystic, Connecticut: Marine Historical Association, 1948.

SALMINEN, Sally
Katrina. Translated by Naomi Walford. London: Thornton Butterworth, 1937.

SHERIDAN, R B
Heavenly hell: the experiences of an apprentice in a four-mast barque. London: Putnam, 1935.

THESLEFF, Holger
Farewell windjammer: an account of the last circumnavigation of the globe by a sailing ship and the last grain race from Australia to England. Translated by M A Michael. London & New York: Thames & Hudson, 1951.

VILLIERS, Alan
By way of Cape Horn. London: G Bles, 1930. London: Hodder & Stoughton, 1952.
Falmouth for orders: the story of the last clipper race around Cape Horn. London: G Bles, 1928. London: Patrick Stephens, 1972.
The last of the wind ships. London: Routledge, 1934.
The sea in ships: the story of a sailing ship's voyage around Cape Horn. London: Routledge, 1932.
Sea-dogs of today. London: Harrap, 1932.
The set of the sails:the story of a Cape Horn seaman. London: Hodder & Stoughton, 1949. London: Pan Books, 1955.
The voyage of the 'Parma': the great grain race of 1932. London: G Bles, 1933.
The war with Cape Horn. London: Hodder & Stoughton, 1971.

VILLIERS, Alan & PICARD, Henri
The bounty ships of France: the story of the French Cape Horn sailing ships. London: Patrick Stephens, 1972.

WALLACE , F W
In the wake of the windships; notes, records and biographies pertaining to the square-rigged merchant marine of British North America. London: Hodder & Stoughton, 1927.
Wooden ships and iron men; the story of the square-rigged merchant marine of British North America, the ships, their builders and owners, and the men who sailed them. London: Hodder & Stoughton, 1924.

Plate 202 *Viking*, *Passat*, and *Pommern*, laid up in Mariehamn during the Second World War. (Ålands Sjöfartsmuseum)

Index

SHIPS